TIRAN

A TALE OF CROWS AND KEYS

D1519767

BEN LYNCH

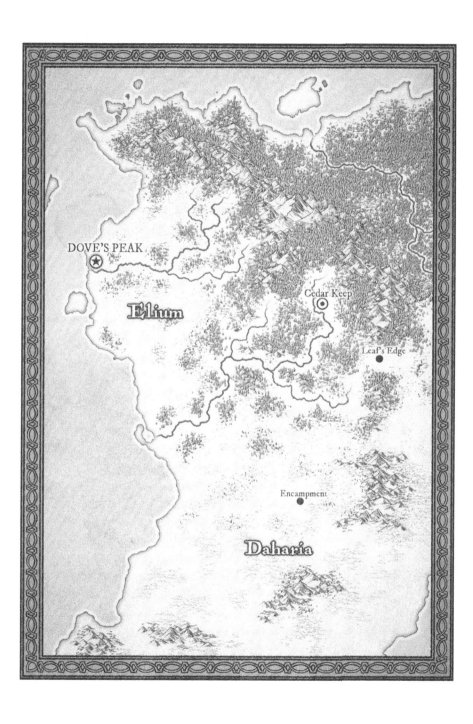

TO THOSE WHO SEEK TO INSPIRE,
THE WORLD AWAITS.

Contents

AMON
SOMEWHERE IN THE SAND

One year prior…

Harsh, coarse, and full of malice is the sand as it whips throughout the desolate and vast desert. Rigid and rough conditions for our journey, the only bright side is the sun, which beams down on the desert below. Amidst the sand, the only color in sight is the near-blinding arrows of light that dash through the torn cloth of the tattered carriage cover. The carriage itself is empty, aside from where I sit in silence.

Leaning upright against one of the worn down, arching support beams, the sun gleams off my sand-covered steel chest plate. Sitting still with bread in hand, a worn black hood extending from my cloak envelops my hanging head. I can't tell what's falling from my weary hands to my brown boots, as the wood shakes with each turn of the wheels: the crumbs of hot, stale bread or the sand finally peeling off my every limb. At this point, it matters not, for both are useless, whilst my hunger needs to be quenched.

The sun peeking underneath my long, black curls forces me to pull downward on the cloth to avoid the blinding rays. Yet, still, through the cloth hood fighting to hide my face, strands of light surely reveal the long and rigid scar over my blind left eye.

Pathetic how I sit here and eat crumbs diluted by my environment and aged past any nutrition. Not because of a want but rather a need. *Because of a need to eat or rather a want to not die?* Hmm. I continue pondering the thought as I pull off a handful of bread, chew, and swallow.

My focus breaks from the stray pellets falling downward onto my black pants as the beating hooves of the horse neigh to a halt. A swift whip of cloth catches my eye as the back flaps to the carriage opens and the sun pours in. Whilst my good eye adjusts to the harsh light crashing through the opening, a silhouette of a man stands still, blocking out most of the rays, the figure outlining a tall, broad, and towering nature.

"Fuck's sake, it smells of piss back here," the shadow bellows in a gravelly tone.

My eye finally achieves clarity soon after he speaks, noting long ginger hair down to his wide shoulders and beard. The man grins, his orange beard covering his jaw from ear to ear, as he releases a dirty smile. My eye wanders from his teeth to the lower mass of his beard tied together.

"Care to join me? Or are we still nibbling on that dreadful bread," he asks, bearing a brown cloth cloak that covers everything but his outstretched hand.

"The next time you blind me like that, I'm going to take my dagger and cut your good eye out," I reply, referring to his right eye that wasn't covered by a black eye patch.

"Oh, your demeanor is as refreshing today as ever, I see," he banters back, shaking his steel chest plate with his laughter.

"Where the gods are we, Sylas?" I mumble whilst glaring at him for a brief moment.

"Welcome to the Gallery of Rays, mate. Daharia—the sea of sun," Sylas says with a grin as he pulls my outstretched arm forward.

Hopping out the back of the carriage, I observe the scenery around me. Throughout our trek, all to be seen was a bleak and barren desert. Now, however, I find it full of color and life. Dozens of tents varying in sizes and shapes fill what was once an empty void of sand. Living amongst the cruel sea are hundreds of people, from the local olive-skinned Daharian to the lighter shades of refugees from Elium and Savar. All living in peace, with a multitude of vendors to our east, armorers to our south, and families with children abound.

With citizens roaming freely, the Daharian guards watch and patrol, ensuring safety, sporting short-sleeved chainmail shirts, brown leather pants, and leather sandals, the sand kicking up with each of their strides.

Breaking the focus on our new environment and pondering the lives that live here, I say, "Where in God's name do we find the man? Why did we even take this bounty? I shan't believe you dragged me down here for mere information."

Sylas quickly fires back. "Ha. The Crow is too good for a retrieval contract? Oh, pardon, don't tell me you're mad at the sun blessing your skin? Looks like you need it," he teases.

I spare him an angry glance as he chuckles. My counterpart turns his head from me, then, looking off into town, and after a few fleeting moments, he says, "I believe that's the spot the guide detailed," eyeing the tents in the distance.

"Perhaps you can be more specific," I say, looking at the cloaked ginger.

"There, Amon," Sylas says with his finger directing upward toward the towering black tent with gold trim in the very center of the rag-tag civilization.

"Ah, I see. What a spot to hide in. I never would've chanced it," I say.

"Ha. We better get moving then," he responds.

Returning our gaze back to each other, he advises, "Keep those tucked away," looking at the scars on my left cheek. "Don't need another strike against the guild,"

I nod as we both pull up our cloth masks and stride forward toward the center of the town. No one gives us a glimpse on our walk toward the open-air, makeshift civilization. Perhaps we blend in perfectly with our sand-stained cloaks, or, more likely, they don't care who we are. After all, most here are too caught up in something, someone, or somewhere to notice us outsiders.

We pass by families playing in the sand, people eating together in the open, and the occasional tent filled with 'single suitors.' A seemingly peaceful and harmonious commune of people, this place has presumably never known turmoil or anguish, as 'tis deep into the Daharian desert. The only red liquid being poured out here today is wine, with an exchange of words and smiles.

For me, however, this is not my first trek into this nation. Many moons ago, I sought to bring refugees to safety at the border, mostly for coin. However, I had never been so deep into the sea of rays until this moon. We found our way here due to Sylas and his charm. We bartered with a Dahrian guide at the border a week ago and acquired his services in order to find this place. After a night of drinks and an exchange of gold coin at a town called Kyme near the border, we secured our guide, and then traveled for two moons under the beating sun. Eventually, Jesfer, our Daharian counterpart, fell off the wagon stone-cold dead in the midst of the dunes. After his departure, with the assistance of the crudely drawn map found in his pocket and Sylas's compass, it took us weeks more to find our way here. I fear it nearly took our sanity with it, although I don't believe Sylas ever had that.

Gaining ground on the extravagantly massive tent, we pass through the avenue of traders on either side. Bustling in business to our left and right, we make sure to keep our heads down and clothes donned. From freshly cooked food, clothing, and jewelry, all the way to spices and herbs at the very end of the line of stands, the traders offer just about any need or want one could imagine.

Getting ever so close to the opening of the pitch-black, wide tower, I make eye contact with a vendor. She is intently looking at me with her hazel gaze as she stands smiling behind the wooden table. Short in stature, wearing a sandy brown cloak, cloth covers her from head to toe, except for her kind eyes. She stands close by behind her spice stand, awaiting customers.

"Can I help you find anything, sire?" she asks in her Daharian accent.

Smiling back, I shake my head no. I can't risk being outed attempting to buy spice with my Elium accent. Breaking the shortlived conversation and paying her no further attention, my mind stays sharp and focused on the entrance directly in front of us.

Upon entering the tent, a darker setting takes hold. The interior is dimly lit by an array of scattered candles placed on tables. The massive pole lifting the overarching cover in the middle also bears a torch on each of its four sides. 'Tis a lively scene inside the giant, cloth pyramid. A tavern of sorts made out of wooden tables, a bar stocked full of wine and ale, and a kitchen out back in another tent that the service keeps visiting.

It isn't necessarily quiet, but not nearly loud enough to drown out my inner thoughts and scattered observations, even with the multitude of people dining and conversing.

Walking over to our left and sitting in the corner nearest to the entrance, we cherish the reprieve. However, I refuse to lose focus mentally as my eyes grow heavy in the soft seat. Even after weeks on only straw and wood with little rest, Sylas and I promised to remain vigilant, for our lives and mission are at stake.

Thinking of our promise and objective to gain information from our target, I look at Sylas, who is about to speak. Before doing so, a long, blue-and-purple tailored dress appears in front of us. Her dark olive skin, accompanied by her long, wavy brown hair, catches our attention.

The beautiful Daharian woman stops in front of us and asks, "Food, drink, or girls?"

I say nothing but deliver a simple wave to shoo her off in response.

Whilst the woman nods and leaves, Sylas stares at me in displeasure and says, "No girls? Fine. At least ale, for fuck's sake,

Amon. 'Tis been weeks."

"Sylas, you damn well know this is no time to be social," I quip, staring back at him.

Silence falls between us as the tension from our journey runs high. I look off into the crowd of people in the quiet for a moment before turning my attention back to Sylas, who seems rigid. I lean over and whisper, "What's wrong?"

He takes a deep breath before turning to me, saying, "I find it hard to believe we are the only ones who know where this man is.

I worry it shall be more difficult to get the information than at first glance."

"We both know this won't be easily pulled off. Give me solutions, not problems," I whisper back.

Sylas scoffs and shakes his head whilst I break eye contact to scan the room and observe.

"Middle of the room, isolated, long blonde hair, scar from the right corner of the mouth to his chin," I say.

"Dagger under the waistbelt, knife clenched in his hand from dining. He's scared and mindless. He'll be on edge with every movement," Syals fires back. "Give it time, till dusk, when he goes back to his tent. Acting under the moon's light is favorable for us." "Hmm," I groan and nod.

With sand and time passing in front of us, we sit in silence, observing the subtle changes in the open, dimly lit space. Drinks were ordered and delivered, food was played with and eaten, and women were seduced—or attempts were made—by both Daharian men and women.

I stare off. I can't tell if the darkness arching above the mass of bodies is from the shadows of the candles or a genuine wickedness inside the tent.

Looking at the ceiling closely, my trail of thought is broken by Sylas saying, "I'm going for ale. I'd ask if you want any, but I'm not paying for you. Be patient, Amon." With a heave and multiple deep breaths, Sylas rises to his feet.

Before I can even respond, evil enters the room in the facade of a woman. I don't know if it's her movement or the look in her hazel eyes that draws my gaze. With a couple steps and tugs at her cloak, she blends in with naive customers and folk whilst gliding toward the center of the room with haste, as though she's racing something, or someone.

At first glance, I don't understand, until I see where her steps are taking her. The race is against me, but one in which the sand is grabbing around my ankles. Paralyzed, I watch her meticulously planned movement. The woman treads lightly on the ground as she gains headway on her target, and I simply watch.

Rising to my feet, free from the momentary shock and now aware of the woman's wicked intentions, I attempt to warn Sylas. Alas, it matters not.

I don't know what came first: the stillness and peace of the moment as the air sits frozen in place, looking at each other with a locked, frantic gaze... or the slice of the knife.

Chaos ensues. The once lively area is now torched by emotion and panic. Our mission, in one act of violence, is set aflame as the man we were contracted to receive information from is keeled over, dead. Before I even move from my trance, Sylas grabs my shoulder with a thrust and firm tug. We find ourselves hurrying outside the towering tent as others scramble out.

The tranquil setting is tossed into utter and complete chaos, the vendors leaving their stands full of produce, jewelry, and clothing. Families dashing to their tents and carriages. The armorer puts out his flame, whilst the guards are dashing toward the tent amidst the confusion and hysteria pouring out.

Too slow, is all I can think. *We were beaten to the job.* But why? Why now? Why cause this panic? Why not before we even arrived? Why in the very middle of the tent?

While pondering my thoughts, trying to replay what had occurred, the environment burst into moving parts. We step swiftly between the tents, people, and guards as the sand shifts and sags with every step. When Sylas and I arrive at where the carriage once sat, we stand in shock at what we now see. Our transport and its wheels were engulfed in flames. The fire shone off the sand, making it an impossibly hotter and more dire circumstance. We turn and run while frustration sets in my skin, harsher than the sun beating down from above.

The surrounding tents catch aflame on either side of us, with the echoes of screams and disarray sounding throughout the desert, causing my mind to race.

"Amon, this way," Sylas yells as he darts toward a makeshift stable made out of wooden poles and cloth covering.

Almost reaching my targeted mare, I notice a shifting figure from the corner of my eye. It feels planned, as if she wanted me to see her.

"Amon!" Sylas yells again as I divert away from the stable and make it to where I last saw the assassin, knowing it could damn well be a trap.

Rushing and pushing past Daharian citizens whilst dodging the guards, I make my way back through the tents set aflame. Hundreds of bodies streak by, thousands of voices ringing, and the same blinding light beams from above as I scan the chaos. It's daunting to spot her among identical dirty cloth masks and cloaks stained by sand, and I stand still for only a moment, taking it in, before preparing for my next step.

About to propel myself forward, back to the stable, the wind and sand hit my back, and the cloth of my cloak being cut jolts me to the side. I turn to face the thrust, finding the woman assailant now standing in front of me. Her features are hidden, aside from the now frigid hazel gaze, her maliciously extended olive arms holding a curved dagger.

The craftsmanship on the blade is impeccable, as it bears an inscription from its red leather grip to the steel tip of the weapon.

We lock eyes as I pull my sword from underneath my cloak. No cross guard needed, as the leather down to its onyx hilt supplies grip for my hand. From there, we start our game of chess.

Moving her piece first, she lunges with a fierce thrust, breaking through the dry air. I instantly parry away to my left as I shift right, about to strike. I, however, can't act on my instinct, with another thrust coming from my right, revealing the second dagger in hand.

Gods. This time, the dagger slices across my forearm, revealing red. I release a deep breath in pain as we refuse to exchange words. Rather, we seem to let the steel speak and sing.

Her words fill the air as she thrusts with wickedness in a tone of hatred, mine now filled with aggression and questions.

Strike by strike, our duel of wills and intellect comes to a standstill. That is until one of my questions is answered. We lock steel, face to face, with both of her daggers using their curved edge to block my strike. Quickly, I release and roll behind her as she falls forward, turning to me with a look of confusion. With one downward slice amongst a sluggish reaction, the cloak of disguise is cut down the middle. The strike reveals a stunning figure of a Daharian woman, sporting only dirty-white cloth apparel. She flings off her hood as the rest of the tattered cloak falls to the ground, glaring at me with a stare as if upset I'm not returning the favor.

Amidst the panic and citizens fleeing, we stand still for a moment, and I ponder the many questions floating in my mind as she catches her breath. The dullness of the moment wears on me, however, with patience not being among my values held close to heart. Accordingly, I advance my steps, keeping a sharp focus on the opponent in front.

Attempting another downward slice, a swift roll behind me rebuffs my approach and seemingly catches me off guard. She, using the very same act of attack I had beforehand, outwitted me in this duel. Rotating back around to meet the consequences of my impatience, I brace for a swift strike as I ready my blade to parry.

But it seems my punishment will have to wait another day.

"Piss off," Sylas lets out as he strikes his round golden round against her head from behind.

The beautiful yet treacherous woman falls to the ground, whilst I turn my attention to Sylas. "Thanks," is all I can muster, trying to collect my breath.

"We have to bring something back. This was for my other eye, not you," he says, looking down at the woman on the sand.

"Gather the horses; I shall be but a moment," I respond after a laugh and sheathing of our swords.

Sylas nods before he ventures off back toward the stable. I turn my attention to the figure at my feet, bending over to pick the assassin up. The motion of her hand tossing sand in my face doesn't register at first. Seeing it too late, I turn my face sideways in hopes of blocking her attempt. The siren would normally succeed in the attempt to blind one's eye, but it happens mine is already useless. The bits of grain dash across my face and left eye that's out of commission. She sits in confusion only for but a moment before a quick motion of my fist sends her back to dreaming.

Reeling from the pain my knuckles endure, a shift catches my attention. The breeze flowing through my hair and scalp whilst feeling the sand within sends a shock of angst throughout my body. My hood had unknowingly fallen off amidst the fight, and as if the Gods were playing a cruel game, a guard rounds the corner. I imagine he can now clearly see the guild markings on the left side of my face. The three symmetrical lines, with the first extending and angling over the top of the other two as if creating the letter E. "Bounty Hunter," the Daharian guard exclaims before yelling in his native dialect as three more guards round the corner behind him. "You did this!" he yells.

Unsheathing my weapon once more, I realize this is no time for words of diplomacy or compromise. In the midst of their steps closing in, I ready my blade to be wet with their blood. Before I can do so, though, I hear the galloping of hooves breaking the wind.

"Quickly, Amon", Sylas lets out, riding an amber horse with another one in tow toward the guard.

I act, dodging and rolling from the blades aimed at me with vicious intent. Narrowly escaping their vengeful thrusts, I climb upon the identical mare to the one Sylas rides, rushing through the flames and soot of what once was a joyous, safe place. Daringly, we race away, leaving the burnt town behind.

I can't help but feel defeated, having lost all hope of hearing the urgent message—one of mystery, as we were not informed what it revolves around but rather that it would carry political influence. We also managed to lose the assassin, get pinned for the atrocities, and, as a result, flee toward a journey of misery with no civilization on the horizon and guards chasing behind us.

I think of the women left behind as we push on, and the revolving questions that shroud her in mystery.

Days pass by as Sylas and I walk over the blazing sand while guiding our horses, giving them a reprieve from our weight on their backs. It seems the guards gave up chasing, as if they knew we would be lost and left to the desert for punishment.

We dig up the small trees, littering the sand for the sap that lies at the roots. Day by day, we drink and feed on the gathered liquid whilst also using it to keep our horses nourished.

"One week's journey to Elium. North, just over those dunes in the distance," Sylas says as he ties our horses to a dried-out tree, "If we return with nothing, you know the consequences. The guild always takes payment," I reply. "And I won't lose my other eye over this."

"Amon, we've spent the last moon deciphering the events that occurred. There's no sense in making out of it; we were bested and beaten to the target," Sylas says with a tired yawn.

"Yes, but I can't help but ponder why. What could the man have possibly said that warranted his death in the middle of the room? Who are we even up against for this?" I ask. "She had to know we were coming, Sylas. Why wait otherwise? She knew who we were. Knew our carriage. 'Tis more than just luck; it was planned... By her? By the person who requested this contract? By the guild? Gods know who!" I panic.

"And if we don't? If we don't return? We'll be hunted down till the end of our days," Sylas pronounces with a stern glare. "You damn well know the agreement. You don't just leave the collectors guild. If we don't report back by the next moon cycle, we end up like the others who have tried to flee. It seems you forgot about our friends; Gaya tried; arrow in her heart. Jervis just pondered the idea; poison in his wine. Even Kyler was found sleeping with the damn lionfish in the Silver Lands after he'd left for nearly three years, Amon. This isn't even something to consider."

"I know," I say. "There just has to be some sense made out of this. We just saw hundreds of homes being burned to the ground for gods' sake, Sylas. It can't be by chance; it was by design. That doesn't make you boil? That we've been used? And you're just moving on? Letting it go? Not giving a damn?"

He let out a sigh whilst the sun set on the never-ending desert, sitting around a fire of dried-out tree limbs.

"I'm not. You know I'm not. I'm not one who forgives and forgets, but if there's anyone who knows what just happened, 'tis the same people who gave us this contract. And if it happens that they set us up, then there are clearly larger forces at play here. Especially for a man to be executed and a town to be torched to cover tracks. We must be diligent, and most importantly; we must be patient," he says, staring off into the setting rays.

I look at him for a second as he speaks before breaking concentration and shifting focus to the darkened sky on the horizon. He's right, but my curiosity and anguish from the pain caused overwhelms my mind. The scream and panic of the people, the blaze and pain of the families who lived there playing on repeat through my skull as I let out, "Fine, but there's one more stop I want to follow up on first before I go back."

He looks at me for a moment with his forest-green eyes and carefree expression, sitting in silence before breaking the still, dry, air. "We all have dues to pay, Amon. Some pay them sooner than others, some don't pay for a long time, but it shall always be collected. Whether we collect or fate does, whoever started this shall pay in abundance..." He pauses for a moment before continuing. "But you can't just let your emotions overrun you and become your master, Amon. It can be the end of you. Or worse off? You could end up like the ones who plotted this; filled with such rage and wickedness," he says.

I look at him and nod in agreement, although my mind still races with flickering images of the town erupting into chaos. 'Tis not a thing some would so easily forget with the sights of the hellish spectacle. However, soon after, we allow our dreams to take shape, for when dawn breaks, we'll prepare for our separate journeys.

RAMSES
CEDAR KEEP

10th year of Our Elder's Reign, present day...

The daylight is covering the busy stone streets whilst the warm breeze flows throughout the market where I stand. The second day of the moon cycle is as enjoyable as ever, standing in the busy square. The hold is filled to the brim with bustling citizens while safe in the arms of the stone walls of Cedar Keep.

Amidst the busy day, I found myself often thinking about the keep and what it holds, wondering what I admire more: the massive mountainsides, lush in green from the cedar trees behind the hold or the burgundy painted stone that brings to life the egregious castle. Both beautiful, with shadows cast below.

Drifting in and out of thought with a lack of attempt to sell produce, I focus on the walls that keep us safe. The color of the clay, mortar, and stone making up the safeguard matches that of clouds that carry Loria's tears. Massive in size and length are they, holding ample opportunities within, as 'tis one of the largest cities in all of the continent of Tiran and only second to the capital in the nation of Elium. Or at least that's what I've heard travelers often say.

The walls of Cedar Keep that separate us from the abundance of green trees and farms reach five horses high and two horses wide. The nearest wall shadowing above the market seems to be slowly cracking, as the age of the walls vastly predates my own years. Atop the stone edges of safety, I spy the guard overlooking the citizens both inside the walls and out in the farmlands. Peace and prosperity being their mission, with a vision of becoming the most harmonious city in all of Elium. A goal set by the Elder residing in Cedar Manor.

That being said, I'm not especially fond of the steel brass who hawk the city with their condescending demeanors. The recent scamming of taxes, food, jewelry, and clothing has the people at a bubbling point in their anger. The shady behavior even affects my own stand from time to time. The hold, often so bountiful in beauty, kindness, and prosperity, has shown its limits in this regard, with most civilians known to avoid the likes of its

'protectors.'

My focus drifts to the opposite side of the market, where homes lie in hundreds, and a surplus of places to worship, dedicated to the many religions held close to heart, line the street.

Studying in detail at my surroundings, I find armorers and their raging fires, hundreds of traders and vendors, 'single suitors' and their place of 'work,' whilst looming above all stands the colossal tower of Cedar Manor, casting a shadow over a mass of the civilization, almost serving as constant shade.

Staring up at the grand building in the sky, I notice dusk about to set behind the manor. My vision comes back down to the wooden stand where cabbage, carrots, and other produce sit still, as I notice a new indention in the wooden table below. Looking beside the produce, I glance at my small cedar box. Lightly glittered in silver and bronze, the box is nearly empty. Alas, another grand day out in the fresh air of the city, yet not quite the best in regard to raking in coin.

Starting to pack up my belongings, produce, and earned coin, I smile at my fellow vendors and other passersby.

"Good-moon, son," a fellow vendor says.

"And to you," I return, brushing off of my face a few strands of my blond hair.

Having picked up all the necessary items to be taken on my walk home, I leave the wooden table behind, striding in my beige pants and worn-out shoes to turn the corner down a cobblestone street, leaving the large market square in my kicked-up dust. I head in the opposite direction of the castle and market and make my way toward the large looming walls.

As I continue my trek, I start to wonder about dinner, as I have become quite hungry over the course of the day. Mother has probably made lamb stew again tonight, as she has for the past three meals. The repetition doesn't nag at me; however, it comforts me in a sense to even have such a simplicity.

Aiming to go through the pointed teeth and mouth that is the large iron gate, I slow to a halt as I approach the guards who stand watch by its side. I am cautious. In recent times, I have heard tales of some guards demanding coin, jewelry, or even other personal belongings. Like a pattern, on all moons, I avoid the guard; however, the one waiting by the gate I consider a friend. Harley.

He stands tall and proud, bearing the keep's emblem. One of which makes out a leaf at the top with a bow coming out of the stem, an arrow hitching itself onto the stem acting as the bow's string. This image is etched into his steel chest plate, over the guard's heart, and shines bright from the little rays of light that still linger.

"Goodness, 'tis good to see you. I'm starved," he says, approaching from beside the gate.

"Good-moon, friend. How goes the watch?" I ask.

"The Loria truly favors me," Harley says. "I have been blessed with standing and watching the damned open air. Did The Loria shine on you today?" Harley asks with a smile.

"That trinity of deities shines on me every day, just not in silver, it seems," I respond, holding out two carrots.

He reaches out to grab them as he extends two silver coins in his off hand. "Perhaps under the new moon," he says, trading coin for carrot. "I've even heard whispers that the royals shall be visiting the market to prepare for their feast."

"Ha, if only they'd grace me with a visit. But then again, maybe under the new moon, we'll both find luck," I say, nodding whilst walking past him.

"Good Moon," we both say in departing as I make my way toward the fields outside the keep.

Traveling through the gate and out into the farmlands that lay in front of the city is always a refreshing sight. Whilst I traverse the outer section of the keep, my nose is filled with the scent of soil, greenery, and food being cooked. This brings me joy, as well as the sight in front of the keep, as 'tis home to the color green. As far as the eye can see, each plot of space is touched by it, whilst tall and staggering wood hides underneath the costume of color. Yet, even closer to the keep is home to hundreds of fields and huts. At every corner, street, and turn in the maze of crops, lives operate their well-being and living situation. The land, meanwhile, is loaded with rich and ripe soil, whilst the crops burst through the earth, creating want and need. Seeing this sight always brings a sense of comfort, knowing I'm home. Continuing my trek, I stop upon hearing a familiar voice.

"Oh, Sir Fike, was the day in the sun that cruel?" the voice of a lady teases.

Turning around to where she spoke from, I see a woman donning a long, brown, dirty farming apron.

"I mean, Mother Fike shall go to war with the Sun and Moon over these red brandings," the girl says, shaking her smaller brown-covered head with each word.

"Perhaps she'll win; her will knows no bounds, as we both know," I tease back to the shorter young lady now in front of me. "Tell me, Erin, would you fight the sun for me as well? Mother may need some assistance with using a sword," I ask.

"Hmm, I shall have to dream on it. I'd imagine we'd need a larger battalion than the three of us, Ramses," she says

A smile begins to come through my pitiful and prickly beard. "Three? Who said I had qualms with the beams of light? I think I look quite handsome like this," I say.

Both I and Lady Erin laugh for a moment amidst the warm breeze that flows through the stone street.

"I shall expect you tomorrow then, yes?" she says, looking at me with her sparkling blue eyes.

"Hmm, I shall have to dream on it," I tease.

Erin punches my shoulder. "Ramses, be honest, don't tease me," she says.

"I wouldn't miss it, I shall arrive with my best top for the gala," I say, this time delivering a serious response.

"Until tomorrow's moon then, sire," Erin says mid-curtsy

"Under the new moon, my lady," I say with a slight bow and giggle.

Both walking our separate ways, I look back once more. To my surprise, she does as well, our longing gaze locking together only for a moment before turning toward our destinations.

Taking only a couple more dozen paces, I see the open doorframe of our hut. Small in overall size and covered by hay, there sits the poorly put-together clay and stone home for three.

I'm genuinely happy to be back after a long day, feeling joy and ecstasy almost. That is until the wind blows upon me, coming in new directions. As quick as a snap, I'm met face-first with the dirt and grass of the fertile land. The boxes I once held spill their innards onto the street as I lie and watch my own stream of blood from my nose. "The Loria's sake," I say, groaning in pain.

The fact I am face down in mud sparks a sense of anger, and looking behind me to see the glimmering water on the stones fuels the spark. All it took was a few wet stones to put me on my back.

I sigh.

"Oh love, what mess you've gotten into," I hear from a woman's voice.

I look up, now covered face to chest in mud, to a middle-aged, blonde-haired woman reaching down with her hand toward mine.

"Come along," she says, smiling with her blue eyes and lifting me off the earth.

The shorter woman pats off the dirt on her gray shirt and black apron as I smile in her direction.

"Thanks, Mum-ma," I say, bending over to pick up the spilled items.

"What a mess, you fool," she replies, whilst we walk through the wooden doorframe of the shoddy hut.

Gliding by the table where I choose to sit, mother walks to the open flame and opens the pot that sits above the blaze with a sleight of hand, releasing an aroma of neatly sliced vegetables and tender, spiced lamb. The room fills with the same smell as the past three moons.

"What, no pig this time?" I say with a grin from ear to ear, teasing mother.

She scoffs as she picks up two wooden bowls from a ledge over the fire. It takes two scoops of the liquid to ready the meal to be served.

"Here, love," she says, walking toward the table with a bowl of stew in either hand. Mother sits down and slides the stew along the boar pelt our wooden table wears.

"How was the square today?" she asks.

"Ten silver coins and seven bronze. Busy, I'd say… more than almost double what we made yestermoon," I respond.

Her bright and kind eyes don't budge with this news, although we both know it's far from the best collecting we've had.

"Perhaps The Loria shall shine on us tomorrow," Mother says after drinking some of her soup.

"Perhaps the Royals shall visit the stand," I say.

Mother smirks. "Hmmm, that too, maybe Lady Sylvia? No, no. Lady Illia, she is the epitome of beauty. Her and Erin, of course," she says.

Glaring at mother from across the boar's pelt, I drink my soup as we lock eyes.

Mother giggles.

"Well, Ramses, let's get you cleaned up," she says, putting down her bowl of half-finished stew.

Drinking the remains of mine, I rise up to my feet as we both aim for the door, entering out underneath the open black that has dimmed the farms and cedars. Step by step, I follow her around the house to where the well meets the earth.

Torches lining the streets give enough light to see mother pulling the string from the well upward. She takes out a bucket from the open void and instructs me to sit with a motion of her hand. In the time between, which felt slower than seconds, I look off toward the house, and in a glass pane, I see my muddied reflection.

My overhanging hair is clumped together by a mixture of soil and water. Bright green eyes complimented by the dark brown spots and streaks on my face. Golden small hairs peek through the surface of my skin to create a short beard, while my once cleaner beige shirt and pants are now the color of the cedar's bark.

"Ouch," I mumble, seeing the darkened skin on my nose.

The mess and bruises don't bother me; however, the frigid stream pouring over me causes my heart to race.

"For the Loria's sake," I exclaim before receiving a slap over the head.

"Mind yourself," my mother says, her kind eyes dissipating into a somber look with each word.

My words having weight on her heart, nearly always make me apologize.

"Sorry Mum-ma," I say, looking up to match her gaze.

Waiting for a moment before putting my head back down, I allow another flush of the cold, dirtied water to fall.

"All done, love," Mother says and puts the bucket back in the well.

Rising from the lumber used as a seat and wrapping myself with a sheep's-wool blanket, I ask, "Any word from father?"

Avoiding eye contact with mother, waltzing in front of me, we stride back toward the mouth of the house. Upon reaching the door,

Mother says, "Not a pigeon's word. I sent a letter to the East last cycle but nothing since."

"Do you think he's enjoying his time in the jungle?" I ask, enveloped in wool and sitting down at our table.

"I can only hope, dear. Perhaps he'll bring back a tale or three," Mother says.

"Being away for six moon cycles, one can only hope so," I say, smiling.

"I've heard tales of Lymre, of creatures of all sorts that slither and strike. You never know when they'll... pounce!" I say and exclaim, my hands acting like a snake about to bite.

We sit, laughing so hard the flame flickers on the candle set atop the table.

"Perhaps I shall go see him," I say.

"Ha. Then who shall sell the produce?" she asks.

"What's so humorous?" I ask her with a perplexed look.

"Nothing, love, I don't imagine you'd enjoy the passing moons out there," Mother says. "From the tales, 'tis barren of life aside from the soldiers who patrol it. I couldn't imagine how lonesome the lives of most of the men posted. Bless the Loria for their vigilance."

"You think Father's alone?" I ask.

"I don't think he would mind being alone for your safety. I think he is often busy protecting the ones he loves," mother says in a cheerful tone.

Sitting for a moment, both of us enjoy the flame from the candle on the table. "Ramses, what's weighing on your mind?" she asks.

"What do you mean? I'm grand, right? We could do better with silver from the stand, I suppose..." I trail off.

Mother snickers. "That as well, but no," she says. "Wanting to leave? Head in the sky? Not to mention using the Loria's name in vain."

I smirk and pause whilst looking down at the dark red boar skin, then return my eyes back up.

"I must admit I do not like that you know me so well," I say, smiling at her. Drawing in a deep breath, I exhale. "Don't you dream of more? More to do? Explore? I find it hard to imagine you settling with being party to the guard's tricks. Or only ever knowing the land of this keep," I say.

Sighing and grabbing the wooden bowls off the tables, mother walks away to place them back on the ledge from which they came, then turns and glides back toward the table, asking, "Shall I ever need more than the roof over our head, the food on our table, or the love I hold for you and your father?"

"Is that all you ever want, Mother? Is that all you ever needed?" I ask.

"One day, when you have kids of your own, you shall perhaps gain insight. You are my wants and needs, you are my joy," Mother says.

"I am delighted to live this life, whether or not the guard swindles us, whether or not I never see another landscape. You must understand the things in life that matter," Mother says, sitting at the table once more.

"Mum-ma, that can't be your truth. You have never simply wished for more?" I ask.

"The truth, my dear? We all want more," she says. "That's the truth. For some, more in want. For others, more in need. More in a feeling, a person, time. But we don't get more, Ramses," she says. "We work for coin. With coin, we can provide for our family. With the family we have, we enjoy each other's time.

There's nothing more special than that."

Mother speaks with conviction in her voice, and thus, I know her words to be right, or rather… she believes them to be so.

"Love, I didn't mean to be off-putting with your curiosity, I apologize," she says.

"No, I wanted honesty. And such was an honest answer. It, too, is the right one," I say, breaking my gaze from her.

Rising from the table, I blow out the flame that dances in the middle.

"Good moon, Mum-ma, I'm off to dream of all these wants, it seems," I say, standing beside the table.

Mother gives me another warm smile before saying, "Goodmoon, love."

The moon's time above elapses with dreams of coin, crown, and courage. The town rises to life with the streams of yellow peeking through the panes of glass in their homes.

"Bless the Loria," I sarcastically release, pulling myself off the straw on the floor.

Looking around the vacant home, I notice no signs of life. Mother snuck out before I awoke by the looks of her apron and tools missing from their usual resting place. Typical 'tis for her to have an early morning reaping the crops before heading to cook in the manor.

Rising off the floor, I crack my back. Upon releasing the stress from my aching bones, I walk toward the box of produce left on the dinner table from the night prior and pick up the large wooden crate with new scratches from the fall and let out a heave. I then head toward the door and exit with a motion of my hand and a push of straw, a diluted sky of gray and blue appearing above.

"Hmm," I mumble at the sight of the overcast sky. How strange 'tis to see the half dimly lit sea above, having not seen color other than blue for much time across the horizon. As half the rays beam down, whilst the others hide behind gray, I walk the stone streets, navigating toward the entrance of the walls.

Arriving at the gate, after a short walk, I stop. A line to enter the walls creates a snake, full of those seeking passage inside.

Curious to see the holdup, I peek around to the front of the line. "What in the Loria is going on?" I mumble.

With no choice but to wait, I stand patiently and think about my upcoming plans. *Work, clean, change, Erin,* I repeat in my head. *Work, change, gala, Erin?* I smirk, but the chainmail rattling from underneath a silver steel chest plate rings in the nearby air, causing a pause in my thoughts. His hand is extended out to motion "stop," causing an abrupt end to my steps. "Five silver for entry," he says. "Five silver? Why, sir? " I ask.

"The Elder's tax to enter," the steel-covered guard says.

"Tax? What's the meaning of this? We pay our tax at the start of the moon cycle, do we not?" I ask.

"If you wish not to pay, you shan't enter," the guard says, looking down at my box of produce then back up to my eyes once more.

During our animated conversation, a man approaches from my left, unnoticed by the guard or me, and slinks into our vision from seemingly out of nowhere.

A few long strands of black hair hang down his face to meet his tan cheeks, and the man looks at me with his dark gray eyes. Wearing black and silver-lined robes with the keep's insignia laying where the collar meets the neck, he looks at the guard. "Good-moon," he says.

"Lord Bale," the guard says, bowing his head in a sign of respect. "What's the manner of this," the lord asks.

"Sire, I was just informing this man about the new taxation per orders of his Elder," he says, head still bowing.

"I see," Lord Bale says before returning his gray line of sight to match mine.

"Is your Elder asking too much out of you? Is the tax for safety amongst these walls such a steep price?" Lord Bale asks.

"Sire," I say, bowing my head. "'Tis not the Elder's will I am concerned with, rather my lack of coin."

We three stood after the words left my lips, still as the mountain range behind the keep under the multicolored sky. That is until the midnight-haired man strikes a chord of surprise and mystery, handing the guard five silver coins from his pouch attached to his hip.

"Go along," he says, looking off behind me.

"Thank you, my lord," I say with little thought in regard to who he is actually speaking to.

Noticing the thorn-shaped hilt attached to the black leather grip peeking out of its scabbard, I make a note of the kindness he afforded me. Thoughtful is he for paying my toll into the city, but quickly, the focus from his action shifts to the curiosity of the new tax.

Slipping by him and the guard, I pass the gate. *What is the need for such a steep price? For the gala, I suppose? Was that just another scam?* I pray it does not last every day, for there is no way I shall be able to afford such a cost. For now, however, I approach my destination.

Coming upon the dark cedar stand, I notice the already busy market square. Lifting upward with a thrust, I place the crate, packed to the brim, on top of the stand. My carrots, beets, onions, and the rest of the crops line the darkened cedar top as my day truly begins. Customers perusing and citizens walking by, I find myself in a trance as I stare off at the looming manor not too far from the market square, dreaming of life inside, imagining my place amongst the ruby halls. The fresh boar and pig to be feasted on, the plentiful amount of wine poured for events and quenching thirst, and a crown with emeralds and lapis awaiting to be donned by me.

I haven't even noticed who is in the market square midmorning, as my focus rapidly returns with their words.

A white-haired man gazes at my stand with his brown eyes. "What do we have here?" he says. "Hmm, tell me, lad, how much coin for the beets?" the cloaked man asks at the front of my produce stand.

My eyes grow wide whilst my mouth is paralyzed to answer his questions.

"Pardon, son? Are you alright?" the emerald-eyed man asks. "Jov, is he mute?" he says, turning to the tan, white-haired man in identical robes.

"No, my Elder!" I say, breaking my stunned silence. I look at the produce. "Uh, it varies, how many would you like?" I ask the disguised Elder of Cedar Manor.

He grins and says, "All of them."

"Um. Well. Honestly, your Elder, I wouldn't know. This has never occurred," I say in disbelief.

"Shall this do?" the white-haired robed man asks.

He sets a hefty bag of coin down, shaking it as it rests on the table, before me.

"Heh. Certainly, my lords," I say, bowing my head in gratitude.

"Lovely. Lord, if you wouldn't mind?" Elder Elovis says, prompting Lord Jov to place all the beets into a crate.

"Shall you be in attendance tonight?" the kind Elder asks as the lord picks up the beet-filled crate. "Yes, my lord, it shall be my honor," I say, nodding.

"Wonderful, I hope you rather enjoy yourself. The Loria bless you," Elder Elovis says before walking off, tugging at his hanging hood.

Stunned at who I had just encountered, I could only laugh for a brief moment at the bag of coin sitting in front of me.

From there on, time flies; from unpacking more carrots, cabbage, and radishes to selling potatoes and onions. My happiness knows no bounds.

My recurring customers bring me even more joy, even as the gray clouds above shift in a position to cover the whole sky.

After a few and far between exchanges of coin after the Elder's visit, almost another full day in the market passes. The fleeting thoughts and daydreams of the gala with Erin fill my mind as I still bear a smile. The excitement and hope I hold for the night ahead fuels me to push through my tired moments. Ultimately, the smile I dawn from the events earlier in the day wears weary, even with the new pile of coin, as drowsiness sets over me. Watching passersby, a grungy older bald beggar passes along before me in the square. Swiftly, a prompt grasp and pull of nearly all my carrots from my stand gains my full attention.

"Thief!" I scream in a panic, trying to get out from behind the stand, with other vendors to my left and right. Whisking away with no shoes or guilt, the bald, dirty, shit-stained shell of a man shows no signs of slowing. Feeling empty of hope and care, I give up chasing only a few steps from out behind the cedar wood. Shockingly, before the thieving beggar could get more than twenty steps, he crumbles to the cobble. A tug of his shirt and a quick whip of a hand over his head causes him to fall to his knees. The carrots sprawled all over the dusty and dirty stone. Briskly, I jog over and pick them up. Turning my eyes from the orange of the vegetable and gray of the street, I see the figure who's holding the man's shirt in hand.

The man stands tall with his gray, tattered cloth hood over his head. His brown robes seemingly wrap around his body in the color of soil, while his hair hides underneath his lowered cloth. Scars on his left cheek protrude out in a red and pink fashion, accompanied by a long, matted, orange beard.

Walking toward the man, I smile and hold out my hand to be shaken.

The mountain of a man reaches out with his right hand, letting the thief go with a shove and release of his left.

"The Loria bless you, sire," I say as the beggar recedes away into the crowd of bystanders.

"Tell them to bless another; don't waste their words on me," he says, walking past me.

"At least partake in food, sir. As a token of thanks." I attempt to gain the stranger's attention before he drifts into the sea of passersby.

Looking at me now upon hearing my words, the man lets out a deep, mumbling laugh, looking at the carrots in my clutches.

"I assume not the ones in your grasp," he says.

Now, locking looks, I laugh in response. "Ha. No, indeed not," I say with a waving of a hand as if to follow.

Reaching my wooden stand, only a few steps away, we look over what lies on the table.

"Richest vegetables in taste. Harvested before the rays even dare peak over the ridge of the mountains," I say to the possible new customer.

The brooding man looks up at me with a slight grin before going back down to the table.

"Here," he says, passing two gold coins along the coarse layer of wood.

"Bless the Loria, where did you get this?" I exclaim, inspecting the newly grasped coins.

"I earned it," he says, this time not even cracking a wry smile from his cut and dry lips.

A sense of truth and honesty pours out from this man like a flowing river in the Silver lands. Charisma and genuineness emit from under his cloak of mystery, naturally stirring my curiosity.

"How does one earn such a reward?" I ask, admiring the indentions making the woman's face on the coin.

"Reward? No. This is sacrifice, my friend," the man says.

"What do you mean by sacrifice? What did you sacrifice for this?" I ask with a perplexed look.

He looks at me with only one good eye. "So many men chase riches, son. Riches of a different life than their own, and oftentimes end off worse for it," the figure says. "For now, enjoy this honor, in this moment," the ginger-bearded man advises, turning away from the table.

"Sir! Wait! You have forgotten to take the crops you bought!" I say before he can take his next step.

He turns once more to look at me. "Just because it looks pure of malice and full of taste certainly does not mean it is. Keep the coin, keep the crops," the mysterious figure says before walking in the direction of the manor east of the market.

Sparking every node of curiosity in my blood and bones with his words and actions, I watch him go, and carrying a new sense of adventure, I decide to leave my stand behind and pursue the enigmatic figure. Step by step, I etch myself deeper into the lanes of people and carriages now passing by my limbs only a breath away.

"He's from the manor," I mumble, continuing to scour for the tattered cloth he bore. "There," I whisper, seeing the man now only several dozen steps away.

Watching closely as only a few strides away, the man takes a swift change in course of direction, from navigating toward the manor to now aiming for an alley between a blacksmith's workshop and rows of rundown housing. The last thing I see is him disappearing into the shadows cast by an overarching tower attached to the manor, my intentions of trailing the kind man cut short as I find myself face to stone for a second straight day.

Dark red rushes out onto the stones where my nose now sits. Swiftly, I come to my senses and pick my head up from its rest on the ground, scanning only to see a guard on the ground opposite me.

The guard rises swiftly to his feet, brushes off the dirt on his shoulders and chest, before walking over toward me and mumbling, "Bastard."

Only now, I realize, as he towers over me menacingly, the long beige cape whipping the ground in the wind, silver chain links connecting the ends together whilst a key hangs from the middle. This is no guard but a member of his lord's keys of the keep.

"Sir Valincias!" a voice exclaims, ringing throughout the now heavily eyed scene.

Looming over top of me whilst blocking out the gray above, the honored captain of the Elder's guard stares while guards sprint to accompany the knight, circling around me as panic creeps into my mind. "Captain, are you in good health?" A guard asks.

I rise to my feet and look at the captain, who holds a cold smirk.

"Apologies, Sir, I am a fool, not looking where I was going," I interrupt with my head hanging low.

Lifting my chin, the captain processes my words whilst his cape flutters from his clean silver armor that shines from head to toe. A look of joy enters his brown eyes, or at least that's what I assume before he speaks. The captain wipes the dripping blood from his mouth, turns to his fellow guards, and says, "Take him."

His words shake me. Shake my mind, my bones, the air in my lungs, and my mouth goes dry upon hearing the knight.

"Wait, sire, I must beg for your forgiveness," I say, getting on my knees.

The captain bends over and says, "And how much are you willing to pay for this so-called forgiveness?"

Turning my head upward to meet his voice, I say, "I have two gold coins, sir. Please, 'tis all I have."

Staring at me intently with his dark eyes, he produces a soft smile and laugh. The captain nods to the guard as he turns to walk away. I can only process the words being said for a few moments as I kneel in shock.

"By order of the Elder, for the assault on his royal Captain of the Peace, I hereby place you under arrest," the guard who firmly grabs my hands says.

I freeze in a trance as three guards drag me away, my mouth silent. No desire to run, no desire to fight; I stay still as they haul me off. All the while, floating through my mind isn't emotions of anger, sadness, or confusion but rather intrigue. I can only think of the mysterious man I stalked moments prior. That is until my focus shifts to the long, heartbreaking look coming from the crowd.

"Erin," I mutter.

LORD BALE
CEDAR MANOR

The Twentieth Celebration of His Heir

Observing shapes and outlines, I allow my senses to take in the scenery. Although my eyes have been of no use to me for as long as I can trace back, I have strived to find peace of mind on the balcony of my room in the manor. Using my nose, ears, and limbs to navigate, I draw my surroundings in my head of the life below. Bakers baking bread, children running around, blacksmiths bartering prices, and above all else, the metal uniforms of the guard clattering against their limbs. Smells of freshly chopped wood, open flames raging, the soil beneath each hoofing step, and even the unpleasant shit-stained corners of the city float by with each passing whiff. The passing air whistles as the fresh scent of dark cedar fills my senses, along with the rambling noises of the keep. I stand still, overlooking the roaring city, taking it all in.

Reaching the ever-elusive peace of mind and stillness of body, I stand immovable, taking in the scenery and all it offers. My peace of mind lasts ever so shortly as it slowly breaks off into pieces, with my attention turning to the footsteps drawing near.

The creaks of wood from the floorboards grow with each step as it comes closer. Louder and louder, the groans grow, coming to an abrupt end to my right.

Out in the open, a new smell lingers, closer than the rest. One of sweat, steel, and wool cloth in arm's reach. Not bothering to look, as I know the familiar stench, I try to remain mindful. "Brother, taking in the new sun?" Jov asks.

"Simply escaping to find solitude," I reply softly, shifting my head rightward. "How are we this moon, Jov?" I ask, putting my hand on his shoulder, feeling a similar fabric to the robes I wear.

"Good, brother. Better if I find a date for the gala," Jov says with a snicker.

Jov seems to be full of jokes, as usual. He always has been the one blessed with an upbeat mood between the two of us. I wonder why he continues to check in on me. Is it our bond? Or is he just bored? I turn my attention back to delivering a response. "Hmm, so soon forgetting about your last date?" I ask with a grin.

"Well, she did have two lazy eyes and two hands for feet, so I don't believe dancing would be her strong suit," Jov laughs.

"I didn't know you took a liking to sloths, brother? Now that I mention it, she did act a bit off," I tease in return.

We both laugh for a moment before he asks, "And you, Bale? How are you this moon?"

"All is well, brother. Implementing a new tax in the morning and a grand ball at night; truly, I am blessed," I say.

"Ha. Don't joke, we both know you dread tonight, you'd rather stand and tax all day," Jov exclaims. "If that is the Elder's will',' I say, grinning at Jov.

Whilst still facing my brother, a new pattern of hums appears. Much heavier steps and much shorter breaths enter the room behind us.

"Captain, good of you to join us," I say, peeking over my shoulder.

"Lord Bale, Lord Jov," he says.

"When did you notice me this time?" Captain Valincias asks.

"Valincias, you draw breath so swiftly it could steal an island's breeze. I could hear such heaving if you were all the way on the mountainside," I tease, whilst Jov snickers.

"I see. I hope my breaths do not cause too much disruption, my lord," his voice falters.

"He only teases, Captain; what's the manner of this visit you honor us with?" Jov asks.

"The Elder has requested your presence in his chamber," Captain Valincias replies.

"After you then, Captain," I say, turning toward the odor of wine and steel coming from the direction of Valincias's voice.

His strides, almost heavier than before, lead out of the room and turn left before halting as he waits for us.

We leave the balcony and are met by the maneuvering of maids and servants scattering throughout the long, echoing halls, the aroma of roasted pig cooking for the gala ahead filling the nearby air and causing my mouth to water. The sound and smell of the sweet and crisp wine in the manor being poured, drunk, or spilled in nearly every room we pass float into my ears and nostrils.

My favorite, above all, is the light shining through panes of glass, warming my skin upon its touch and giving me an idea of the time of day. Meanwhile, women laugh and men converse as their words float through my mind before being disregarded.

My internal processing rapidly sifts through each and every different situation as we come to a halt. We had ventured only a couple dozen paces, up a flight of stairs, before arriving at our destination.

The loud creaking and gust of air reveal the size and stature of the grand door in front of the three of us.

Opening with slight screams of the wood, I now realize the room we approached.

"Pardon, Elder, I bring Lord Bale and Lord Jov," Captain Valincias announces before shutting the doors as he exits.

Within the room itself, I smell a blaze roaring, smoke sitting in clouds, freshly poured wine, and a new figure. This outline smells heavily of metal, sweat, and wine, with no vibrations until a groan of wood reveals two footsteps aiming in our direction.

"Your Grace," I say, bowing my head.

"Bale, my friend, please do not bother yourself with that, how many times do I need to tell you?" Elder Elovis says. "And I am no king, so I must insist you address me by my name."

"As you wish," I say, keeping in mind the true power he holds. A power that makes him answer to no other man except the king himself, as Elovis governs with full authority over one of four holds in Elium. "How are we this moon?" the Elder asks.

"Well, my lord," Jov says, smacking his hand together with the Elder's in a shake.

"And you? Lord Bale?" the Elder says with his steps approaching my stance.

"All is well, Elder," I say, holding my hand out.

"Tell me, lads, what are your thoughts about the night ahead?"

"I'm quite looking forward to it, my lord. The free wine especially," Jov jokes.

Elder Elovis lets out a laugh while his arm quickly smacks against me as he pats me on the back. "And you, my friend?" the Elder says, still giggling a little.

"I think Lady Illia shall love her celebration, my lord," I say with a smile.

"Ha. You blind bastard, you damn well know she'll find something to complain about," the Elder exclaims. "That girl acts like a mare on fire at times. Even the king would have trouble trying to rein her in." We all let out a laugh for a moment before the air was filled with the voice of the Elder once more. "Well, friends, I must admit, I brought you here for more than brief pleasantries," he says, catching my full attention. "In truth, I brought you here for a favor," he says as his creaking steps wander toward the smell of the flaming wood.

"In what regard, Elder?" Jov asks.

"With Lady Illia's celebration of birth comes political invitations being sent out. Pigeon's traveling to keeps all over the nation. With that comes many guests that need security," the Elder says.

"Of course, my lord, we would be honored to help with the guard," I say.

"And I value your willingness, friend. At some point today, the king's brother and his wife, Duke and Duchess Arys, shall arrive from the capital. I need not stress the importance of their safety in their time here," Elovis says, before pausing for a moment to pour the smell of wine into what sounds like a metal cup.

"I would like you both to oversee their safety whilst they attend the gala tonight. I entrust Valincias and his band of brass to keep them safe until then within these walls. But I trust you two shall see to it that they enjoy their time while under your guard," Elovis asks. "It shall be done, my lord," Jov says.

I stand quiet amidst the burst from Jov, raking my thoughts, consumed by angst.

"My thanks, then, friends. I shall see to it Valincias informs you of their departure for the ballroom when that time arrives," the Elder says before taking a sip of the wine.

"My lord, if I may, I must insist you allow one of us to be by your side tonight. Allow Jov or I to shield the duke and duchess," I say, halting his sips.

"Bale, I admire your will to protect me, but the captain shall see to my and Lady Sylvia's safety for the night," the Elder says. "This is not a punishment, only the need for safety for our capital counterparts. I would ask anyone else, my friends, but I trust none more to do this task than my twin peacekeepers," he says, taking his last sip and setting down his chalice. "Besides, a good showing of respect and protection shan't hurt or be forgotten in the capital's eyes either."

Elovis puts his hand on our shoulders and ushers us in the direction that we came.

"Oh! One last thing. Jov, I shall meet you out front of the castle at midday. Otherwise, I shall see you two soon, I'm sure," he says.

"Brother?" Jov says when we take the spiraling stone steps toward our rooms, "What pains you so deep to guard the duke and duchess? It should be an honor."

"It is. I know it is. However, we owe it to the Elder to shield him—" I say, as he strides through the halls.

"I know," my brother says, cutting off my trail of words and bringing our steps to a halt. He sighs. "I know we do, brother. But this is much different than a mere guest from the city," Jov says. "This is an honor from our Elder and friend. We shall take it as such. Nonetheless, you know the importance of the duke and duchess being here," he says.

"And I agree, brother, but this is no mere favor and no normal night. Everyone within the walls of our city is invited, meaning the risk of danger is that much higher. Besides, lest you forget, Jov, he saved us from tragedy, from war. He saved us from slavery when the battle for the Isle was over. For the gods' sake, he gave us a home in a castle, he gave us positions as advisors, he gave me purpose even with my eyes being flawed. So, yes, I'm worried.

Any sane man would be with the amount of guests we're allowing in," I say.

Jov says nothing in return as I turn my dark and hazy gaze from his face to the steps and continue our descent. Once reaching the floor below, we both take only a dozen strides, Jov stopping his feet a carriage length away from where I do the same. He opens his cedar doors, proceeds to enter, and then closes the room's mouth once more. Aiming to go into my room, the frame squeals as it opens.

"Apologies, my lord. Just dropping off your new clothing," an unknown voice says.

"No apologies needed. Thank you," I say to the tall, bleak outline.

As the servant's steps echo away, I stand still, and in my head, I unfold a map of the bedchamber.

Table and chair to my left in front of the opening, where flames often dance. Shelving and desks straight ahead beside another entrance that leads to the open air. Bed diagonally to my left, as my wardrobe oppositely mirrors it to my right. Smells of cheese and wine emit from the center of the room where, presumably, the maids have laid fresh food on my dining table.

Stepping toward the bed, I place my hand out to feel the soft silk hanging off in front. I hold the robes up to my face to smell, noticing the metal key-like shape at the top, buttoning the two sides of the fabric together. Feeling the four blades of the key, I retreat my nose downward until reaching the cloth before setting it down on the bed once more. Upon doing so, I turn and stride to my chair as I sit and close my eyes. I only want a moment's breath before I continue with the tasks of the day. As I sit, I begin to regain the peace of mind I have been longing for since losing it earlier this morning. I find myself going in and out of sleep, cherishing the silence around me. That is until the doors of my chambers fly open.

My eyes open in haste as I rise to my feet and grab my blade's grip, only to release it upon smelling the captain's odor.

"Damn you, don't you know not to rush in on a near-blind man?" I say with a small, dry laugh.

Valincias releases a deep chuckle. "Apologies, my lord, but we're needed in the key room," the captain says.

Leaving my chambers, we venture on a short trek down to the opposite end of the eight-room hall before finding the entrance of another doorframe, where I hear people gather.

Valincias opens the door and says, "After you," as I walk in.

The key room itself seeks to bring all the keep's trusted advisors together in a conference room of sorts. Inside, the gathering place bears four heartbeats, and if my memory serves me well; four chairs, open windows emitting the breeze inward, and my favorite: the long, detailed, metallic table weighing down the center space.

"Oh, brother, how nice of you to join us," Jov says.

The space erupts in brief laughter with four different pitches.

I hear the lord, Jov, the captain, and one I hadn't heard in years.

"Hamzi, my friend? When did you arrive?" I ask.

"'Tis good to see you too, lord," the Lymrian voice calls out as his heavy steps draw near.

Embracing for a brief moment, the smell of grease, perfusion, and perfume nearly overpower my nose. His velvet robes brush up against my hands as we let go.

"I arrived just moments ago with the lead carriage ahead of the duke and duchess," Hamzi says, his steps backing away toward his seat.

"And the Loria bless us for your return, we dearly missed your wisdom, old friend," Elder Elovis says.

"As I have missed yours, all of yours, to be quite honest," Hamzi says, pulling his chair out beneath the rectangular table.

As we all glide to our chairs and sit, the Elder clears his throat. "My lords, I would like to apologize for pulling you in today on a day of celebration, but our returning friend here has made me aware of news he wishes to share," the Elder says. "Hamzi, would you please?" Elder Elovis asks as I run my hand along the ingrained table that maps out all of Elium.

"Of course, lord. 'Tis great to see you all. However, pleasantries aside, I rode ahead to bring a manner of business," he says.

"Way to keep us on our toes, waiting," Valincias chuckles.

"Of course. I bring a request from his royal majesty and an urgent message," Hamzi chuckles.

Intrigue sets over the mouths of those in the room, as the prospect of a favor from the king is not something to be taken lightly.

"Pray tell, friend, what does our king ask of us?" Jov asks amidst our stunned silence.

"'Tis a time-sensitive request, my lords. His grace..." Hamzi pauses.

Eager to hear the next words, the Elder teases, "Well, go on then, friend, do not leave us hanging on your lips waiting for your words."

"Ha. Of course, my lord. His majesty... has asked for the Lady Illia to give her hand in marriage... to his youngest son, Dedric Arys, my Elder," Hamzi says. The mood shifts in the airy room.

"Does he now? This is truly an honor," Elder Elovis says with contemplation in his tone.

"My lord, if I may," Hamzi says, "I believe this to be an opportunity that benefits us all, especially in securing our legacy at this keep or even beyond."

Sitting back and patiently waiting to hear the other responses in the room of keys, Captain Valincias says, "My Elder, I must agree. The Lady Illia is due for an arrangement, and with the king asking, 'tis not something we can simply say no to."

Pausing for a moment, the Elder replies, "You both make valid points, friends. Bale? Jov? What are your thoughts on such a favor?"

"It would be hard to make a case against this, my lord. It seems to be everything we could need or want in a marriage for Lady Illia. I would trust none more than the royal family to deliver her safety and a full life," Jov says.

"I agree with that sentiment. Thank you, my lord," Elder Elovis says. "And you, Lord Bale?"

My fingers stop rubbing over the table's etchings as I focus on my thoughts. Taking in a deep breath I respond, "I believe you need to ask Lady Illia, not I, my lord."

Captain Valincias scoffs. "Lord, you can't truly believe that she shall make a clearheaded decision about this," he argues.

"I did not say it was her decision to make, as 'tis neither of ours," I say, whipping my head in his direction across the table. Pausing before looking back toward the head of the table to find the Elder's blurred outline, I say, "The points made are too thick and full to disagree. In my own mind, this makes political sense in every way, my Elder. I only caution that dealing with the likes of the royals may be more troublesome than we admit. If we heed now, then the favors shall never cease," I finally conclude. "Bale, mind yourself, you speak of the king," Jov says.

The Elder intervenes, "No, my friend. Lord Bale makes a tried and true point. This is something I must give thought."

"Think not too long or too hard, my lord, for Prince Arys shall be arriving with the duke and duchess in much haste to hear your decision. Such is the reasoning I rode ahead to give you warning," Hamzi says from his cold, stone seat.

"I see, we mustn't waste time then," the Elder agrees. "What's the other manner of business then, Hamzi?"

"Well, my Elder, as we know, Elium has been in a time of peace for many moons. However, his grace has urged me to share that there have been uprisings at the border just east of here." Hamzi says. "Uprisings? Of what sort?" Valincias asks.

"It seems some of the refugees have formed their own militia at the Savarian border. They seek passage and land in Elium, as they have made it clear they shan't back off their advances and looting until the king grants them this," Hamzi explains.

"Hmm, and what would our king have us do then? I'm sure he requested a course of action, correct?" the Elder asks.

Hamzi gathers his breath for a moment before saying, "He wants you to… deal with them, my Elder."

The Elder quickly responds in displeasure, "Hamzi, do not come in here and tell me our king has asked me to massacre refugees? I beg of you, there has to be more to this. I cannot act so wickedly."

"His grace has been informed that there are many exinhabitants of the Isle of Reeds…" Hamzi stops momentarily.

"Go on. You are of no bother to us," I say, acknowledging mine and Jov's origins to the Isle.

"Very well. The king wishes us to wipe them out, he fears another war on the horizon with the disgruntled people. It also happens they've picked up many others on the way. They are no army, but they shall be a formidable force, our scouts say," Hamzi adds.

"I see," Elovis says, his tone clipped. "For now, we focus on Lady Illia. We shall revisit the other matter tomorrow. Jov, please show

Hamzi to his quarters and then meet me out front near the stable. I shall see you all tonight; perhaps I shall have an answer by then regarding the proposal," the Elder says as his paces recede from the sun-filled room.

"Way to make an entrance," I laugh, screeching my chair against the concrete floor.

"Ha. We can't all slip in with the shadows like you, friend,"

Hamzi jokes. "Tell me, lord, how is the keep? My mind has not forgotten these walls since I left to study at the capital's library."

Gliding toward the doorway, the heavy steps of the captain produce the words, "Safe and sound, my lord, the guard let no threat within a league of the keep," the captain says.

"You mean the guard can fill a lake with the amount of coin, jewelry, and more they've swindled," Jov says with a tinge of seriousness in his tone.

Making our way out into the torch-lit halls, we talk for a moment.

"Ha. Captain?! Do not tell me you have allowed your men to stray to thievery?" Hamzi says with a hint of laughter.

"I admit there are some bad berries in our ranks. We've caught a multitude stuffing their pants with jewelry or coin under the guise of 'taxation.' I myself have been returning to the market to reimburse goods found on some of these culprits. "They've been made examples of, I assure you, lord," Valincias says.

"I trust in you, my friend. This place is far cleaner of such actions than the capital. I believe in you to sort it out," Hamzi says.

"Time shall tell, my lord," the captain says before his brisk steps lead him away. "Shall we then?" Jov asks.

"Indeed, my friend, I need rest after the two moons cycle journey. Bale, would you accompany us?" Hamzi asks.

I shake my head no. "Go along, my friends. I shall see you tonight. Rest easy," I speak as their steps carry them toward the stairwell only paces away.

Standing still, I indulge myself in the moment; the noises of flickering torches, the smell of my three counterparts drifting away. Alas, nearly half the day has gone by in a flash.

Feeling an overcoming sense of drowsiness, I depart from where we three stood in the hall on a trip toward my room. Reaching my doors once again, I push the metallic hinges to open before closing them once more.

Trying to secure time alone, I lay on my bed and doze off to sleep.

I awake to a jostle as my internal system brings me to a panicked awakening.

Fearful I had missed my duty of escorting the guests from the capital, I run toward my window to see if I can still feel the sun's heat, and my panic subsides as the weaker warmth of the rays still come through the panes of glass.

Turning my attention to the silk robes dropped off before, I change and ready myself for the night ahead whilst wisps of fresh roses and dandelions fill my nostrils. The aroma is so sweet, I can almost taste it.

"The finest material. Worthy of its wearer, some may whisper," a woman says.

"Don't you have celebrations to attend to, my lady?" I say, turning my stance around and bowing my head. "Although I am honored by your presence, Lady Sylvia."

"The honor is all mine," she says as the sounds of her steps echo on the wooden floors. "How goes the day?" Lady Sylvia asks.

"The day is well, my lady, but if I may ask, what's the honor of your presence?"

She giggles. "Always straight to the point, Lord Bale. I come to ask a favor," the lady says with her steps guiding toward the fire pit.

"A favor of what sorts?" I inquire, creasing my brow in confusion.

"Well, I've just come from seeing Illia. It seems her escort has vanished into thin air, although I assume she scared him off," she chuckles. "On my walk to my husband's chamber, I thought of who I trusted the most to escort her for her introduction. Between you and Lord Jov, it was close. However, he has only two good eyes. You command a thousand," Lady Sylvia says, unmoving in front of the flame.

"My lady, I am honored, truly, but the Elder has already asked for me and brother to protect Sirs and Lady Arys," I respond. "You shan't worry about the Elder, my dear," she says, turning around and continuing with, "I shall inform him and Lord Jov of the changes; do not fret. Just see to it that Illia arrives promptly, you know how she dallies," before pacing her way out the door.

Kind yet firm is she in her request, or rather demand. Getting a word in is not wise with the lady of the keep, as she always gets her wishes fulfilled. Therefore, I set my mind toward escorting Lady Illia as I walk toward the open doors to close them once more.

Before too long, I find myself in the maze of halls yet again. This time, there is no sun warming the skin, as darkness has presumably set outside. Instead, the flickering of torches that are lit aflame every time the moon comes out replaces the sun's warmth.

This tends to be my favorite aroma in the entire hold, as it reminds me of the day Jov and I were brought to the keep. I do not remember every detail of the day, rather I just remember how cold I was at the time before being warmed up next to the fireplace in the Elder's chambers. Nevertheless, I shake those memories away, as I have made it to my next destination. I stand in front of yet another identical cedar door in the manor, a floor above my own. This door leaks a peach and lavender scent, which only grows and flourishes as the doors open with a pull of my hand.

"By the Loria, where did I put my necklace?!" the voice of a lady says, as frantic steps pace all around the room until eventually they come to a full stop.

"Lost necklace? Lost escort? Lady Illia, it seems you must be losing your mind," I smile.

"Lord Bale? Making jokes? Amongst being my escort? I ought to lose more if this is the result," Illia says.

Both hers and my laughter fill the air for a brief moment, until she says, "Ah! There it is!" and paces off.

As she goes to gather her necklace, I say, "I hope the celebrations of another year of life have been grand so far, my lady. Any presents that you favor?"

"Hmm, let me ponder. Perhaps my necklace from the capital father got me? New Daharian horse from Lord Hamzi? Or maybe the marriage proposal from the capital?" she says.

"Ah yes, I see you found out. Where did Prince Dedric end up? I'm patiently waiting for him to drop out of the wardrobe, hands and feet bound," I say, aiming to improve her mood.

"I sent him to the mountains to retrieve me the bluest flower he could find. I hope that gives me enough time to get through most of the evening," she says.

"Shall we? We must make the most of this time then. In addition to the forewarning that we mustn't be late," I propose.

She wraps her arm underneath my outstretched limb as we leave the room, navigating our way three floors below. Stopping our strides, we arrive at the ballroom as the noises and scents only grow in size and stature.

The great, large doors creak to an opening as the royal announcer exclaims, "May I introduce our lady of the hour? Lady Illia Elovis, first of her name and only child: heir to the Cedar throne."

There is a roar of hands coming together and voices whispering as we descend the grand staircase with my left hand gliding along the railing. Torches lining the walls emit smoke. A large chandelier casting light onto the room with each rattling of the chains it hangs from. And a mass of guests with heavy breaths of crisp wine scattered throughout. Gliding through the room, I feel my own heart rise to a higher beat, gripping the leather handle of my blade with my thumb resting on its sharp hilt. Lady Illia must feel my senses and nerves overloading, as she takes the lead in guiding us through the people.

"Mother, father... Captain, looking as grand as ever in your uniform," Lady Illia says as our steps come to a halt, far away from the crowd.

"My dear, you look like you're worth every gold coin in the capital," Lady Sylvia says after a laugh.

"It's true, my dear, you simply look priceless," Elder Elovis says.

"Lord Bale, you have my thanks," Lady Sylvia's words flow in my direction. "The honor is all mine, my lady," I say in response.

The crowd and our conversation come to a standstill in silence as the royal announcer hits his cane on the floor once more.

"'Tis my honor to introduce to you, Prince Dedric Arys of Doves Peak: Second of his name, third in line to the throne," the voice exclaims. "Loria's sake," Illia swears under her breath.

"Lady Illia!" a squeaky voice yells, coming through the ballroom doors.

I snicker for a moment as rapid steps decline the long stairway into the mass of bodies watching.

"Lady Illia!" the high-pitched voice cries out again amidst the now clamoring crowd, approaching where we stand.

"Lady Illia, one moment," the prince says, heaving for breath as his outline bends over.

"I have... returned... with the bluest flower from atop the mountainside," Prince Arys says, reeking of sweat, drawing many breaths between each word. "Elder Elovis, Lady Sylvia. My deepest apologies."

"Ha. My prince, 'tis Illia, who apologizes. She can be rather off-putting with her affection at times," Elder Elovis says mid-laugh.

From what I gather from the situation, the prince seems to be in high spirits about his return with the flower in hand. A triumph of sorts. Knowing Illia, however, it seems to be just a ploy to scare the man away.

As if planned, the sound of an angelic harp starts to play a slow tune, causing the crowd to drift into pairs as they begin their slow steps, side to side.

"It seems I arrived with perfect timing after all, my lord," the prince says, jingling the multitude of bracelets and necklaces he'd donned.

"Lady Sylvia, I would be honored to have this dance with you," he says again as his outline bows.

With a tug of my arm, I sense her true emotions amidst the gentleman's proposal. However, I can not hide my delight in the situation as a grin starts to poke through.

"That would be delightful. Lady Illia was explaining she wished you back by now," I say.

A swift and harsh kick to my left ankle causes pain to rise through my body.

"Wonderful," the prince releases.

"And Lord Bale, you have my thanks as well for accompanying her beauty in my absence," Prince Dedric says as I sense him put out a hand to shake.

"Oh, Loria, I'm dreadfully sorry. I meant for us to have a shake of hands, it slipped my mind—" the prince says as I cut him off with a grasp of his hand and firmly shake.

"I know, My Prince," I say. "And the honor is all mine."

"Wonderful... well then. Shall we?" the prince asks as Lady Illia lets go of my arm to imaginably accompany his.

Even without my sight, I can almost feel the glare emanating from Lady Illia in my direction as the couple's steps immerse me in the crowd.

"Come along then, Bale. There are some guests we shall attend to," the Elder says as I turn my head away from where the two disappear into the multitude of guests.

Both I and the captain follow Elder Elovis and Lady Sylvia step by step whilst the Elder seems to greet each passerby with a

"Good-moon," until we come to a halt.

Elder Elovis and Lady Sylvia stop their movements as I feel three unique sets of vibrations waltzing our way amongst the hundreds of others.

One I know for certain to be Jov, as the pattern of his heart thumping is ingrained in my mind, while the other two vary in size and noise with each step. One vastly heavier than the other, while the steps behind the larger paces seem light as a feather with almost no creaks in the wood beneath their strides.

"Duke and Duchess! How nice 'tis to see you both again," the Elder says.

"Oh bother, 'tis our pleasure. 'Tis been too long, Duggan. How wonderful to see you again, and of course, your lovely wife," a Daharian woman's voice exclaims.

"Ah yes, Duchess, truly it has been. I believe 'tis been nearly seven cycles of the moon passing since? What was it? Your coronation?" the Elder says.

Releasing a smell of roasted lamb the man must've eaten, the duke replies, "Indeed it was, friend, but now we celebrate your

lovely Illia." Standing still in the ballroom, the four converse.

"I do hope you both are in good spirits? Please tell me, how was the journey?" Lady Sylvia asks.

"Ah well, bringing the wine from the capitol had to be the best decision we made," the Duchess says whilst laughing. "It at least made the trip memorable."

The four laugh for a moment before the Elder asks, "And your time here? I hope you have been well taken care of?"

"All has been more than grand, Duggan. This event, the wine, the service. Although he seems to be living in our every shadow," the duke teases regarding Jov behind the pair. "And you, my lady?" Elder Elovis asks.

"The manor has been quite wonderful, I must say," Lady Arys says in her native Daharian accent. "A nice change of pace from the gaudy castle, the smaller space has been a wonderful experience, as I feel we've been visiting a lovely cabin for days now," Duchess Arys says.

I raise my brow in disbelief, receiving a nudge from the captain to regain composure behind the respective conversation.

"Ha. Well, I'm delighted you have enjoyed yourselves," the

Elder says. "We shall leave you to it, then. Please find us if you need anything. Jov shall assist you in any way needed; all you need to do is ask," the Elder says as we begin our walk away

During our strides from one guest to the next, from one politically polite conversation after another, a distinct smell rises out of the rest, identical to one earlier in the day. It comes in the form of rattling glass along with the quick repeated question, "May I take this, sire?"

It seems to be a servant assisting with the event going on. Yet, at second glance, the outline of the tall man emits a smell of wine coming off his breath.

Odd it is, as the servants in bedrooms do not often serve at our social gatherings. This leaves me with no choice but to probe the figure further amidst my suspicions. As I closely listen, I notice the steps of the 'servant' are too light to be an underweight and starved member of the help. Furthermore, his breath reeks of wine, which all servants know they are not permitted to drink within the walls of the keep.

I could very well be overthinking this situation, but I cannot shake the feeling of something being off with this man, as he has now gained my full attention.

"Pardon me, Elder, I seem to be parched. I shall only be a moment fetching some water," I say, masking my concerns.

With an agreeable "Hmm" and pat on my shoulder, the Elder releases me from his and Lady Sylvia's guard as the pair glide away with Valincias in tow.

My mental state takes a turn as my mindset shifts from protector to hunter. With each tread on the wood, I gain ground on the subject, stalking the man. Trying to walk parallel to the heavy set of paces and shadowed tall outline, we mirror each other in our steps. Attempting my best to blend in amongst the crowd, my sole focus lies on observing the man's actions and listening attentively.

In my mind, I make note of the growing list of things that don't sum up for a servant. Another one to add is his unbothered disposition by the entire event, almost displeased in his tone as the repetition of his questions grows silent.

Even more alarming is the small metallic clanks coming from him, too quiet to know what it may be. I suppose that's what causes me to act, but not before the royal announcer bangs his cane and voids the room of noise once more.

"Fine, ladies and gentlemen, would you now turn your attention to the center of the floor," his voice rings.

"'Tis my honor to present Lord Duggan Elovis, Elder of this manor, first of his name and ruler of Cedar Keep. He shall be accompanying his daughter, Lady Illia Elovis, first of her name and heir to the Cedar throne, on this dance to commemorate her celebration," the voice bellows.

The high-pitched sound of a harp envelopes the silence in the air with each tug of its strings. Playing a sweet and melancholy tune with each pluck as Lady Illia and her father slowly drift, step, and turn in their dance.

Meanwhile, a dance of my own is ensuing, as with each two steps forward 'tis followed by one step back from the imposter.

Twirling and turning is my mind, observing the quick movements of his hand picking up and placing glasses down. We both waltz between guest after guest until his steps become heavy and his breath becomes repetitive.

Fear and uncertainty fill my mind, but only for a moment, as I lose the man among the guests. Picking up on the trail once more as his voice projects closer, this time asking, "May I take these plates from you?" the voice almost sounding in arm's reach.

To my surprise, the familiar tone of Duke Arys replies, "That would be grand of you, but perhaps bring me another glass of wine?"

"Of course, sire—" he responds.

"Of course, Duke," Jov interrupts. "Of course, Duke," the voice replies.

"That'll be all," Jov says once more, just a few paces from where I listen.

With the heavy footsteps retreating toward the kitchen, I hear the man muttering beneath his breath. For a moment, upon reaching the steps, I think, *Leave it, 'tis simply a disgruntled servant,* but my curiosity nags at me, and dropping it is simply not in my nature. Deciding to take action, I follow the hefty steps that lead me back to the grand staircase I once descended. Only this time, entering underneath where the servants' tunnels open from behind a doorway. Crossing the threshold and stepping into the tunnel, an unease sets into my skin, overtaking the emotions of the joyous event.

"Turn your attention, ladies and gentlemen, to the front of the room for the opening of gifts," the royal announcer says, only this time much weaker, as I drift into the torchlit halls.

Smelling of dirt and moisture, I reach out with my hands to find the narrow walls close by.

Aiming to track the man I once stalked now seems hopeless, with what sounds like thousands of steps echoing in the brick-and-mortar hallways. I'd nearly forgotten about the size of the servants' staff that worked to upkeep the manor, and now trying to find one imposter amongst hundreds seems daunting.

I feel an overwhelming amount of paces wandering the small and shallow halls, all unique in pattern yet so similar in scent and words.

"Good-moon, my lord." "What brings you here, my lord?" I often receive, gliding past each person, putting themselves to work.

In all truth, I do not know what brings me here. I do not have the answers to their questions. I cannot decide between a concern, a curiosity, or a desire? It all seems so silly standing in this small hall, chasing the shadow of a man who has done no wrong. On what?

Instinct? Belief? Noises I only think I heard through an ever-clamoring crowd? Gods, am I even chasing the right fleeing steps?

Upon these worries crossing the front of my mind, I stand for but a moment before turning my hips around and brushing the walls with my hands as I navigate back to the doorframe. Not knowing what awaits me on the other side, I take a deep breath, ready to absorb all the noises and smells thrown my way. However, with each step, the buzz and crowd grow louder; with each step, the groans and nature of the emotion pouring from the room become clear. The door swings open as I expect a massive celebration; instead, I find groans and screams of mass hysteria.

In the chaos, I can hardly decipher anything; in the hundreds of raging paces, I can't identify who is who as they move so fast and recklessly.

"Please show restraint and calm yourselves," I hear the Elder scream far off.

It seems rather hopeless of an ask, though, as none seem to slow their panicked movement nor quiet their groans of fear. The roars of screams and feet shuffling grow louder than any applause given all evening as I dash into the room in search of clues. Pushing and shoving through the crowd of guests reduced to chaos, as with each step, they disregard their cares for anyone other than themselves.

Now, in the stampeding crowd, I surf through the vast amount of bodies, attempting to locate the Elder and his family. During the moments of slipping and dodging the jabs of disregard, I hear a familiar low baritone cry out, "Breath, damn it!"

Hearing this, I am able to locate the cause of the commotion and head in its direction as even more voices produce wails for assistance. In a short time, I come to find the gathering of bodies around the scene in my blurred vision.

"By the gods," I mumble.

AMON
BETWEEN THE LEAFS

I can hardly see with the rain pelting down as my eye fixates on the driver speaking to his partner. "Gods, that's cold," the back of the guard holding the reins says, pulling his brown hood over his head.

"Damn right," one of the transporters in their beige cloak replies. "'Tis frigid, and I'm fucking starved."

It's hard to tell who is talking as the pair situates themselves facing away from us on the wooden bench. I close my good eye to increase my chance of listening in.

"On the bright side, 'tis only a two-moon journey from here. It doesn't hurt that we've already dredged through most of the thick of the storm. Should be just light drops from here on out," the driver says.

His compatriot scoffs. "This is light drops to you?"

"This is nothing compared to the isle, sire. It would rain for months, flooding the marsh and lands in between at times," the carriage driver says.

"Seems even the powers above wanted that damned island to be overrun, whether by rain or by steel," the fellow guard says, jingling his chainmail with a shallow laugh. "The Loria bless the souls we lost to those devils."

Interrupting our captor's conversation, a fellow prisoner sitting across from me asks in his Savarian accent, "Say, you don't think you could stop for a piss? Mentioning all this rain seems to have stirred something in me."

A harsh bash of the cage causes the moisture on top of the steel bars to drop.

"Shut your mouth," the guard turns to us and says, revealing the officer's pin in his cloak.

As the officer turns back around with a clank of his armor, the guard continues to shiver and mutters, "Damn Savarians, snake-tongued creatures. Piss yourself to sleep."

The officer isn't the only one displeased, as those of us in the cage cry out with each dump of water. I, however, feel nothing but rage sitting upright against the bars—void of any other emotion and thought except ones of unleashing my anger. In my red haze, my eye gravitates to the ragged and tattered group of vagabonds. Each man and woman seemingly broken, bruised, or cut, with half of the ill-fated bodies hanging their heads out of the cage, heaving.

Neglected and beaten by those who entrap us, half of those who started this journey met an early end before we reached the looming needles of the cedars.

The figures who made it thus far aren't far better off. It seems nearly everyone who sits all around suffers injuries. From a bloody toe to losing a hand, even the unfortunate man holding his own right foot. Each city has its own take on how to deal with thieves, murderers, and criminals alike—some appearing excruciatingly painful.

Looking in all directions at the cruel punishments that abound, one would think I may be grateful to be fully intact, but nay, the harsh treatment of others only fuels my inner fire and desire to fight back. Nevertheless, we all huddle together in our rage and sorrow.

Whether by the thought of creating body heat or due to the fact that we are bound and locked to our respective spots. Ropes tying our limbs and chains around our feet, reminding us that we belong to those who navigate between the lush trees and droplets of water.

In my dire circumstances, my eye intriguingly watches the rough-edged rope sinking into my skin, too tight to shimmy free of and too thick to bite through, even the sharpest of weapons would struggle to saw through the coarse thread. However, not too long into my pondering of the bindings, I jolt back to reality as the leading officer breaks the silence. "Do you see that? The smoke coming through above the trees?" the officer asks.

In return, his compatriot responds, "I pray 'tis a spot to eat and get some ale."

The officer looks at his compatriot, guiding the horses. "As do I, but be mindful, it could be any number of things. We must proceed with caution," he says.

"Caution to what? Bandits? This deep into the keep's land?" the driving guard asks.

"Hm, foolish if so. I don't know, but there's far worse than bandits in this forest. Just keep a lookout," the officer says as he glares toward the road ahead.

As if their conversation has pissed off the powers above, the rain begins to pick up with much ferocity, and the wind starts to blow with so much force, the guards on horses around us struggle to calm their steeds. In response to the heavy hail and struggle to manage the mounts, the officer sends out orders to his men. "Damn this, Eigor. Pull this thing off the road, we'll make camp for the night," he demands.

The steering guard asks in return, "Are you sure you wish to yield tonight, officer? We may be better off just pushing through for the last two days."

With a deep breath, the officer mutters, "'Tis about damn time for a good night's rest, even the prisoners need a reprieve from this rain. It already cost us enough lives."

"As you wish," Eigor says, pulling the reins, steering the hoofing steps in a new direction off the road.

With little care for the life they haul, the trolley hits every hole and rock, causing more and more prisoners to empty their stomachs.

"For the gods' sake, get ahold of yourselves," I mumble to myself as the men and women around me moan in misfortune. These souls know nothing of true pain. I've survived countless situations worse than this. Living off of swamp vines in Lymre for a moon cycle, escaping the Daharian desert, even living through the bone-eating frost at the very tip of Elium.

Yet now I am trapped and caged amongst the weak-willed, filled with defeat and disgust. I feel like a fool. I feel a slave to my emotions and numbness to be in a situation like this. Not only because I am bound but also because of the information I uncovered shortly after leaving Daharia. However, that seems pointless now, between my days traveling to follow a lead and being detained, I lost count of the moons after twelve. I lost hope after ten, but my anger only grew under each passing light of the moon.

I can't help but think about my partner almost every day and what he's been up to. I left Sylas in the desert as we both went our separate ways. I can only hope he brought the Collectors Guild a semblance of something to show for our contract. That or at the very least, bought us some more time. If not, everyone in this cage sitting around me could be met with a doomed fate at the hands of one of the guild's hunters.

Breathing in the cold air to match my frigid disappointment in myself, Silas, and the guild, I observe the life around me releasing mist with each heave. All I can see are the dirty and almost lifeless bodies shivering, who now squarely sit next to the trees as the guards hop off their steeds to tie the horses' leads.

Whilst the guards make way to set up camp for the night, the tan-skinned Savarian speaks once more, smiling underneath his black stache. "About that piss then?" he asks.

A few snickers come from the dozen or so guards who attempt to pitch tents and make fire. That is until the lead officer speaks. He giggles under his breath as words emit from the mouth swallowed in matted black hair, "Piss, you say, friend? That's what you need?" he asks as he motions his hand to one of the steel-covered men. "I believe one of the guards can help you with that.

Don't want you to feel neglected, after all."

Per the lead guard's request, a steel-covered man pulls down his chainmail and begins to piss on the cage, catching everyone in it. Uncaring for the pleas of the prisoners to stop, the man makes life in our steel box that much more unbearable. Coming to an end of the stream, the officer jokes again, "Did that fulfill your desire?" before snickering once more.

To the guard's surprise, the prisoner fires back once more in his foreign accent, "Not really, looked a bit lacking, but who am I to judge."

The mood and facial expressions shift as quick as the rain falling on their armor. With looks of disgust and disregard, they turn their back once more to fix their spots for the night. Sleeping under their tents, safe from the cold, the guards dream of better weather and safer travels, except the two guards who would change watch every now and then throughout the night.

Left alone to think in the darkened and moist forest with the dwindling number of prisoners, I escape to my thoughts. *Twelve moons and no help from him. No. More than twelve moons and not a sign of help.* Yet what else should I expect? Why would Syla come? How would he even know? I'm on my own; I've always been on my own. That's all I've ever known.

If I can just get my hands on a weapon, I could possibly escape. Alas, none have come close to my reach since being caught and detained months ago.

Losing myself in the resentment of my situation and feeling full of loneliness, I turn my thoughts to those around me. 'Tis utterly disappointing that no words come from the bodies of thieves and murderers during the guards' slumber. I would think their true character, their will to live, their desire to survive would rear its head, but alas, their spirits are broken—or at least that's what it seems on the outside. None even give the slightest indication of trying to hatch an escape, their wills truly diminished.

It seems pointless to continue the plotting in my head, as all life around has dozed off, even those who stand watch waver in and out of sleep. Sighing in frustration, I refuse to lose focus mentally as my eyes grow heavy in the mobile prison. Even after weeks on only straw and wood with little rest, I fixate my mind on staying vigilant in case action is needed. However, I eventually cannot compete with my weary eyes, and I give into nature and try to find comfort in my slumber.

Opening my eyes once more, I find myself at a crossroads. Sand waving in the air as it slowly recedes into brush, reeds, and eventually solid soil. The air thick in heat but not nearly as hot as when I found myself engulfed in the desert. Looking around, I am all alone amongst the vast land stretching ever so far off in all directions. Lush trees on fire to the north, streams rushing swiftly with what looks like wine to the east, and lastly, rolling thunder with humongous tidal waves underneath approaching from the west. They all seem to be heading on a collision course ever so quick, converging at the border where I stand. Rapidly, they all approach, and with crashes and clatters of all the environments coming down on top of me, I awake.

With my eye flying open, angst causes my heart to race. Slowly, I come to my senses, allowing my racing heart to ease into a slower pace as I find familiar surroundings. Alas, I am still locked in the metal cage, the wheels turning once more, the hooves of the horses trotting along. I can't decipher what is more disturbing in this moment, the dream that I just had or the unchanging circumstances of the iron box and heavy storm.

Yet my thoughts are not alone in speaking as the rain continues to shout and squeal with each drop onto the lives below. An unrelenting storm brewing above, not yielding in quite some time as we continue our venture toward what the guards call 'justice.'

The driver, Eigor, speaks while my senses adjust to the rude awakening. "Raging hell, this damn rain is causing the horses to kick up mud," he says.

Which leads to the officer rudely joking in return, "Ha. I think you look better that way. It covers up that damn island skin."

Only adding to the tension, a voice cries out, "God's, you're a prick!"

The officer whips his body around in haste and screams, "Son, you're in for a fucking beating when this carriage stops. Do not think the Elder shall even bat an eye about a lowlife like you having a couple of extra bruises and scars." Looking at the tan, black-haired prisoner who made the comment.

"How about you take these bindings off and we find out?" the bound man across from me exclaims once more.

The officer scoffs and spits into the cage before turning his body back around to face where the horses lead.

The tension in the air is as thick as the bark we pass with each trot of the steeds. More hooves ride along the muddied earth as the carriage wheels keep churning with each whip of the dark, wet leather.

Although the guards surround us from every angle, I put my now aware and awake mind toward hatching an attempt to flee.

The bars' separation behind the guard is too narrow. It's too rash to cause a commotion in the cage. The transporters and their blades are too far away.

Unaware that my eyes are tracking opportunities for release, I hear a voice. "Not now, friend," the foreign troublemaker whispers.

Turning my head from the guards sitting in front, I meet his gaze. The downpour makes it hard to shed light on his features beyond his tan skin and dark hair.

"Be patient," he says again, as if he hears my plotting thoughts.

"Quiet!" a guard riding behind the transport shouts, hitting the bars once more, causing an excess of water to fall downward.

While I feel numb to the droplets, I find myself rather curious about the man who seemingly read my mind. I sit and watch as I try to uncover more about the mysterious figure who so boldly challenges our captors.

His short black hair and goatee are riddled with dirt and grime. His torn, soiled garments are identical to the rest of ours, as we all wear the same brown shirt and pants. Nothing is too distinct about the man himself aside from his accent.

Although, as I examine the Savarian, it seems he feels me sizing him up. Noticing my gaze, he gives me one more glare with his dark brown eyes before turning his attention down to his rope-bound hands and then the road ahead.

Whilst processing the man in my mind, the horses carrying us toward our sentencing abruptly stop their hooves and neigh in dismay.

"Whoa there!" Eigor yells.

"What's the meaning of this? Are you blind?" the lead officer yells at the steering guard.

Trying to see the cause of the commotion, I peek through the iron-clad bars. Unsurprisingly, I can't see a damned thing but rather hear a voice call out toward the carriage from a distance, "Pardon me, sire. Amongst this rain, I could hardly see where I was going."

The officer in front whispers under his breath, "Fucking fool," as he hops off the wooden bench.

I only catch a glimpse of the ongoing conversation in front of the multicolored mares as their heads sway back and forth. The rain falling on the tree branches and clanking onto the steel armor plates makes it deafening and certainly impossible to hear what they say far ahead.

Seeing the cloaked figure reach out and hand the guard coin, I assume they struck a bargain as both the guard and the soaking wet robes enveloping the person make their way back toward the carriage.

The first fast-approaching figure I assume to be the lead officer, wearing a chainmail vest and pants, while his long beige cloak is now muddied from treading the soil. The figure in tow is wrapped in a black cloak, concealing most of his characteristics. "What's the matter of this, officer?" the guard at the reins asks.

The guard on foot replies, "He needs passage to Kindwood. It'll be on our way to the keep. Only a day's journey."

The officer signals for the mysterious figure to climb up the side of the carriage first. With his ghost-like skin, he heaves himself onto the carriage, the color returning moderately as he grips the wood in order to climb up next to the driver. The officer who struck the deal doesn't follow suit, saying instead, "One moment," as he approaches the back of the carriage. The officer yells once more, this time in an angered tone, "Someone bring me that shit mouth from out of the cage!"

Suddenly, at the officer's orders, the cage door flies open. "If any of you move an inch, I shall cut you down with no remorse," the guard shouts as they rip the foreigner, who had warned me moments prior, from his position and slam the door shut.

"I told you what would happen if this carriage stopped, filth," the officer says as they kick out the legs of the prisoner.

"Aw, how sweet, you remembered me. Must really have made quite the impression on you," the prisoner says.

Jumping off the front wooden bench amidst the Savarian's words, the guard who is navigating us exclaims, "Sire, what is this? What are you doing?!" hollering against the sounds of the loud falling rain.

"Eigor, shut your damn island devil mouth. Get on the front of the transport before I beat respect into you too," the officer says, looking at the questioning guard.

As the guard leads his steps away, turning his back on the unfortunate prisoner, a furious kick to the stomach keels the troublemaker over. "Filthy swine," the officer says.

I watch as the man who has just been knocked down, leading to his face meeting the earth, picks his chin up and spits on the officer.

"What is he doing? He's going to get himself killed, the fool," I mumble.

The Savarian's actions seemingly only fan the flame of the officer's rage as he yells, "Pick him up!" before another guard, who had been riding behind us on his horse, picks up the poor bound man as the wicked officer strikes him across the face a handful of times.

"Next time, I won't be so merciful," the officer says, delivering one final blow and heading back to his seat.

Amid all the injustice and prejudice, I notice that the shadowy passenger doesn't budge an inch from his stance, looking forward. 'Tis incomprehensible to me how he doesn't turn to see the proceedings, but then again, 'tis in the nature of most men to not want or need to witness such things.

As the now-beaten and bruised prisoner is being placed back into the crowd of bodies, the cage door slams shut once again. The man who delivered the punishment returns to his seat as if nothing major had just happened and bellows, "I wouldn't get too close to the likes of them. Believe me, they'd eat the skin off your bones."

Turning to us for only a glimpse, the man reveals his green stare before turning back around and scooting away from the cage. During his brief glare, I take mental note of the short blade of a dagger peeking out from underneath his wrinkled cloak on the bench. Shaking it off, I know 'tis not uncommon, as nearly every traveler brings some form of ensured safety. But then again, there is a feeling in my gut I shan't shake.

My intuition aside, the driver sends a short glare toward his commanding officer before saying, "Right then. Off we go," lashing the horses almost as hard as the punches the officer threw.

Once again, the wood creaks beneath us, this time from the horses moving their feet rather than the shifting dry heaves of the ill bodies. Our journey is so close to being over, and I believe we all, in some way, wish to arrive at our destination. Whether that is for reprieve in a bar or, for most of us, reprieve in a cell, everyone who has taken part in this trek seeks rest and warmth.

Before too long, the swift steps of the horses come to a pause, but the noise does not cease as the officer says, "Guess we found what was emitting the smoke."

Hearing his words, I look to the side, out ahead of the horses, to see what the officer is referring to. A small stone hut, living amongst the rather large trees, emitting smoke out its chimney. Upon drawing closer, we could clearly hear the chatter and banter coming from inside, even over the loud storm looming above.

Gaining ground on the tavern and eventually arriving, I watch as the guards who once strolled behind and ahead of us climb off their horses and tie them to a wooden post. All three who sit on the carriage climb off and make their way to the ground in hopes of finding a quench for their needs within the wooden doors.

The cloaked stranger, still revealing no features, is the only one not to go straight for the door as he makes his way into the forest before pulling down his pants to relieve himself.

The words "I need ale, a shit, and a pie" from the driver draws my eyes from the bushes to the guards on the opposite side of the cage.

"Ha. Go find a spot in the bushes then, you and Gregory are on first watch," the commanding officer says.

The pair of guards grunt in agreement to the order, not as if they have a choice.

"We'll make sure to relieve you in a bit. Or perhaps not, 'tis up to the ale," the lead guard jokes as he walks away, making his way to the door with guards and the stranger in tow.

The pair of guards sigh in frustration as the handful of steel enters the smaller tavern along with the cloaked guest.

Looking at my less guarded situation, whilst the two captors take relief sitting on a stone bench facing away from us, I decide to act. Subtly, I place my bound hands around a grainy metal bar, attempting to saw through the rope. For mere moments, I act with haste, grinding the rope against the rigid bars. The thread slowly shaving off bit by bit with each thrust and pull, but not nearly enough to break free as the Isle native turns his head toward us. Retreating my hands back to my lap in a swift fashion, the guard stares at me. Thinking repercussions are nigh, I sit vigilantly in watch in case action is needed as the guard stands and approaches the carriage.

"In good spirits, I offer mercy," the short and thin guard says, speaking into the ironclad box.

Noticing the conversation and rising from the stone bench, his fellow tall and bulky guard in watch asks, "Eigor, what's the manner of this?"

Unrelenting in his approach amidst his brother in arms' question, Eigor continues, "Plead guilt now, and I shall allow you inside to get food and ale," he says, looking at the crowd of prisoners.

Sizing up my chances, I analyze the guard. He seems not to lack confidence in his words; however, he is lacking in muscle and height. Yet he stands proud, wearing a heavy set of steel and speaking with conviction. The guard, shorter in stature with bronze skin and black hair sweeping across his head, watches attentively with his brown eyes, monitoring for any sudden movement within the cage.

"Do not think me so naive of an escape. I or my fellow guard shall cut you in half should you attempt to run," he speaks once more.

His words bring my attention to his hand standing at the ready, holding the leather grip of the standard steel blade every guard is paired with.

"Eigor, you must quit. Officer Pekins could come out at any moment, and you know what he'll do to you if he catches you saying this," his fellow guard says.

Eigor turns to his fellow compatriot. "God's sake, do you wish for them to starve or freeze to death before they face punishment?"

In short response, the bulky man says, "At least that would lighten the load and we can be done with this god-awful trek."

Having heard more than enough from both guards, I turn my back to the bickering pair. Upon doing so, I face the inhabitants of the prison transport, only to see the mustached prisoner with his hands free of his bondages.

Stunned to see his freedom, the man holds a curved dagger in hand, nearly identical to the one the ominous passenger had flashed. The numbness of my emotions dissipates with feelings of anxiety and worry. I fear the guild found me, as I am well over my timeline for return. Perhaps I can explain my circumstances. Perhaps if I tell them about what I have uncovered and they shall be understanding? No, no. I'm afraid not. They could care less about what I have to say. At least not a hunter sent to find me. Shit. I'm at his mercy, there's not a move I can make.

Yet amidst my thoughts, contemplating the Collectors Guild sending out a hunter for me, I make an upbeat realization as I sit in silence, leaning upright against one of the worn-down, arching metal beams. Feelings not felt in many moons wash over me as excitement and adrenaline flow effortlessly through my veins. The cause for this is my sense of the tides turning when, out of nowhere, the bushes start to rustle with branches snapping in abundance.

However, I'm not the only one to notice, as Eigor interrupts his argument with his fellow guard, startled by the noise.

"Wait. Did you hear that?" the driver asks, taking his gaze off his compatriot and turning them toward the thousands of trees sitting behind the carriage.

Taunting his partner, the other steel hawk approaches the ferns and leaves. "What's the matter, Eigor? Not afraid to carry around criminals but afraid of some rabbits in the weeds?" he says.

While observing from inside the carriage, I can see what the guards cannot. At first glance, it looks like the bark is alive, mobile, and, most importantly, armed. Concealed beneath leather masks and hoods, a group of individuals awaited our arrival, disguised in a variety of attire, from steel plates to cloth cloaks. They've positioned themselves behind the bark of the cedar trees lining the roadside near the tavern. At least twenty strong in numbers, if not more, men and women preparing to strike.

"Gregory, get back here," the driver pleads to the man deep into the row of trees, but it matters not, as his words are too late.

Happy not to have to rely on my patience; before the bold and rash guard can turn to his compatriot, an arrow glitters in the air with its steel tip. Floating in the passing wind for mere seconds, the arrow finds its new home in the eye socket of the naive guard.

As the soulless body of the guard hits the cold earth, Eigor's voice rings throughout the air, "'Tis a trap!" whilst he draws his sword.

To every ablebody's surprise, the tavern door doesn't swing open hastily. It seems they can't hear the rumblings of an escape happening a few paces away. Or at least that's what I shortly believe. As Eigor reaches the wooden doorframe, it slowly creaks open, only for a thud to follow. The body of the once-cloaked passenger falls out of the door, now impaled with a sword in his stomach. Dark blood spills from his wound, contrasting sharply with the grass of the earth.

Only moments after the lifeless body hits the ground, the guards spill out of the tavern, wielding swords and reeking of ale, a few bodies lighter in numbers than before. Meanwhile, women and men emerge from the forest, some devoid of steel plates, armed with an assortment of weapons, launching their assault on the transport's protection.

I quickly shake myself out of the confusion and panic of the moment as emotions of relief wash over me with a clank of the gate opening. The Savarian, free of his rope and chains, kicks the door open. Hopping out and facing the onslaught of vagabonds, the man clasps arms with one of the bandits, as if in greeting.

"Good to see you in decent health," the woman says to the escaped prisoner.

"And to you. Perfect timing, it seems, friend," the shorter, dark-skinned man replies.

"We would have attempted it last night, especially after watching you take that beating, but Jyn insisted on having patience," the bandit responds.

"All is well, friend. She picked the right time, don't fret, but for now, we must be swift," the mustached man says.

With both nodding to one another, the Savarian turns back to the cage and addresses us. "Listen to me. My name is Leonard DeHall. I am simply a man offering you freedom. You are free to go as you please, do as you like. We ask for nothing in return. If you do wish to join our band of traveling misfits, there is more than enough ale and certainly an abundance of coin in your future. But if you prefer to meet your maker, by all means, stay here," he says with a laugh.

"Free them," Leonard says to the man he embraced moments prior.

The bandit climbs up into the entrapment and, one by one, cuts the ropes and unlocks the chains with his blade. With little hesitation amid the ongoing fight, the mass of prisoners exit the steel cage. Through all of this, I feel a rush of adrenaline along with a mixture of hope. With no insight into why what's going on is going on, I rise to my feet as the last to leave. I feel my bones pop and ache beneath me whilst I hunch over as I head to the exit. In my process of escaping, I can't help but glance at the chaotic scene outside the cage. Men and women falling to their knees with grievous injuries, guards being choked and beaten with clubs and morning stars, arrows whizzing through the air, seeking their resting places in the skulls of the guards, and the dirt being littered with iron armor and red blood.

Exiting the back of the carriage, I grab our rescuer by the arm as he helps me down to the blood-stained soil below. He extends his hand for a handshake and asks, "What's your name, friend?"

"Amon," I whisper, shaking his hand with my own.

"Nice to meet you, Amon; call me Leo," he says with a smile. The man then grabs the sword embedded in the fallen Gregory, pulls it out, flips it up, and grabs it by the blade.

"Well, Amon, the choice is yours," Leo says, offering me the sword.

I don't feel the need to answer with words but rather a nod of my head and grasp of the iron blade as I turn to face the ongoing fight. Concentration makes my mind as sharp as the tip of an arrow as I dart toward the mass of battling bodies.

In front of me, two guards widely approach. Sliding to one knee, I swiftly sever the leg of one of the steel-plated opponents.

As he crumbles to his knees, I rise and slice open his throat in one fluid motion. Seeing his counterpart fall so fast, the other guard tries to run away. A coward, one who will not escape my grip.

I pick up the blade from the dispatched guard and hurdle it toward the fleeing steel plate. Making almost no noise at all, the blade embeds itself in the back of the scared man's neck.

Admiring my toss, I'm quickly brought back to the scene around me as a guard lunges at me from out of my good eye's peripheral vision. Quick and cunningly, I grab his arm as he thrusts, allowing me to deliver a devastating gut blow with the steel of my own.

Immersed in the frantic and chaotic scene, I can't help but smile at my newfound freedom and the chaos rushing through my blood.

At least during battle, I can feel something. Feel alive, be able to experience something other than my deep numbness and anger. With that thought, two more guards in steel plates approach but fall just as fast as those beforehand. With two downward slices after a bull's charge, their bodies lay lifeless on the earth.

Whipping my head around in all directions to observe incoming threats, I notice I am one of the only prisoners still fighting. Yet that won't be the case for long, as my body starts to give way with the lack of water and food. Having been caught up in my dramatically changing scene, I have become unaware of the bandits retreating back into the natural cover of green leaves and towering trees until now.

With my limbs feeling weak and my body rather exhausted, I lean into my rage, as 'tis the only thing that fuels me. Continuing my fight due to my lust for blood and retribution, I hear a voice repeating itself. "Shit. Shit. Shit."

I turn to see the guard who had offered a deal before being backed into a corner against the stone wall of the tavern. Two newly released prisoners, armed with a club and a dagger, close in on him from both sides. It feels cruel, unfair, and unjust, yet I find myself simply watching as the two narrow in on the frightened guard.

"Fine. Fuck it, let's do it," I watch the guard Eigor exclaim, assuming a defensive stance with his blade pointed toward the pair. The two prisoners laugh at his claim and one of them says, "Where's our deal now?"

"You know, I think I'd like to make my own deal now," the other prisoner chimes in. "I shall take that sword, and in exchange, we'll kill you quickly."

Looking like his fate is sealed, I can't help but intervene in the bleak scene. Moving with haste, I plunge my steel through the back of the prisoner who holds the dagger. A crimson liquid bursts through his chest as my pointed tip protrudes through the other side of his skin. In confusion, the other newly freed man whips around in shock before meeting his demise as his head rolls toward the door.

Not knowing why I took sides with the guard, I stand silent. In my mind, it just felt… necessary to save him. It feels… important.

Interrupting my inner examination of my actions, Eiogr screams, "By the Gods!" as he is taken aback by the splatter of blood on his uniform.

We both stand still, meeting each other's line of sight in silence. I guess at this very moment, we are processing what has just occurred: I went through with turning on my criminal comrades and he realizes his life was seconds from being nipped short. Nevertheless, the quiet is broken as he looks at me to say, "Thank you," as I glare back at him, bloodied sword in hand.

Before I can even nod in response, I am struck with a force so strong it reminds me of the time Sylas and I were run into by one of our bounty's horses.

Due to being knocked off my feet and hitting the earth, my senses go awry. Yet while my ears ring with pain, I hear Eigor as he shouts, "Wait!"

Looking up in my daze, I see two hazy figures of guards.

"He saved me!" the Isle of Reeds native yells, stopping the guard looming above me from completing a downward thrust of his sword.

The guard aiming his sword at me with deadly intent sighs with displeasure as Eigor reaches down with his outstretched arm to help me to my feet. Now standing, I find the battle over, a carnage of dead bodies, and only four guards left of the transport. Surrounded by the same leaf and bow emblem that had entrapped me before, my feelings of hate and disappointment return, strengthened by the fact that the cruel officer is still alive. His armor and once beige cloak now stained in red, brown, and yellow. Gazing into my good eye, his voice rings out, "Bind this man," while his hand points his blade toward my face. My cheek meets the steel tip of the officer's blade as he draws blood. To calm my nerves, as well as his, I slowly raise my hands in a peaceful motion.

Placing himself in between myself and the blade, the driver says, "Officer, I must plead for his well-being. He saved my life." "And by the Loria, we are all grateful, but this man just slew a handful of your brothers in arms," the officer says, unmoving, with his outstretched blade now pointed toward his fellow member of the guard. "Now step away, son, so I can bind this man."

As Eigor looks at me and reluctantly steps aside, the remaining guards encircle me, their weapons at the ready. The leading officer approaches from behind, holding a length of rope in his hand. The tension in the air is palpable as he stands just inches away from me.

Without a word, the officer swiftly loops the rope around my wrists, binding them tightly as the guards maintain their watchful positions, their eyes fixed on me, burning with suspicion and the lingering resentment for the fallen comrades I dispatched as we head back to the iron box the horses carry. In my thoughts, as my paces are tugged toward the cage, I wonder if this shall forever be my prison. Forever be my punishment. A man locked away, isolated in rage.

THE ELDER
THE GRAND BALLROOM

Not able to see over the herd of guests, servants, and royals, I make my way toward the aisle of tables nearest to ours at the front.

Voices engulfing the open room in panic and dysfunction rings throughout. Not knowing of the cause of the havoc, I cry out to the crowd, "Please show restraint and calm yourselves," but alas, it falls on deaf ears. Instead of dealing with the stampeding guests, I approach the scene where a multitude of people has crowded. Passing by gown after gown, I realize the request I made moments prior is far beyond conceivable as I stand horrified. As still as my necklaces, that show no sign of shaking their leaf pendants. I stand, not stunned at the crowd raging like wildfire or the eyes that gleam with pain and shock. Rather, I stand mute and watch all the diligent work as Elder to build a safe haven collapse before my very eyes.

The Loria save us.

Amidst the chaos, I notice the mass of weary and scared faces looking at me and feel as if I could reach out and touch the radiating emotions of sorrow and fright pouring from the eyes glued to me. However, I don't reach out, I don't move. I instead just stand, observing in a room designated for the celebration of my kin, frightened at the sight before me as the devil on my shoulder whispers in my ear, *The end is near*.

The end is in sight on a day that signifies a new year of life. How ironic. How cruel.

Taking in the scene, I look at the form of a lifeless boy. No foam of the mouth, not a blade in the gut, or even blood coming from any opening of the body; however, the royal family has a crucial limb snipped, as what remains lays on the grand ballroom floor—void of a heartbeat.

My thoughts spiral as I watch Prince Dedric lay lifeless after many heaving breaths for help before eventual stillness of movement. There is no more deal with the king of this nation, there is no more guarantee of legacy, there is no more safety.

Jolting me back to the present are the whispered words, "May the Loria have mercy on us all," from my wife in the background.

Turning my head in every direction, I find everyone looking for answers, looking for leadership. Even I ponder the drastically dire circumstances as the tragedy of royal lineage sprawls on the grand cedar ballroom floor. Upon seeing the body, however, I come to my senses as the fate of my family, my friend, and my keep lay squarely in my hands.

Before I can act, yell, or even pray, I hear, "Elder!" being called out by an accent of the Isle. Grabbing my shoulder, Lord Bale stands firm in his grasp of me as we match worrying facial expressions. "My Elder, what's going on? I do not understand why all I hear is screams and gasps," he says.

I bring my friend closer as I whisper in his ear the tragic news. Pulling away from the side of his head, I see his eyes widen in horror as his face goes pale. Yet, that doesn't stop him from speaking once more, staring intently with his worried golden brow.

"My lord, what do we do?" he asks.

I stand for a moment, trying to wrap my mind around the endless thoughts and outcomes as I, Lords Bale, Jov, Hamzi, and the duke and duchess, huddle around the center space of the room. "Give me a moment," I whisper.

Shit. I'm at a loss at this moment. All I can do is wipe my face with my hands repeatedly and try to think of something quickly.

Not hearing my request for moments of peace, a voice rings again. "My Elder, please. Give us an order," Lord Jov says.

Raising my head out of my hands, I see now that the looks around me are of those who need a true leader. One of action, one of wisdom.

Yet I find myself feeling void of any of this. "My lord?!" Jov says once more.

Accordingly, my voice rises and echoes throughout the decorated room. "A moment! But a moment! One must carefully, carefully approach this," I say.

"My lord, the longer we wait, the faster whomever has done this gets away!" Hamzi exclaims to my left.

I take a deep inhale before exhaling the words, "Captain, shut all the gates. The manor's and the exterior walls. No one gets in or out, I don't give a damn who it is. No one leaves."

Per my request, Captain Valincias nods and scurries away with haste as I turn to Lord Bale and Lord Jov. "Jov. Find the apothecary and order him here. I don't care if you have to rip him out of his slumber," I say, turning my attention to his brother. "Bale, scour the manor. Every single inch until we've checked every corner of this place. If there's someone at fault for this, they'll still be lurking around."

In the midst of my barking orders, I notice Jov looking at me curiously.

"What is it, Jov?" I ask.

"My lord, we won't leave your side if there is a chance an assassin is still in the walls," he says.

My mind fills with frustration at his comment. "For fuck's sake, the Loria has damned us. If we do not act now, and swiftly, my life and all those here shall meet an abrupt end from the royal executioner! If you care so much for my life, do as I ask," I say.

With the same motion as the captain before, the pair nod and hurry off to execute their respective duties after voicing concern. Whipping my head to face the trio of Hamzi, Duke Arys, and the Duchess, I ask, "My lord and my friends, I cannot offer my utmost apologies. There are simply no words to correct the unforgivable that has been done. I only ask that you three retreat to your chambers and stay there until word comes that the manor is safe."

he pair of Arys' utter no words, their eyes still wide as they stare at the body beneath our feet. Hamzi, however, bows.

"Of course, my lord. I shall see to it they get to their rooms safely," he says, guiding the pair toward the grandiose brown door they entered at the start of the night.

The remainder of my focus trails to my daughter and wife, who stand still in their beautiful, long dresses. I slip by each guest with my eyes set on the locks of black hair of both women in the front of the room next to the pile of gifts, while the guard slowly regains authority and allows the attendees to leave the room less frantically.

Striding toward the two, my breath grows heavy. Not from the heaves of my steps but rather the fear that takes over my mind, the fear that takes over my nervous system and every limb. A fear not held for myself or my position in this keep but for the two blue-eyed women and what the future may hold after this celebration of life.

Unable to reveal my true emotions as I reach my family, I say,

"My loves, we need to get you out of here at once."

Illia looks at me with tears in her eyes and says, "Papa, what did we do to deserve this?"

My wife grabs Illia by the hand and pulls her in close. "My dear, we'll be alright. Go do what needs to be done," she says, staring at me.

I lock eyes with the two as I wave my hand to signal a guard to come near. "Sire?" he asks as he steps closer.

"Please take Lady Illia and Lady Sylvia to their chambers. Do not stop for anyone or anything on the way. I must stress the importance of this," I demand.

"Of course, My Elder," he responds.

However, before they can take a step, I speak once more, "Guard. Once you're done, bring me Rylan when he's done here. I shall be waiting for his word in the key room."

"Yes, sire," the guard in his full silver armor says again before he whisks my beloved wife and child away.

As I watch the steel-plated bodyguard steer my blood and legacy out of the room, I escape to my thoughts. My next steps can either save the keep or ultimately be its downfall, I must act with much thought and care as I plot and scheme for the safety of those both inside and outside the halls of the manor.

With that in focus, I set out for the meeting room a handful of floors above as I ponder the delegated courses of action I gave to each of my keys to the castle. My Iron Key, Valincias, looks to bring a total lockdown to the hold. My Key of Snow, Jov, seeks out medical assistance within the manor, whilst the Golden Key, Hamzi, is escorting our guests to their room. Lastly, the most indispensable: Lord Bale, the Key of Shadows, is currently searching the entire castle with help from the guard to find the perpetrator of these crimes. I feel at ease as I rake over my thoughts of those carrying out my will and continue up the staircase. Passing by each hurrying and dutifully working guard with each step I take, I aim for the etched table with a map of Elium, finally arriving at my desired floor. Taking only moments to quickly reach my destination, I open the door with the four-blade key insignia above the entrance and approach my seat. In the dark room, I wonder if there can be mercy. Will His Grace show us kindness? Would I?

I should have known with talks of marriage and massacre, the Loria would not smile on us. Who are we to give and take? Who am I to even consider the idea of luxury in legacy yet still weigh the possibility of wiping out those who only ask for simple needs?

Unable to shake the thoughts, the door I sit watching impatiently flies open and does it for me.

"My lord," the Jov says with a bow of his head before walking in with our apothecary covered head to toe in vials. "We have finished our examination," Jov says.

"Thank you. If you would, go join Lord Bale's efforts," I ask. He nods and leaves, shutting the cedar door behind him.

"Rylan, sit. Speak. And with haste," I demand.

"Certainly, I shall, uh, make this quick, My Elder," the bald apothecary says as he jingles the glass vials on a strap across his chest, his steps taking him to the seat closest to my right.

In response, I give him a nod, signaling him to proceed.

"It didn't take me long to find the cause of death, all it took was a closer glance at the body. It seems the prince... well... suffered from a multitude of things," Apothecary Rylan smirks.

I lean forward in my iron chair, over the indentations of the table. "Rylan. I don't care about his ailments from who he slept with. Get on with it," I say.

"Oh, of course! Forgive me… I was just giving you the full story..." he trails off.

"Rylan," I snap.

"Apologies. You see, my lord, there were multiple bruises on the prince under this shirt. Not only that, but very small puncture wounds," Rylan says.

"Puncture wounds? Was he stabbed? I don't follow, there was no blood on the floor," I ask.

"No, My Elder, the wounds are tiny. Almost invisible to the naked eye. At first, I could not find any indication of what caused his death, but with a closer glance with my magnifier, it seems to be something quite precarious," he says. "Okay, go on," I pronounce.

"Now, I must admit that this may sound quite crazy… but I am under the assumption the holes are from stingers," he says.

Scoffing, I say, "A bee?!"

"Not a bee. No mere bee could be so deadly, but..." he trails off. "Go on," I say, matching his gaze.

"I've been studying a specific type of insect, a, um, phantom... now, they only frequent the mountainside but can be, um, quite deadly, especially with how many times the prince was apparently stung. The insect itself is named after their ability to kill almost anything, with the poison lasting not much longer than a day. However, 'tis stinger can look almost identical to any other bee, so I can't be a hundred percent certain," Rylan says.

I feel the blood rush away from my face as my thoughts of saving my family from the misfortune of the king's anger dissipate into the shadows hiding in the corners of the room.

"Thank you, Rylan. That'll be all," I say with a motion of my hand to leave. "Elder," he responds, bowing his head.

Before reaching the cold iron handle of the door, I call out once more, "Rylan…"

He turns himself around and replies, "Yes, my lord?"

"Not a word of this to anyone," I say, matching my serious emerald gaze with his. "Of course, my lord…" he says as he leaves.

My will folds with the door shutting, as I am left alone with this newfound discovery. I can't help but think about Illia in this moment; such a strong mind, such a ferocious will, my pride, my legacy… she has unknowingly doomed us all by having the prince fetch her flowers.

With my head in my hands, I contemplate what the future holds. Not just mine but also my family around me, my loyal advisors, and my loyal subjects. With this in mind, I say a short prayer.

Loria, help me, guide me. I beg.

Upon releasing my prayer, or rather a plea, the cedar door opens once more. In front of me, I now find my dear friend, one of foreign home. A man blessed at birth with his skin being kissed by the sun whilst complimented by his buzzed black hair and a short goatee. "My Elder, forgive my intrusion," the Lymrian voice calls out.

"Hamzi, my friend. You need to find safety in your bedchambers; we do not yet know when this evil shall rear its head in the manor once more," I say.

Pulling the handle of the door to a close, he says, "I know, my lord, but if you so bravely wish to be unguarded in your attempt to sort through this, I too wish to join your efforts. It won't hurt to have two minds sifting through this, at the very least. After all, this is what you sent me off to study." "Murder and treason?" I return.

Hamzi chuckles. "No, indeed not, but strategies and tactics are from the same family, some would say," he says.

After a moment of processing his words and inclining to agree with my Lymrian counselor, I point to the seat nearest to my right and say, "Alright then, take a seat."

"That was easier than I thought," he remarks. "In truth, my lord, I was worried about you. What's going through that mind of yours?"

At his question, I rapidly try to decipher what to tell the man. If I tell him the truth, he has a duty to tell his grace, but shall he? Shall he have mercy? Shall he understand?

"My Elder?" Hamzi's accent breaks my focus.

"Apologies, friend. I'm just thinking over what apothecary Rylan informed me," I say

"You should have led with that! What did he say was the cause, my lord?" he asks, looking at me intently with his brown eyes.

Pausing for a moment before I speak, I seal my and my family's future.

"Not a clue," I say.

"What do you mean? You don't have a clue what he said? I'm confused," he asks.

Still pondering whether or not to entrust the truth to my old friend, one I have seen grow since a boy, I say, "No, friend. Rylan simply found nothing."

"But how is such a thing possible, my Elder? It cannot be as if the Loria themselves have struck down the prince of this nation?

A prince devoted to his divines? No, no, I shall go drag Rylan back to the body by his hair if I need to," Hamzi says, rising from his seat. "No! Sit," I exclaim.

He looks at me, confused, in a mid-standing posture before he relaxes his body once more into the chair. Locking eyes in the dark room, I decide not to cower in my lies and to be the leader this time of tragedy needs: one with honesty and integrity, admitting the bleak reality of the situation.

"In truth, Rylan did—" I manage to get out before being interrupted by the clank of the cedar wood against the stone wall.

"My Elder!" Jov exclaims in his heavy breaths, eyeing the pair of us. "We found him!"

Never having moved at such a fast rate, I succumb to being uneasy in my balance as I rise to my feet. It matters not as I keenly push through, my thoughts squarely on delivering justice, or rather a cover-up for the sake of my bloodline.

As I rush through the halls alongside Jov and Hamzi, I begin to wonder whom they have caught. I can't help but bear a puzzled mindset as we descend the staircase at the end of the hall until eventually arriving at the very bottom.

Briskly, we make our way to the circle of torches out in front of our large stable. Pushing aside the guard who huddles in front, we enter the stable, spotting my loyal advisor and personal guard.

Long strands of hair lay over his face whilst the rest is trapped in a bun; Lord Bale stands in front of us with his weapon drawn. The long, silver blade bearing no cross guard resembles that of the traditional weapon of those who once lived on the Isle of Reeds. He holds the black leather grip tightly, the single-edged, curved blade standing vigilant at the accused's throat.

Lord Bale's grayed eyes shift from the cloaked man on the ground to match my curious gaze. Unrelenting in his pressure with the sword-bearing down with lethal intention, he says, "My lord, I found this man cowering behind the barrels of wine in the cellar... I also found this on him."

With a whip of his hand, the lord tosses over a glass vial, which falls into the hands of his brother behind me. "What is it?" I ask, turning behind me.

Jov uncorks the top of the vial and takes a whiff. "Ugh," he says, scrunching his face as he caps it.

"Coral snake venom, Elder," he says, handing the vial to Lord Hamzi.

"How The Loria can you know that?" Hamzi asks, inspecting the vial.

"We had a pet one growing up on the Isle. Friendly things, except when startled, they spit acid. Much like the manner of men," Jov responds.

Furrowing my brow in part confusion and part amazement at the talents of my child of war, I come to three realizations. Firstly, there is still much I do not know about my own pair of refugees and their arsenal of rare talents. Secondly, I have no time to get wrapped up in my curiosity about the lord, as a man carrying deadly poison sits in front of me. Which leads me to my third epiphany: Who? And why does this man carry a venom that is not even used on the ill-fated royal?

Yet the words I produce are, "I want Rylan's eyes on this now."

With a nod and bolt of his body, Jov darts toward the grand doors of the manor as I shift my focus to the man down on his knees before me. "His hood," I say.

I watch as Lord Bale bends down and rips the black, tattered cloth back, revealing a bronze-skinned figure with long, sleek, black hair amassing into a ponytail.

The man's head hangs low as he utters no words, waiting for us to deliberate his future.

"What's your name, sire?" I say, bending down to get on his level of sight.

Raising his chin, he stares at me with cold and stirring brown eyes. Upon meeting my face, his facial expression transforms from blank to almost as shocked and befuddled. His eyes wander in a wide stature, taking in my face as disbelief creeps upon his brow. His head falls downward once he takes a deep look at me, his eyes closing whilst doing so.

"Your name," Bale reiterates as the sharp edge of his weapon readjusts itself at a higher angle, forcing the man to look up.

His head now lifted toward Hamzi and me, a thick male Savarian accent says, "I am only the bearer of a sole purpose, we have no name."

"We? Who sent you? Why did you kill the prince?" I ask.

The copper-skinned face looks at me puzzledly for a moment before saying, "It matters not, I guess. You, indeed, are the fool they described. Men like you, ever so meager in thought but always ever so entitled in want. We have already won, it seems..."

"Won what? What do you think you've accomplished here?" I ask.

In the midst of my questioning, the man acts. With urgency, his movements send waves of profound shock, as with a thrust of his hands, he grabs the blunt edge of Lord Bale's blade, and all in one motion, the man's throat opens from the honed edge of the sword being pulled across his own skin.

My thoughts sprawl from the scene I just witnessed in the stable only hours prior. The twists and turns in the day have tugged at my heart and my sanity, from mass panic in the ballroom to being told my daughter is the one at fault for the death of royal blood, and ultimately, the demise of a wrongly accused yet vile man. Yet through all this, I sit upright in my grand bed while my wife, not batting an eyelash, lays fast asleep.

A fool? A fool to what? To whom? I ponder these questions as I rise out of my spot in the feather-filled blue sheets.

My mind is not the only thing racing, as my paces, too, are swift in action to leave the room. Finding myself amongst the stars outside the walls of my chamber, I stand still on my balcony beneath the sky engulfed in black, the moon beaming its rays down, whilst I continue to ponder in turmoil.

To what end? To what greater scheme? What battle has already been won that, in reward, he sacrificed his own life? Yet what I greatly wonder about is what he meant by 'we.' We who? Savar? No. No, a quarrel with Savar would be with the king, not I. Which makes me question: why poison? A poison not even used on the prince? And if not him, who was the target?

In my muddled concentration on the prince and the assassin, the soft skin of a hand reaches out, touching my shoulder while wisps of faint perfume flow in the open air.

"Love, please come back to bed," Sylvia says, hugging me from behind.

I turn and, with no words, tell her all she needs to know with a raise of my brow and a soft smirk.

"I know," she says. "But your mind must get a reprieve, my dear. There is no one better equipped to lead and lead wisely… but only when fully rested."

With her words holding sense, as I always heed my wife's advice, I nod my head and follow her back into the great, wide bedroom before finding solace in my slumber.

Falling into a deep sleep, my eyes open as I find myself surrounded by new terrain. Floating through the sky, the wind and breeze whip against me, my wings outstretched, soaring through the air as below is a large body of water. Above me, I feel the pellets of water being shot down as I continue my journey over the water. Gliding and flying, I feel free, yet at the same time, such a heavy pressure on my back as I keep flapping my wings. The last sight I see is the totality of the environment: an immense ocean with no end in sight while heaven and hell rain showers on the never-ending sea. With a brush of my overhanging brown hair, my eyes open to reality.

"Good moon," Sylvia says, smiling as her gaze meets my own squinted eyelids. "Night terrors, my dear? I felt you flinching all night."

"Mmm mmm, all is well," I say, letting out a yawn. "Just another vision of the typhoon before arriving at the Isle."

"Ah, I see. Well, that's behind us now, my dear," she says, kissing my forehead. With a nod in response, I groan, rising out of bed.

Dressing myself for the busy day ahead, I pick out my usual royal garments: blue robes and pants of silk, white shirt of cloth, sandals for my feet, and I don my leaf pendant necklaces.

"Hmm," I grumble, looking in the mirror that sits atop my wardrobe. Dark circles are apparent under my eyes as the figurehead of Cedar Keep stares back at me. No amount of sleep would rid me of the dark undertones, as I fear they do not come from a lack of slumber but rather a bad omen for the days ahead.

With a deep sigh, I approach the door of my room, setting out to deal with the urgent matters at hand as well as attending to the mysterious and probing questions from the day before. Running over the list of things to do, I contemplate them all in my head; *Find Rylan, gather the advisors in the key room, talk to Illia. Find Rylan, gather the advisors, talk to Illia.*

As I repeat the list, I cannot help but feel lost and scared. Whether that is caused by the traumatizing events that have so recently occurred or from my dreams is up in the air. All I know to do in this moment is pray.

"The storm, my eyes, my little girl. The Loria, I beg for your mercy. I beg for your grace. I ask for strength to guide me through this," I mumble, walking the dark-brown planks of the halls. Alas, my prayers matter not in the moment at hand as I descend the spiral staircase of the manor. With each step and foot forward, my outlook gains positivity. "Duggan, you are the key. You can be the savior. You need to be the savior. You have to be the savior. Not just for your people but for your little girl," I mumble.

Continuing to attempt to raise my own mood, I arrive at the second floor of the eight-story manor. Meandering the halls lit by the sun's light, I come to the door belonging to the room of my apothecary.

With a slight and simple knock, I am greeted by, "Who goes there?" coming from the other side of the wooden frame.

Without wanting to bring much attention to myself, I lower my tone, "'Tis me, Rylan."

Briskly, the door flies open. "My lord," the clean-shaven, green-eyed man says before bowing. "I would have saved you the trip from coming down here if you had only simply sent word."

"I know, my friend, but I was already out and just decided I should stretch my legs a bit more," I say, entering the small room. "I'm on my way to meet the others in the key room, I figured I should stop by to see if anything more came of your analysis on our departed prince… You must have a better room, my friend, this won't do for a friend of mine," I say.

"Oh, no need, my lord, I actually picked this out myself. A man of small needs; however, if we're talking favors, I'm sure I could write up some wants on a list for my experiments," he says, cracking a smile. "Besides, I do not wish to take a gift of pity and bribery, my lord."

Stunned and wide-eyed at his remarks, I snap at him, "Watch your tongue, Rylan, I simply offered out of kindness."

"Of course you did, my lord," he says, wandering over to his bookshelf.

"Rylan, say your piece, I am in no mood for sharp-tongued words or accents of satire," I say, staring him down.

With a deep breath and exhale, with a sigh, the apothecary turns his white cloak back around, clinking his vials as he says, "Forgive me, My Elder. I, um, simply do not wish to be a party to being silenced or, uh… bought. It goes against every value I hold."

My head draws back in disbelief. "My friend, I wish not to buy you. I simply wished to make conversation. But if you have more to get off your chest, then please do so," I say, sitting on the wool sheets of his bed.

"No, no, no. No, I feel like a fool now. I didn't mean to offend my

Elder. What brings you here? I must say I'm a bit more than curious. I guess that's what caused me to speak out of turn..." he responds.

Lowering my facial expression out of my outraged state, I speak, "Honestly, 'tis more of a hope, a prayer... did you happen to find any indication of the venom being present in the body? Any trace? The slightest hint?"

Taking a seat by the long cedar desk, he gives me a stern look.

"I looked. Two times over, in fact, but there was none that my eye could see, even after the closest examination. However, without being able to fully dive into the body, there is quite frankly no telling. I'm afraid the cause of death in my eyes would still be the phantom stings. Which makes me wonder who this was for," he says, picking up the vial of poison off his desk.

"I see... is there any way to cut open the body without raising the suspicion of the king's apothecary?" I ask.

"I'm, uh, afraid not. That would be, um, impossible, or at least a practice I have yet to learn," he responds.

"Hmm," I grumble. "I need another favor then, Rylan..." His eyes look at me tentatively.

"I need you to take out the stingers and inject the prince's body with the vial we found. Once you're done, dispose of all the evidence," I demand.

Locking eyes and exchanging pleas with my gaze, he nods. "Of course, my Elder," he says as I rise from the bed. "But..." he stops.

Turning to find the man in his chair, I stare intently.

"I must ask. To what end?" he asks. "Pardon?" I return.

"To, uh, what end? To what goal? What is the, um, outcome of this if we do, my lord? I mean, the trespasser found with this was, uh, Savarian, correct?" he asks. "Indeed," I say.

"Well, this shall be war, my lord. This is the death of a prince. Blood shall have to be shed over this; the king shan't have it any other way," Rylan says.

"And whose blood would you rather it be? Illia's? Mine? Yours? If we tell them the truth about Dedric going to the mountainside, you, I, and this keep shall burn to the ground, and that would be a merciful showing of his grace's justice," I say.

Rylan exhales deeply before saying, "Hmph, you know where my loyalty lies, my Elder."

Taking one last glance at the short man, my intrusive thoughts float across the forefront of my mind. Loyal? Loyal to who? His values? His Elder? His king?

Alas, I attempt to ease my mind upon entering the ruby corridor. Why even worry? Not only has he stood by me and served me without any want or need since my coronation but he also stood by my side through the entire dread and horror of sieging the Isle, even when looking utterly bleak and damning.

Whilst my angst dwindles with each passing thought of confidence in my friend, I stride for the key room lying two floors above. Taking the same route as before: down the hallway and up the pale, white-stone stairs, I pass the torch-lit entry. My steps halt at the sight of my fellow compatriots conversing outside the room I aim for.

Peeking behind the fellow key he converses with, a Lymrian voice yells at the sight of me, "My lord!"

Quickly approaching me is the well-dressed Hamzi in his white and orange garb, while Valincias clinks and thuds with each step his silver armor takes.

"Hope I didn't disturb any talk of importance," I say, shaking hands with the pair.

"Of course not, Elder. Simply sharing perspectives on the night prior," Valincias chimes in.

"And?" I ask, passing the two, aiming for the metallic handle of the door.

"Some townsfolk were displeased, inconvenienced, and spooked, but a good showing of steel calmed their nerves," The captain says. "Besides, with the gates down and it weighing ten times more than the largest horse in all of Elium, there wasn't much they could do."

Behind the captain paces our recently returned advisor, who chimes in, "And I was just explaining how maybe a good showing of calmness and honesty might have been the better approach, like how it did when I handled the duke and duchess's erratic nerves. However, I do believe I still have the markings of the duchess's claws from her nails being embedded in my skin—"

"Hamzi, you cheeky bastard," Valincias says, grinning.

"Ha. No. I would never; they're simply from guiding her and Duke Arys to their room," he says.

Turning to the pair behind me as we reach the frame of the door,

I say with a stern glare, "Gentleman. To put this kindly… the prince lies lifeless in the basement of this keep. Our walls have never been so close to crumbling. Our lives are ever so close to meeting an end, and by a breath, and possibly sheer luck, we kept our legacy alive whilst the royal lineage has taken a detrimental toll on theirs. Yet we stand here, laugh, tease, and admire our actions prior when there is so much more to do. I plead, focus on the agenda at hand," before opening the door to the room where we all are set to gather.

Upon pushing open the cedar, we find two more advisors waiting for us within the walls of the key room.

"Lord Bale, Lord Jov. Thank you for getting here with haste,"

I say.

The subtle accents of the two natives to the Isle linger in the air as they both greet me. "My lord," they both pronounce with a bow.

We waste no time getting settled in our seats as we prepare our minds for the discussion ahead. The five of us exchange glares for but a moment before I void the room of silence.

"My lords, I shall waste no time. With the untimely death of both the royal prince and the trespasser found within these walls, we are left in a dire position. One of which I ask you all to stand firm in. As of this very moment, the prince's body is being carted away, where it shall be placed into a carriage and driven back to the capital. Upon doing so, they shall find the same outcome of death as apothecary Rylan: death by poison. From there, I can only imagine the king's response, with the Savarians to blame," I say.

"So, we do believe 'tis Savar responsible for this attack?" Jov asks.

"At this moment, nothing is concrete. However, I feel that is the likely conclusion his grace shall come to," I say.

"And shall his majesty be so merciful to us for letting this happen under our protection?" Bale asks the room.

I don't know... 'tis possible this... may very well be the last of us sitting in this room... all together, I think to myself but instead say, "No. I presume there shall be consequences that we shall face. I shall face."

"My Elder, you are not alone in fault with this, we all share the blame for the events that occurred," Hamzi says.

Looking over to my friend, I say, "I appreciate your support; however, there's no guarantee the king shall see it that way... though I have come to the decision to be proactive in sealing our fate, or rather lessening our punishment."

"What do you mean by that, my lord?" Captain Valincias asks.

With a deep inhale and exhale before speaking, I draw my focus on my next words. "I have decided to grant the king's request to rid the border of refugees. I feel, at this time, 'tis best to carry out his grace's wishes," I declare.

Quickly but unsurprisingly, due to his sense of honor and roots, Lord Bale interjects, "My Elder, I must advise against this, we do not know what exactly we are walking into with that. Not to mention 'tis murder, cold-blooded murder."

I find my head swiveling over to meet his line of grayed sight. "I'm sorry, my friend. My mind is made up on the matter. And for the sake of this keep, those within our walls, and your own peace of mind, I do hope that you too shall come to an understanding of why this decision is being made," I say.

Disappointment reeks from the pair of grown-up orphans as my words rest on the passing humid air. Yet my own mind finds comfort in the fact that this is the only opportunity to prove worth, loyalty, as well as sincerest apologies to our king. If slaughtering a hundred displaced refugees, not to mention those who have displayed criminal behavior, can save my daughter, wife, and, unknowingly, those within this room, 'tis a decision I shall make a thousand times over.

Nevertheless, without them being made aware of the prince's true cause of death, they sit void of noise with stunned expressions across their faces.

"Jov and I shall travel at dawn for the border along with an infantry of guards, our Bannerman, and wagons supplied with a full moon's cycle worth of rations. Hamzi, how much longer are you staying for?" I ask.

"After what just occurred? I refuse to run. I shall stay until you force me to leave, my Elder," Hamzi says.

"Very well, I shall leave you in charge of overseeing the daily operations of the keep. Bale shall inform you of all that needs to be done, as he'll stay here as well. Valincias, tighten down on security until we return," I order. "That is all. Thank you."

With a motion of my hand releasing them from their seats, the four keys rise to their feet, while I turn my line of sight onto the man I consider a son. "Bale, stay for a moment," I plea as the four others exit the room one by one.

Rubbing my face with my hands, I wait for the others to all completely leave the room before looking up and saying, "Friend, I know you may not see this as the best course of action, and I respect that. You are not the soul who would so maliciously jump to this decision, but I feel and know this to be our only hope of walking away with our lives intact."

Bale stands with a blank facial expression and offers no response, which leads to me asking, "Can I ask you a question?" "Of course," he says.

"Do you know the history of Elium? The royal family tree?" I ask.

"Well, yes, you taught me and Jov that yourself," he says. "If I remember correctly, you said history was the only thing that mattered, whether telling its tales or writing it down, history is the only thing man can learn from. The only thing man can grow from."

Smirking at my pride in him, I respond, "That's correct. However... do you remember the last time someone of royal blood was assassinated? In someone else's keep, mind you?" "Mmm... no..." he says.

"Precisely. No king, no queen, no prince, nor princess has ever, ever met the fate of Dedric. None would dare to even try, as the repercussions would be immeasurable. As you very well know, the last time someone even thought about questioning our king's power, they were wiped from their land, wiped from their life, and wiped from their legacy," I say.

Watching closely, I see Bale's face wince with the mention of what happened to those living on the Isle of Reeds. Even if he was a mere child when the massacre happened, one does not forget the sounds of an entire kingdom and its people being burned to the ground.

"Apologies, friend... I simply am trying to make a point that we are in a position no one has ever found themselves in. We must tread lightly," I say.

"Of course, my Elder," he responds. "Shall that be all?" "There's one more thing... I need you to keep a close eye on Illia until I return. In truth, Bale... I need you to vow to me that no harm shall befall her," I ask.

"Illia? My lord... of course, but what's the meaning of this? What's the cause of this request?" Bale asks.

"Bale. Promise me," I say firmly.

Not for a second do his blind eyes flutter or waver as he says,

"I promise."

"Thank you, friend. I shall hope to return with good news. Until then," I say, rising to my feet and holding my hand out to shake.

He stands and grabs my hand to pull me in, sending a shock through my veins. However, his warm embrace is a pleasant surprise, lasting only a few fleeting moments before the release of our hug. He looks at me to say, "May the Gods be with you," then leaves the room.

RAMSES
THE MOIST CELL

The day before judgement

My bones ache from the hard stone surface. My mouth is dry from the need to ease my thirst. My belly roars in its want to sustain all life within. My skin crawls at the sight of spiders, insects, and vermin in the cold, square room.

I sit silently in my habitat, worse off than my days clamoring for a better life. At least then, I witnessed the lively scene of the market and fields, while here, life only passes by the steel-clad bars a handful of times within the day. Once for food, once for a check-in, and once for the exchanging of guards under the moon's light. My newfound routine is excruciating to take in as my reality, and yet my mind escapes, wandering off to reminisce of the days when I had food on the table every night, of my kind-hearted mother, of my dull but quite fulfilling days selling vegetables. But mostly reminiscing about the sweet, comforting smile I'd often receive from Erin. I cannot imagine how both she and her mother are taking my disappearance. I only hope those at the market who saw what occurred inform them of my whereabouts.

Alas, all I can do is look back on such times and be thankful, for the days I have recently been through have been the opposite of my once blissful life. Undergoing fowl and cruel treatment from stale food, being beaten, and even having to defend my life against my former cellmates. Each coming for my soul with a different weapon in hand. The first time, a sawed-down stick, the second, a spoon broken in half. Each time, my wicked captors ironically come to my rescue as I screamed and pleaded for help. Unfortunately, even with my yelps, I still managed to be poked, prodded, and now scarred, as I took my fair share of stabs with each makeshift weapon. Some murmur me weak for not wanting to fight back, but I don't care, as I'm willing to do whatever it takes to get back to the simplicities I once knew.

Sitting here, I wonder why I even came to meet such circumstances, as I must be extremely unlucky to endure such acts in only two nights under this moon. Perhaps I snore loudly? Or was it my weeping during the first moon? No. They are just acts of evil men. Men who seek to take their anger out on others instead of processing it themselves.

Trying to rationalize the deeds I have survived, my iron door screeches open, and new life entering the small room forces my head out of my lap as I raise my eyes to meet my visitor. Entering is a guard dressed head to toe in chainmail, donning a silver helmet with the keep's insignia ingrained in the middle.

I push my weight up against the wall, trying to position myself far away from the guard with my hands up—not wanting to give any reason to receive a beating.

Scoffing, the steel enforcer says, "Ah, Loria's sake. Calm yourself, I'm not here to hurt you, muck."

Upon hearing that sentence, I lift my chin, allowing my line of sight to peek through the crevices of my fingers. Doing so, it seems my sense of time looks to be lost, as with the words, "Don't you move a fucking inch," the guard looms over top of me as he bends to put down the slosh and sludge they serve every day. I feel disoriented, as I could swear it wasn't the hour of the day I am typically fed. Looking quizzically into the bowl, I see the yellow and green makings of porridge, smelling unfit for the human body. However, I don't give much thought to it as I grab the bowl and scurry back to my spot in the corner of the room.

Eating the slush, I find my focus drifting to the brown wooden bowl, much like that Mother uses for her infamous stew. She must be ill with heartache. *I'm sorry Mum-ma... I'm sorry.*

In my sorrow, overwhelmed with dejection, I succumb to tears filling the slits of my eyes. I need to get her a message... to let her know I'm fine... or even that I'm alive.

With that very idea in mind, I scoot close to the door of iron poles as the guard proceeds to exit. "Guard," I whisper but hear no response. "Guard!" I say this time with a slight rise in my voice. This time, the clanks of his armor churning down the dimly lit hall of the prison halts for a moment, then proceeds again, this time drawing closer to me. The metallic thuds stop right outside my door as one of my captors stares down at me menacingly.

"What?!" he says.

With little hesitation, I rise to my feet and grab the bars. "I need to get a message to someone," I say.

Alas, the guard shows no interest, as he laughs wryly and starts to walk off.

"Wait!" I yell once more. But again, it falls on deaf ears as he keeps pushing the meal cart past my cell, disappearing to the side of the walls of stone and mortar.

With a sigh, I slide my back down the bars. *I just want them to know I'm okay.* Even if all I feel is far from okay as a sense of foolishness washes over me for being caught up in a curiosity. Caught up in a want to chase a different life and, in turn, following the man who represented that—only to lead me here. A place where I'm losing time, I'm losing coin, I'm losing life each day I sit here. From what? My own mistakes? My curiosity? The treachery of the guard? I guess it doesn't even matter now.

Sitting and pondering in the cell, I leave my anguish alone as I glance toward the barred window near the top of the wall in the small enclosure. Standing up with a bowl in hand, I look through to the open air outside the prison. Having to get up on my tiptoes, I can see the street level, the stable, inner gate, and the abundance of guards. I realize where I am now. Funny, it is, as I always wanted to see inside the manor, I guess just not like this.

Eyeing the surroundings through the jagged opening, my sense of curiosity overwhelms my anguish as the guard shouts at the sight of two steeds being ridden by more guards of the city and a carriage in tow. "Transport arriving!" I hear as the beating hooves of horses draw near. Seeing this spawns my sense of question, as 'tis not the protectors entering the keeps. That strikes me as bizarre, as a multitude of guards have come and gone in my two nights here, including a large mass of the steel hawks leaving at first light yestermoon. However, this one seems different, as it arrives in the form of a carriage loaded with a large, metal cage. I watch the wooden wheels come to a halt in the courtyard of the manor, but much to my dismay, a handful of guards surround the carriage. The bodies do not allow my gaze to see who or what is in the cage, thus my small portion of entertainment is cut short as I relieve my toes of the stress, resting my heels on the straw-covered stone.

Sitting down with my back against the iron bars, I wonder about the great deal of traffic within the inner gates of the keep. Perhaps I never really took notice before of how busy the manor actually is with transports. It seems to never end, as I hear the trotting of each mount throughout the majority of day and night. However, these noises are the only comforting things here, the only familiarity, and the only reason my mind hasn't lost its sanity completely. The sounds often remind me of the days Father and I would go out to the fields and I'd watch him try to tame the wild horses. Even though we'd never actually managed to wrangle any, he always just seemed to be happy with the adventure. I guess that's where I get it from. This idea of always looking for an exciting opportunity, a new challenge. However, my mind wanders from my past with Father to how he's managing in the present. I wonder what he's been doing in his watch over the border of Savar. I wonder if he'll be mad at me when I tell him about this when he gets home... if I even get out of here.

I shake off the notion of not returning to life outside this steel with my thought of Father taking over the forethought of my mind.

"Hmm," I snicker. *Perhaps this time he'll actually bring back something useful once he's done with his watch. Just not anymore damned cups and bowls. Why is it always cups and bowls?*

Amidst my mind finding solace in my recollection and questions about Father, I hear the metal scrape against the mortar.

"Take him to the end of the hall," a guard says, coming from outside the cell.

Standing up and turning around from facing the window, I approach the black, iron door, shifting my head to the side and trying to angle my eyes to see the approaching footsteps. A handful of paces gain ground on my cell, and I back away from the door, my eyes locked to the sight passing in front, not halting their movement as they waltz by my designated room. The guard pushes on the shoulders of a figure of a man, and I briefly see long, black hair hanging over his face, accompanied by bound wrists and chained together feet. The man in soiled beige garments takes a dozen or more steps as I watch through the bars to see them place the prisoner in an iron-doored cell. The guard sets the man inside, then closes the door. Having no visible line of sight in or out of the cell, I can only observe the pair of peacekeepers shut the black iron, turn, and walk back toward the hall's end.

So strange. No one was in there when I got here, nor has one been placed there for the past two days. So why him, I wonder.

Breaking focus on the man behind the door, a woman's voice rings throughout the dirt and grime of the dungeon as it says,

"Don't want to get put in there."

Directly across from me in an opposing cell is a small woman.

Her blonde hair dangles down in front of her blue eyes as she says, "Only seen a handful of people make it out of there alive. They usually are left to rot… or worse; hanged off the tower."

Puzzling is the prisoner counter to me, my brow furrowing at her comments. "How long have you been in here to see all that?" I ask.

"Oh, sweetheart, I'm a bit of a regular here," she says, turning away from the door and sitting. "Apparently, stealing hearts is a crime, or maybe 'tis relieving them of their coin? All the same, I suppose."

"And the guard doesn't get fed up with that? With you always winding up here?" I ask.

She chuckles a bit before saying, "It depends, I guess."

"Depends on what?" I ask, getting my hopes up for leaving this small captivity early.

Picking at her fingernails, she responds, "On what you have to offer, hun."

My eyes gleam at this newfound possibility. "And what would one have to offer to get out of here?" I ask.

Taking a momentary break from attending to her fingers, her sapphire eyes look me up and down. "Love, unless you've stockpiled more wealth than what your life warrants? You weren't born with that, I'm afraid," she says, sitting in her stained, brown dress.

Caught up in my thoughts of what I could offer, I ask, "Born with what?"

Raising a golden eyebrow, she says, "Oh, honey…" "Oh," I say as my hope dwindles.

"'You really are a confused little thing, aren't you?" she says.

"How did you even find your way in here? I can't imagine you'd make much of a criminal."

Embarrassed, I turn away from the cell door and respond, "Chasing wants, it seems."

"Don't we all?" she asks, stopping my steps. "I mean, that's what got most of us in here. 'Tis what puts bodies into all the iron-plated uniforms, not to mention how our beloved Elder got to his position of power."

Continuing my motion of approaching the wall, I ask, "What's your point?"

"My point is, just because you chase your desires doesn't mean you're a bad guy," she says.

"What then, wise one?" I return, sitting with my back against the dingy stone.

Scoffing, she says, "There's no need for your sarcasm, I'm just trying to share some hard-earned advice."

"My apologies, I'm just not feeling like entertaining philosophy from a thief," I say.

"You little shit. I guess your small frame can be a bit brutal. Maybe you do deserve to sit in here after all," she teases.

I roll my eyes at her while she just plays with a strand of her light-auburn hair.

"Oh, come on, lighten up. 'Tis not like you have much choice, but you're more than welcome to sit here and wallow in your sorrow," she says. Sitting in silence for a minute, she breaks the stillness. "What's your name?" she asks. "Ramses," I say.

"Nice to make your acquaintance, Ramses," she projects between the bars.

Raising my brow in question, I respond, "You?"

"Nyssa," she says.

Nodding, I reply, "You too, Nyssa."

With silence enveloping the corridor once more, I relax my body and eyes. Thank the Loria, she's done. However, even with my facial expressions showing signs of unwillingness to talk and wanting to rest, the reprieve in conversation is short-lived.

"So, what is it?" Nyssa asks.

"For the Loria's sake... what's what?" I return. "What's the reason you're in here?" she asks.

Opening my eyes, I stare across the dungeon. "Seems I knocked over the wrong person," I say.

Her face sets into a puzzled expression as she asks, "Who in the Loria's name did you knock over to get yourself thrown in here?"

I sigh before saying, "Valincias."

Nyssa's eyes widen. "Oh boy, you screwed up big time, huh? You pushed over the captain of the guard? Guess you're not so little after all," she responds.

"Guess so, huh?" I manage to say amidst my eyes becoming heavy.

"Hmmm," she says, smiling as she looks back down to her worn-down nails.

Finally she's done... however, a new sense of curiosity jolts my mind to race again.

"What did you mean?" I ask, my eyes half-cracked.

"Hmmm?" she grunts.

"When you said chasing your wants doesn't make you a bad person. What were you getting at?" I ask.

"Oh, now you want to know? By the Loria, I'm honored you asked," she says, smiling.

Rolling my eyes once more, I say, "I deserved that." She giggles. "Mmhmm... I meant 'tis not the chase that's evil, 'tis the desire... what are you chasing? Coin? Legacy?

Relationship? 'Tis always the desire that gets you in trouble, not your want to chase something... just has to be the right thing." I crack a smile and cover my mouth, attempting not to laugh.

"What?!" she asks.

"Nothing, nothing," I say. "No, now you must tell me!" she demands.

Smirking and raising my eyebrows, I say, "Nothing... I just wouldn't have guessed you were so thoughtful... I mean for a thief, of course," I say.

"Oh, hang yourself," she laughs.

Abruptly, a woman echoes throughout the corridor, "For the Loria's sake, just fuck already."

The fellow detained woman's comment causes Nyssa to giggle for a moment, before the door from around the hall's corner screams once again. The slinking of chainmail sends chills up my spine as I await the guard to pass by my cell for the daily check.

However, to my surprise, the first pair of footsteps are accompanied by a second set. "Where's he at?" the familiar voice asks.

"At the very back, sire," the other body responds, clanking their way down the dungeon's walkway.

My body boils with rage at the sight of the beige cloak whipping the ground, the caped man appearing to be the same one I met face to face two days ago. His steps are heavy as he paces his way past my cell, not even batting an eye at the sight of me, with the jailer in tow. As they pass, I rise to my feet and grab the metallic bars of the door. I watch as they make headway to the iron door frame at the very back of the jail.

"Open it," Valincias bellows as they reach their desired destination.

With a nod, the guard, per his captain's request, unlocks the door, pulling the handle to open the doorway. The door, however, stops at an angle, not allowing the iron to come to a full opening nor allowing my line of sight to see the man in the cell as the captain enters. As quick as it opens, it closes again—this time with the captain of the guard inside. Attentively, I listen and watch the door almost as hard as the guard on the outside does. The only noise to be heard is the occasional thud coming from inside the ironclad room. Standing and watching diligently, I wait for any glimpse or noise to come my way. Alas, after many moments of waiting, nothing new is heard aside from the occasional clanks coming from within, and eventually, the captain exits the room, brushing his knuckles with a white handkerchief.

"That'll be all," the captain says with a nod.

Shutting the door once more, his counterpart asks, "Any luck?"

"Mm mm," Valincias mumbles, shaking his head from side to side. "But he'll break soon enough."

With those words, the pair glide back down the aisle with jail cells on either side. This time, as the captain passes by my square captivity, he stares only for a second before giving me that same cold-hearted smile he gave me before taking my coins and ordering his men to arrest me. Balling up my fists, I want to act. However, as the captain passes, I catch a glimpse of Nyssa behind him. Her eyes broad as she signals 'no' with her head. Heeding her advice, I release the tension in my hands and just stare as the two enforcers waltz down the hall and turn the corner.

Unable to contain myself, I turn to face the wall once again. Only this time, I close my hand and hit the bricks with pure frustration. That corrupt bastard causes my blood to boil.

In response, Nyssa exclaims, "Stop that! What are you doing?!

Are you insane? You'll break your hand!"

Caught up in my emotions, I turn swiftly to face her voice.

"What do you care?! For two full days, you acted like I didn't exist.

Even when I was being attacked! You just sat there and watched!" I shout.

"And what did you want me to do? Slip through the bars and strangle them?! Think for a moment, Ramses!" she fires back.

Due to our shouting, a guard bursts in. "What the fuck's going on in here?!" he yells, raising his voice, but none returns any comments back. "If I hear any one of you scream again, I shall take a club to all of you!"

Even with the guard yelling, it falls on deaf ears as I stay locked in my gaze with that of the royal blue that stares back. Eventually my facial expressions drop into one of shame as well as my temperament dropping into one of familiar pain within my situation. With that on the forefront of my mind, I return to my corner, hiding away from the women jailed across from me.

Eventually, even in my sorrow, I find my eyelids heavy and beyond saving as I fall into a slumber. A deep and heavy sleep comforting my bones and putting my mind at ease. Dreams of the small hut on the outskirts of town. Mother and Father both await me inside as I play amongst the arching branches of cedars. Losing myself between the leaves, Mum-ma's voice becomes more and more distant, until finally, I can't hear her soft and comforting tone. Suddenly, with a snap of the twigs in the forest, I awake.

"Oh, come on, love," I hear through the grog. "Didn't you say you wanted to get out of here?"

I force my eyes open and look through my slitted eyes and see a flame dancing from a torch in front of the cell across from me.

I can't help but think it to be a new day amidst the active life, yet as I pan around my cell, I realize it can't be morning, there's no sun coming into my darkened cell.

With those thoughts in mind, the rattling of keys brings me fully awake, perhaps in distant want of the metallic blades being used to free myself.

Alas, that is not the picture in front of me. Lifting my head off the straw on the floor, I watch as one chainmail-covered enforcer tugs Nyssa out of her square cell. She says nothing as he guides her out of the dark, dusty cell; however, she needs not say much as her face tells the whole story. Her expression is blank, aside from the apologetic looks she flashes me before they disappear down the hall.

I don't know what to make out of this. Should I be mad? Should

I be upset? Is this injustice? Should I expect anything less? These thoughts last briefly, however, with the main idea floating through my head being, *Why? Why do I even care?* With that notion in the forefront of my mind, I return to the floor, trying to rest once more.

When my eyes open again, this time, the light peeking through my barred window tells me I face a new day in captivity. Yet even with breathing the dawn's air and being lucky enough that my wounds didn't cause me to pass before this new day, I sit with despair on my lip as I look at the empty square space across from me. Perhaps I expected her to still be there. Perhaps I expected it to be a dream. Perhaps I expected her to be dozing off. However, even in my state of mixed emotion, it matters not as I stretch my arms up high and wide, cracking my back and getting ready for a day of more peril in solitude.

The time passes as the previous three days have; wake up, sit up, wait for food, wait for sleep. My daily routine strikes me as frustrating when I could be doing more, being more. Nevertheless, I sit in turmoil, whether in my thoughts or in the itch to get up and do something. I am on edge most of the day, and as the guard comes to bring me my daily meal, it only builds. My emotions refuse to relinquish their grip on the interest of what happened to my fellow prisoner as he unlocks the metal frame.

"Here," the steel brass says, laying the same foul porridge on the floor as he had the past two days.

"Sir?" I ask.

His fleeting steps stop as he turns to face my gaze. "Listen, I'm not going out of my way to get someone a message," he responds. "No, no, that's not it," I respond.

The guard is still in movement as he looks at me to say, "Okay then?"

"What happened?" I motion my head toward the prison chamber across from me.

I can tell something is afoot as his face shifts into an expression of disgust, more than it already is. "Don't know. The whore must have disappeared," he says.

Disappeared? What do you mean disappeared when a guard was the one to take her away? Instead of asking questions, I blankly look at him. Staring deeply into his hazel line of sight, with no further words being exchanged, he leaves and strides away, delivering porridge to the other prisoners from his wooden cart.

Amidst my newfound curiosity and feelings of grievance, I pick up my bowl of gruel, looking at the slop before deciding to put it down. I can't force myself to take this anymore, even with my insides churning away. Thus, I decide to take action in the little form that presents itself. With my hand moments away from beating on the bars to gain my captors' attention, the squeal of the front door catches my ears. Moreover, the man entering gains my full recognition. The thorn-shaped hilt, the royal advisor's robes, and most noticeably—the dark, hazed eyes gliding through the halls wallop any plans I had. The man being escorted by two other guards is the infamous Lord Bale, the very same man who afforded me kindness at the gate almost a week ago. This time, in a different situation, I hope he may show me the same mercy once looking upon me. However, that stream of ideas is severed in half as he briskly walks past.

Reaching the darkened steel door at the very end of the corridor, he asks, "Is this him?" to which one of the guards responds, "Yes, my lord."

"Very well, make sure he's secured tightly with steady eyes on his movements," the lord commands.

"Yes, Lord Bale," the guard responds before saying, "However, I don't think he's in any shape to do any damage."

The fancy robes of the lord tread across the grainy stone, back toward the entrance from which they came as he smiles and says,

"Even a blind man has tricks up his sleeve. Don't be naive to any

of his." "Yes, sire," the guards both say.

The lord's last words are, "I shall be waiting outside," before turning the corner, and leaving my vision.

With a nod, both guards turn around as one of them yells, "Everyone against the walls! Now!"

One by one, they come into our rooms and lock chains around our hands and feet before guiding us into the halls. I question this approach, however, as I think it easy to get away from the clutches of our jailers, though I simply am not the type to take that risk. As the guards enter the last few locked rooms before arriving at the windowless door in the back, it seems another man had the same idea.

Not being able to see what happened within the cell itself, we all hear a "Ugh!" before the thief who had attempted to steal my produce days ago races away down the hall. Pushing the other guard to the side, he turns the corner. Jealous of his escape, I ponder doing the same, but alas, the pair of guards rise quickly to their feet and mutter, "Damn fool."

I think all of us who stand still in our ironclad line wonder what they mean by those words but shortly after restricting the rest of the prisoners, we are led out the gate by the guards to find the bald-headed man on his knees, pleading.

The blade of the lord aims at the man's chest as he says, "Put him back in the cell... his actions shall make him wait longer for his judgment." Then looks down at the teary-eyed old man. "Consider this mercy, the next time you lay hands on the guard, they won't be as kind."

His words of wisdom don't seem to get through, however, as the beggar cries out, "Damn you!" whilst being dragged back into the hallway of barred rooms. It takes them only a short time to accomplish the task, this time without being bested by the criminal, and with that being done, we are all ready to set out. Looking in front, two guards and the lord steer the way. As I glance behind the serpent figure of prisoners, I see two guards bringing up the rear. All five guards with swords, ax, and bow at the ready in case action is needed. Seeing the sight makes me become a bit more precarious in my emotions regarding where we're being taken. However, that becomes evidently clear as we leave the dungeon only to enter a narrow hallway.

With servants passing by us left and right at a distance, it becomes apparent that we are being guided through the multitude of servant tunnels beneath the manor. We walk down the dark, torchlit halls, but for only a dozen paces, when we reach a new opening in the stone and mortar walls—a spiraling stone staircase.

"Oh, fuck's sake," a woman in front of me moans at the sight of the never-ending well of steps.

After a multitude of heaves, I find myself on par with her attitude as I lose my breath, trying to climb each smooth surface of stone. Unfortunately, our heavy breaths fall on deaf ears as our paces continue to climb to the very top of the staircase. Upon exiting the spiral stairwell, we are surrounded by a beautiful garden. An array of flowers in full bloom covered the ground, the walls, and the ceiling. The petals cover everything but the panes of glass that let the sun shed its beams through. It feels like a maze with the amount of garden beds the guard navigates us through. Looking either way, colors of yellow, blue, red, and purple abound in different shapes and sizes. All the while, I'm not able to fully take the scene in, as the guard pulls and tugs us forward. However, from what I have seen thus far, it is ironic that this is where they deliver judgment. Amidst all this beauty, we are being tried for all sorts of ugliness.

Reeling at the site of retribution, the voice of the prisoner behind me starts to sniffle with each inhale. That is until he lets out a loud and moist, "Achoo!" which lands on the back of my shirt. My body flinches at its impact before he starts again.

"Ah… Ah… Achoo!"

This time, I try to counter by ducking down to avoid him, but between dodging the man's sniffle, staying between the lanes of flowers, and all the while being locked together by chains, I slip. With a thud and clink of the metal against the tower's wooden flow, I find myself lying down on the hardwood. "Loria's sake," I mumble at finding myself facedown.

Picking myself up, I hear, "You clumsy fool," from above me. Soon after the words reach my ears, I find my feet.

Ignoring the comment, I face toward the front of our chain-linked line. Step by step, we tread through the aisles of daisies, lilacs, roses, and sunflowers. Reaching the end of the overhead covering and labyrinthian assortment of flowers, the leaders of the keep stare at us, along with a handful of citizens on either side of the blue carpet walkway. All gather around to watch the proceeding of 'justice,' or, rather—here to witness them delivering punishment.

As the metal scrapes and squeals against the stone being warmed by the looming light, we line up adjacent to the cedar throne. Getting this close with the royal advisors and leaders of the keep, I realize two things. The first comes in the form of a seat with dark-brown accents. The chair itself planted on a silvery pedestal, propped just a step higher than the floor the rest of us walk on. Not seeing the throne up close before, I subside in disappointment; as 'tis just a chair. Perhaps my ideas of grandeur are completely misplaced, as my expectations dwindle with the sight of the slightly larger-than-normal wooden chair. However, swiftly, my second realization takes grip; *where's the Elder?*

Sitting squarely on the throne is the shadow of a Lymiran, whilst in front of the shorter silhouette is the face of Lord Hamzi. Peculiar is it to see him here after many years, it was once said he was the greatest mind behind the walls of Cedar Manor—aside from the Elder, before he left to study in the capital. However, he isn't widely known as a man amongst the people, as neither I nor anyone I know has seen him within the gathering places of the common man and woman.

Alas, my mind, along with its thoughts, screech to a stop when the rattling of the chains finally halts as all prisoners are set into our order of retribution. On the pedestal, Lord Bale takes his place to the right of the throne, while Captain Valincias is oppositely put to the left of Lord Hamzi.

Now ready to begin, the captain yells, "Quiet!" amongst the whispers of the common folk who gather for the proceedings.

With that command, the murmuring stops, and Lord Hamzi takes his seat on the cedar throne. With a motion of his finger, as if asking to draw closer, he says, "Bring them forth." Thus, the trials begin.

As the very first man goes in front of the lords, his crime is read aloud for everyone to hear. "This man is hereby presented in front of the loyal servants of the people's will within this land of cedar and freedom. The crime placed upon this man's shoulders is theft. Caught stealing a jeweler's work from the market square," the royal announcer reads off the parchment paper the jailers hand him.

Accordingly, the judge and jury, in the form of one man, clears his throat, about to speak. "I see... In accordance with the laws of this land, we do not seek such harsh sentencing as our fellow provinces may. In such a perspective, I spare this man's life, I spare this man's hand... but the price and act for committing theft is not one to be forgiven and forgotten. Such is why I order this man to be branded in one eye, as the next time he gazes upon an item he wishes to take, he may be reminded that if he is caught again, he shan't be able to see anything worth stealing," Hamzi announces.

Clamoring and gasps come from the crowd while the man himself pleads and sobs in front of the lord. Yet whilst the delegating official indicates to the guard to drag the man away, the loudest noise of all is my heart racing.

"Losing an eye for theft?!" I mumble as anxiety washes over me.

One by one, the men and women are brought in front of the three delegators of the keep. In prompt fashion, the Lymirian delivers his justice. The charges brought in front of him come in an array of forms. From theft, murder, assault, and public indecency, the three-headed snake of justice hands out their punishment. All murderers receiving the death penalty, those who stole are told to be losing a finger or eye, whilst the ones with similar accusations to mine have had an array of punishments, from prolonged jail time to reparations in coin.

Eventually, it finally becomes my time to go forth before Lord Hamzi. My former jailer pushing me forward nearly causes me to fall. However, I maintain my balance whilst I'm guided by a guard behind me. Walking to the center space in front of my judge, the royal announcer reads, "This man is hereby presented in front of the loyal servants of the people's will within this land of cedar and freedom. The crime placed upon this man's shoulders is assault on his lord's loyal guard."

With fear holding its power over me, I bow my head to the three who rule over the proceedings.

With a grunt and slight scoff, the dark-skinned lord squints his eyes at me and smiles. "What on earth did you get yourself into, young man?" he asks.

Few fleeting moments pass before the voice I've heard before incites anger inside me. "His Lord asked you a question," Valincias barks.

If I tell the truth, would he believe me? Would he see the captain through the same lens of disdain as I? No. It would just lead to more problems for me... for Mum-ma... for Erin.

Therefore, instead, I say, "I... it was a mistake, my lord. I would like to offer my apologies to you, my lord," before turning my head to the captain of the guard and bowing. "And to you, sir.

I did not mean for my foolish nature to lead us here."

I watch as Lord Hamzi and Bale scrunch their faces in confusion before turning their heads to the captain. "He assaulted you?! Valincias? This... man attacked... you?" Lord Hamzi asks.

The captain's face turns red. "Well… I, uh um… yes, my lord," Valincias says.

Hamzi lets out a deep laugh. "So that's why you're here, aye?" the interim Elder asks.

Still smiling and shaking his head, the lord turns his attention back toward me, "Listen, do you promise to keep your nose out of trouble?" Hamzi asks.

Nodding with haste, I say, "Of course, lord."

Looking over at his other fellow counselor, Lord Bale, who nods, he turns back once more to say, "I hereby pardon you of your accused crimes against the laws of this keep. Free him of his chains."

In shock by the mercy after hearing grueling punishment after punishment, a guard comes to free my wrists and ankles of its shackles. Not thinking twice about it, I bow. "Thank you for your mercy, my lord's," I say.

Upon those words leaving my mouth and straightening my posture, I glide away from the eyes of my judge, jury, and executioner. In doing so, I immerse myself in the crowd of people as I try to slink away, out of the tower. Alas, 'tis a futile attempt, as out of the corner of my eye, I spot a familiar sight. Not Mum-ma's golden locks, not Erin's kind eyes, nor Nyssa's charismatic tone, but rather what I see sends a profound sense of surprise through my bones.

The cloak of intrigue I trailed days earlier stands across the sky-blue carpet. The enigma of a man, watches the proceedings, his red beard creeping out from underneath his hood. Frozen in wonder and curiosity, I stay in hopes of confronting the man once the proceedings are over.

My line of sight sticks to the man of mystery; however, when the very last prisoner in the line is brought before the lord, I feel an urge to capture the scene with my eyes. The dark-haired man holding his side as a large red blot covers his beige clothes, along with a multitude of bruises and scars along the skin that is revealed with his back to the crowd.

"Ahem," the announcer clears his throat, yet when he starts to read, the twisting and turning of his brow in confusion sends the whole crowd into a spiral as he reads, "This man is hereby presented in front of the loyal servants of the people's will within this land of cedar and freedom. The crime placed upon this man's shoulders is..." he stops to reexamine the paper and looks at the three lords before saying, "Treason."

With that, the crowd loses all reasonable manners with the amount of gasps and cries of, "Hang him," "Cut his head off!" "Feed him to the dogs!" yelled the disgruntled people of the keep, who are there for nothing more than pure entertainment.

Through all of this, Lord Bale puts his hand in the air with an open palm, saying no words. The crowd goes silent at this sight. None would dare push on with their shouts against Lord Bale's wishes of quiet.

"Hmmm. It seems you've caused quite the commotion, sir," the man on the cedar throne says. Rising from his seat, he walks toward the man in chains and whispers in his ear before grabbing his head and kissing his brow.

"I'm afraid you know the consequences of this accusation. The penalty for such a crime is death!" the lord shouts before returning to his throne. "This man shall be hanged at dusk!"

The fragile man's head stays down, looking at the floor throughout the whole proceedings and announcement. Yet, as the guard comes to whisk him away, he finally raises his chin.

"I ask for trial by duel," he mutters.

Catching Lord Hamzi mid-pace back toward his seat, the words cause him to turn around and ask, "Pardon? You ask for what?"

This time shouting, the prisoner yells, "I demand for a trial by duel!"

Silence falls over the balcony. Stillness of bodies and eyes wide in nature indicate the crowd is caught between two emotions: a flow state of awe from the man's request but also stunned, as the broken and bleeding figure should not dare challenge any swordsman in the shape he is in. With that very thought in mind, the Lymrian lord sits and asks, "Sire, you are in no state, do you wish to die earlier than dusk?"

Not being able to see the man's facial expression with his back toward us the entire time, I can only assume he holds a stern look as Lord Hamzi says, "Very well then. As appointed Elder in Elder Elovis's time away, I would like to appoint Lord Bale as my duelist in the matter..." he says before Valincias chimes in.

"My lord, please allow me to do the honor of taking care of this traitor," Valincias requests.

Looking over toward the gray-eyed lord and shrugging before turning his gaze toward the greasy-haired captain, Lord Hamzi says,

"Very well, it shan't make any difference. I'm assuming you shall be dueling for yourself, sire?" he asks, looking toward the chained man.

Seeing his long hair shake as he signals yes with his head sends chills down my spine. "What is this fool doing?" I mumble.

Alas, the man's wishes, and my hopes, are dashed with a voice shouting, "I shall fight for him, my lord!" coming from the crowd.

Perplexingly, I watch as the man I sought to confront steps forth out of the gathering of bodies and in front of the three leaders of Cedar Keep.

"I shall duel for him," the man repeats, now standing next to the chained prisoner. Turning his head to face the man he claims to fight for, I see the scars protruding from his left cheek as I had in the market, confirming my theory. Then seeing the ginger wink at the captive fuels my inner flame of interest. "And who are you to this man?" The lord asks.

"I am no one, my lord. However, this man is my friend, and I vow to fight in his stead," the mysterious man says.

"Noble. Tell me your name, sire," Lord Hamzi demands.

"Sylas, my lord, Sylas Budd," he says.

"You shall lay your life on the line for one who commits such high and heinous crimes against his Elder and, even more so—the king?" the lord asks. Sylas shrugs in response to the lord's question.

Baffled in utter disbelief, Lord Hamzi sits on the cedar throne and throws his hands up in the air, indicating 'very well.' Thus, the duel is set to begin as Lord Bale signals to the guard to move the man to the side as they clear the area for the trial by duel. Each opposing force between the towering men is apparent; one fueled by anger and hatred, whilst the other is shrouded in darkness and questions. It matters not, as every eye, including mine, locks to the scene in front of us with the fate of an accused traitor hanging in the balance. The captain of the guard fighting against a stranger. A man who seemingly has a death wish, yet Lords Bale and Hamzi stand and watch as the two unsheathe their weapons, unlink their cloaks, allowing them to fall to the ground, and prepare for a test of wills and intellect.

AMON

BOUND ON THE BALCONY

Harsh and cruel is the ongoing image skimming its weight across the stone. Frigid and sterling are the objects in use whilst desires of conquering an indomitable figure stands before the opposing forces. The two whose fate lay in the hands of practice and patience prepare to exchange arguments for the trial. Cases being made for the accused awaiting the judgment of the land or perhaps newfound freedom at the end of this proceeding. A trial which has become volatile and fatal.

Seeing my old friend, with the steel tip of his blade resting on the ground, incites panic and delight in nearly simultaneous moments. My fellow hunter, finally here to ease my burden of captivity and the looming punishment that is bearing down on my shoulders, makes me protrude a grin. Filled with delight, I still speak no words, rather wait and watch the scene unfold in front of my eye.

Circling each other slowly, Sylas is the first to make a move. Scraping the weapon against the floor they tread, he eventually flips it up and strikes down in one, smooth motion. The advance is swift and full of power as the veteran member of the guild shows no sign of letting up, unleashing another barrage of slices—all being rebuffed by the edge of the opposer's sword. With Sylas on the attacking end of the blows, the captain looks to be on the back foot as they both continue to clash metal, unrelenting in their duel. Whilst all bystanders watch in awe at the spectacle, I can't help but notice the truth lurking within the test of skill itself.

The leader of the keep's guard is no match for Silas, shown in every move he makes. In fact, after training and traveling with Sylas for an endless amount of time, I can sense him going easy on the guard, as it seems he's toying with him. Only adding to my theory, the captain advances with a thrust; however, Sylas swiftly kicks Valincias's left leg out front under him as he sidesteps the blade. The larger leader of the keep lands on his knees as I watch Sylas glide behind the man with his double-edged blade now at the ready to cause ill fate on the captain's throat.

Sylas shouts, "Yield!"

Seeing the outmatched man's face filled with disgust and disdain, he exclaims, "Never!" striking his blade against the one that imposes itself against his livelihood. The action gives the captain a momentary reprieve as he rises to his feet and faces Sylas.

As the two throw daggers with their stares, I can feel the rage thickening in the air around the angered commander of the guards. With a near growl and scream, Valincias rushes rashly at the well-trained and battle-hardened opponent he finds in my partner.

As this unfolds, being able to see what happens next while also knowing a victory for Sylas has never been in doubt, I rise to my feet—standing at the ready to be released of my bindings. As I stand, ready to feel victory and freedom, the duel is over in a flash. Sylas, being able to see right through the captain's bull rush tactic, steps to the side of the man for a second time, ripping the blade out of his hand as he lunges past. Once weaponless and moving at a high rate, Sylas gives him a kick in the back and watches as he crumbles to his knees. The fight was quick and clean, with little doubt of outcome as the captain falls to his knees twice in a matter of seconds.

Aiming Valincias's own weapon at the back of the captain, Sylas raises his hand—about to plunge the steel through the guard's cold heart. Yet before Sylas can complete his action, a shout causes a stop in the duel.

"Halt!" the lord on the throne yells before calming his tone. "This trial is over. You may take the prisoner and go. You have until sunrise to be out of this city. If found within these walls after the sun has risen, you will be brought back here to be hanged."

All spectators, including myself, lock their attention to whether or not the fiery-haired man shall heed the words of the interim ruler. I don't know why I would ever doubt my friend, however. He has never been one without mercy and shows such again. He listens to the orders of the lord with a clatter of steel on the floor. Sylas, after dropping the captain's sword behind him, walks over to pick up his cloak. Saying no words nor looking at the lords—who both observe with intrigue, links his tattered robe back on and gingerly walks over to me. Stopping his steps, he looks at the lord on the wooden chair and signals to my chains. With a flick of his finger to the guard, the blades of a key set me free. At long last, I now can attempt to guide myself without having to appease the wills of others.

"Come on, mate," Sylas says. "About damn time, aye?" I banter back.

Laughing through his nose, he wraps my arm around his shoulder in an attempt to pull me along. Passing the witnesses in the crowd, nearly every damn eye is wide open, tracking us as we leave, disbelief written on their faces as we head for the spiral staircase. However, through all of this, the wound on my left side doesn't yield in its outpour of blood.

"Ahhh… shit," I mutter, hobbling down the stairs of the tower. Sylas stops our movement and whips his head around to see the red liquid inking out. "Gods, what'd they do to you?" he asks.

"I shall explain later," I say, wincing in pain as our paces continue. "Agreed. Let's get you stitched up," he responds.

Swirling around the stairs, I struggle to keep pace. The torch's flames flicker on every wicker down the well, and with each passing wave of heat, it gets whiter and whiter. The frame of my one eye only sees Sylas, the steps, and rail in a brighter and brighter fashion.

"Amon..." I hear, but a stinging ringing in my ears drowns out anything more. Empty of light. A Dark chasm.

"Have I lost the other eye? What's going on?" I fret, feeling my way around the black void.

"Amon," I hear, echoing around the vacant space.

"Who's there?" I yell, but nothing returns in response until sharply, the voice yells, "Amon!"

With that, my eyes fly open to a blinding light above me.

"Amon," Sylas says, blocking the overhead beams of light.

"You're okay, fella, just relax." "Uh... what's going on?" I mutter in my weak state.

"Don't fret, friend, we're in a safe space. You just need to rest," Sylas says.

"Sylas, we need to get to the guild..." I manage to get out before the voice of a woman trounces over my words.

"You're in no shape to go anywhere, the Gods favor you for still being able to breathe with the amount of infection and blood you've lost," she says, peeking over where my body lays.

Fuzzy is the outline of the woman, with the sun raining in from above. Upon looking at her blurry face, I ask, "Where am I? Who are you?"

Cutting her off from responding, Sylas says, "She's a friend, don't be worrying yourself with her, she's just here to make sure you get properly healed," he says.

My mind roars with questions, but my body can't quite get them out, as I am plagued with frailty and drift back into nothingness.

Finding myself surrounded by shadows and a bleak emptiness from before, I begin to wander around the space. I notice no shuffling of my feet, no noise coming from afar, and when I speak, nothing comes out. In complete and utter silence, I observe my surroundings, waiting vigilantly for any nightmare that may jump out from the never-ending darkness. To my surprise, no monster, no man, no evil lurks in the plane of empty space, but rather I hear a familiar voice call out, "I see the crow has had his wings clipped?"

Furrowing my brow, I mumble, "Master Kylian?"

The voice thunders all around me once more, "How are we?

Little bird."

At the moment of hearing him again, I attempt to shout, "Master!" yet nothing comes from my mouth.

"Still putting the weight of a boulder on your shoulders, I see. Perhaps, 'tis time, don't you think?" Master Kylian echoes.

Realizing I have no choice but to listen, I don't try to respond but rather wait as Master Kylian says, "Time to let such a burning rage go. You pin the sins of others to yourself, to your heart, and in turn, it has grown black and started to wither."

However, Master Kylian's words seem to get farther and farther away as his last point is made, "...Little bird, it wasn't your fault."

Hearing that statement, I awake to a burst of color, warmth, and light—finding myself sitting up on my wool, having broken a sweat. Panning around the room, I find a smaller space. The brown wooden walls accompanied by a massive mural encasing an entire wall with panes of glass depicting the divine Rol, God of confession. The God is depicted as a man-like figure. His arms outstretched with open palms, whilst a red hawk sits on his shoulder. In the room itself, I can see my bedside table and an entrance to another room. I hold my newly bandaged side, grab my black cotton shirt, put it on, stand, and head for the doorframe. If I wasn't already in a state of perfusion from my dream of my old and deceased mentor, I would be now, as I struggle to make it seven paces to the entrance of the other room, leaning against the frame to rest my body. Now, in front of me and out of the light that beams down through the glass ceiling, I can see my long-time partner and friend Sylas, sitting across from a woman in leather pants and a white blouse. My new surroundings are almost as small as the bedchamber, yet this one holds a cedar table that the pair sit at, more torches, a bookshelf filled with vials, and a long metallic table, on top of which rests bloody rags, a needle, and some thread.

The woman across from my partner gleams up from the table they both rest at with her sapphire eyes. Her curling blonde hair shakes as she stands. "Love, you can't be on your feet right now; please let me get you back to bed," she says.

Whipping his body around to face me upon hearing the woman's words, Sylas too stands. "Get your arse to bed; you need more rest for the elixirs to work," he says.

With his words reaching my ears, in addition to a woman standing to her feet, I shake my head no. "I'm alright. I'm not going back to those damn dreams. Just help me to the table, would you?" I ask the shorter woman in front of me.

Nodding, she places my arm around her as she guides me to the third chair at the wooden table. Sitting, I look over to my old friend. "We need to leave. We need to warn Master Kylian," I say, only to let out, "Ah, shit," as I wince in pain.

Sylas stares with worry at me amidst my pain as he says,

"Amon, calm down. We're not going anywhere until you heal."

Shaking my head whilst holding my side, I say, "You don't understand, Sylas, everyone there is in danger. Gods, everyone here is in danger."

"Breathe, Amon. Take a moment to collect yourself and explain," he says.

With a short glare, I look at the woman listening in seated to my right, only to look squarely back into Sylas's line of sight.

Understanding exactly what I'm getting at, he says, "'Tis fine. You can trust her, she's an old friend. In fact, Nyssa is the one who saved your life, you owe her a debt."

With a grunt and a nod toward the apothecary, I turn back urgently to Sylas to fill him in. "I figured out the intel we were supposed to get when we trekked down into Daharia. The man we were supposed to meet was named Idric Balken. He was a royal servant in Doves Peak, where the king currently resides. He wanted asylum in exchange for his information, but I guess he was silenced for accidentally stumbling across a document coming from Savar. His curiosity must have gotten the better of him, or maybe he did it all the time, but in that letter, it listed talks of alliance," I say. "That can't be; the rumors of war brewing were all but set in stone with the Elder taking an entire garrison to the border only two or three days ago," Nyssa chimes in. "Wait. Just listen," I ask.

As she nods back in response, I continue with my findings. "It was rumored Savar would only agree if the king gave refuge to those who seek land. Specifically, the refugees whose land was taken by the king himself. Those who lived on the isle, the Lymarians, whose land he stole, the Daharians, whose homes he burned, all in the name of expanding Elium."

"But the king must want something in return? He's never been the one to give away favors," Sylas says, standing up and looking at Nyssa. "Hmmm, this can't be a coincidence?"

"Wait, what do you mean? What coincidence?" I ask.

"Prince Dedric was assassinated in the manor only a handful of nights ago." Sylas returns his gaze to me.

Staring at him quizzically for a moment, I return my eye to the grooves in the table. "What...?" I mumble.

"Some rumors coming out of the manor... apparently half the keep witnessed him die in the grand ballroom. They described a brutal scene. I would have seen it myself, but I ran off from the gala before it happened," Sylas responds.

"What were you doing at a gala?" I ask.

"Had this friend missing, miserable one he is, but I was looking for some sort of clue to where he may be," he says sarcastically.

I let out a short chuckle before asking, "Do you know the cause?"

Sylas shakes his head side to side, whilst Nyssa speaks up, "No one knows, just that it caused a mass panic in the walls of the manor."

"Gods' sake... I don't know how that fits... I just know there's something bigger at play here. For the people in this keep and for the guild. If the refugees get this land, they shall just be indebted to Savar. We both know they can't stop expanding their territory when getting the keep. They shall explore all the lands around for the opportunity of wealth and commerce that nature provides. It'll only be a matter of time before they find Fort Kael," I say.

Pacing around back and forth, Sylas waits a beat before asking, "How in the gods' name did you figure this out?"

Thinking back on the harsh and long journey, I say, "It wasn't too long after Daharia. When you set out for the guild, I went back to Kyme at the border. I asked anyone and everyone if they had encountered the informant we were supposed to meet. After a day or two, I had no leads. I felt so angry, so disappointed—and that fueled me to keep searching. So I went north to the closest town, Normun, where I found Daharians offering passage to some misplaced Lymirans. I figured the man we watched get his throat slit had to get himself a guide as well, so, in exchange for a rather large amount of coin, they pointed me to the couple who took him. They both said the only thing that kept the man calm was wine, so they watched as he pumped himself full. I don't know how he lived as long as he did, as, apparently, he would tell tales of the capital quite often when he was drunk. It seems one night, he let a little too much slip whilst traveling in the desert with the husband and wife.

The couple told me all he had told them… but they said he would cut himself short when he realized that he was giving too much away," I explain. "Fuck's sake," Sylas groans.

"The next day, I found my room surrounded by the guard. The couple had sold me out as a bounty hunter because I forgot to cover my damned markings. Unfortunately for the couple, instead of receiving coin for turning me in, they met an ill fate. I saw them both strung up and hanged in the center of town whilst being carted away in the back of a transport," I say. "Fuck's sake," Sylas repeats.

"Who was the man who caught you?" Nyssa asks.

"Don't know. He just stayed until I was caged and bound, then diverted away from the path that led me here. No name, no title, just a leaf insignia on the links of his cloak," I say. "You've been through some shit, aye?" Sylas chirps.

"I'm fine, we just need to get to the stronghold and warn Master Kylian," I say.

"Woah there, love, you're in no shape to even reach the market," Nyssa says. "If you try to make a long journey, you'll bleed out before reaching the outer gate... not to mention after what happened at the trial, the guard will jump on any chance to see you dead and gone, the both of you."

Sylas stops his pacing and leans over his chair. "She's right. You need rest. If you die, any chance of saving the keep from someone else's politics does as well," he says. "In the meantime, someone needs to get word to the officials of the manor here. I don't care if they fucking hate us, they'll want to know this information."

"No... no, if we do that and our intel falls on deaf ears, or even worse, those who help plot this, we'll never get to Fort Kael," I say.

"And if we don't? Thousands of people here could be led to slaughter. Innocent people. Fathers, mothers, children. All of whom will be struck down in the name of 'alliance' and the 'king's will,'" Sylas returns.

"Sylas, you couldn't possibly know that; that's simply the worst case, not something that is set in stone," I fire back.

Looking at me firmly, 'tis like I can feel a second eye burning its hardened line of sight from underneath his eye patch. "Amon. Even if you say this is a worst-case scenario, that still means there's a possibility of a massacre. One that we could very well help stop. I don't know about you, but my conscience wouldn't be able to go on if such an evil act does happen and we did nothing to stop it," he says.

Even in my weak state, I can see there's no budging on this, as Sylas can be as stubborn as a mule. "Do as you wish," I say.

Rolling his eyes, Sylas says, "Nyssa, I need you to stay here with him briefly; I need to send word to the guild's contact in the manor. I shall be but a moment," he says, treading toward the glass panes.

With a push of the lower right side of the glass, a hidden entrance hatches open and Sylas steps through and out of sight. The glass shuts once more, making up the deity of truth, with only two bodies remaining in the room; myself and my healer.

Staring at the picture my fellow hunter exited through, I shake my head. *What a joke. Getting involved in the politics of men, what a fool.*

As if she can read my mind, I hear, "You can't be upset at him for wanting to help."

Glancing over to Nyssa, I tease, "What? You can read minds as well? Wonderful."

"If I could, there'd be nothing for me to read since yours is empty," she responds. "Ha, brutal," I chuckle.

She stands, causing her cedar seat to screech against the stone. "You know as well as I, his heart is in good spirits with this," Nyssa says.

Tracking her as she passes in front of the table, making her way to the long, steel surface with an assortment of tools, I say, "His heart is exactly what shall lead us to demise. We don't meddle in politics. The guild doesn't meddle with politics. 'Tis taboo, 'tis bordering on code."

Quickly, she fires back, "Doesn't sound like code to me. Sounds like a bunch of men who have no fucking balls got scared. Sounds like a heartless, soulless way to carry yourself, especially with what you know," Nyssa says, cleaning off the operating table.

"And you're so sure about this want to survive? To ensure your own safety first?" I ask.

"Loria's sake, you know that's not the same in this situation. Or are you truly blind in both eyes, not just the one?" she whips back. Sternly, she holds me in her trance as she says, "When Sylas asked for my help, he told me his brother was dying. His brother. That's how he views you, that's how much he respects you. Loria knows why..." she says, turning back around to grab the needle and thread.

Her words strangle my mind as I think about my counterpart, but nevertheless, the trail of thought is broken by the tapping against the frame of glass. Having been given what I assume to be a code by the repetition of taps on the mural, Sylas crosses the threshold— this time returning with a look of apprehension on his face.

Upon noticing the facial expression, I ask, "All went well?"

Closing the hideaway entrance behind him, he says, "Mm hm, just noticed the God this place serves to worship on my way back in."

Inciting a quizzical nature inside me, I ask, "I didn't know you were such a religious man! What's with the face? What's the bother?"

"You've never heard the tale of Rol?" Sylas asks, sitting down at the cedar table. I send him a short glare, indicating my answer.

"Right, of course not. What is a God to the great Crow of the guild," Sylas teases. He then turns his attention to the blonde woman. "Nyssa?" he asks.

Carrying the surgical items from the steel surface to the table where we all three now sit, she answers, "Hmmm. If we're thinking of the same story, all I can remember is the need for sacrifice... or Rol was sacrificed? I really should listen more when the priest gives his sermons."

"Ha. Seems like you're not the only one," Sylas says, giving me a short glance before continuing. "He died for his honesty. His brothers and sisters believed his truth-telling nature would lead to a human uprising. They feared Rol would tell man and woman the secrets of the gods, thus there would be no more humans and gods... just gods. So, they sacrificed him to the eldest of the siblings, which we know as the Loria. They killed him out of fear for what he knew and his honest heart. His kind heart."

Silence sits in the room as Sylas ends the tale; however, I can't help myself as I let out a prolonged laugh. While loudly letting out a chuckle, I spot Nyssa and my partner staring at me with somber looks.

"Oh, come on, you both can't believe in this shit?" I ask.

The pair simultaneously answer with a resounding "Yes," and I ease back into my chair. However, even with their collective agreement, I can't help but find them naive.

"Then you are fools. The churches, the gods, they're only here to control the hearts and minds of men. You believe if there was an actual divine, the king would share that with the common man?

That he wouldn't hide that away to himself? For power? For legacy? Piss off," I say.

Cutting the tension in the room with his humor, Sylas grins. "Ah yes, the fools are the ones who weren't captured, beaten, and stabbed by the guard of this land," he says. "You should mind yourself, Amon. What you call luck, others call fate. What you believe is a coincidence, others believe is divine interaction, and that very idea can be more powerful than any man. Any throne. Any crown."

Wise words indeed, words that I know to be true even through my own strong-willed opinions. Belief is power, and that very well may come in different forms and sizes, and it seems I am not the only one to agree with the ginger.

"Thank the Loria, there's at least one intelligent man in this room. You know he was starting to dull my mind with all his negativity while you were gone?" Nyssa quips, looking across to Sylas.

Having taken enough banter and stories for the day, I roll my eyes and stand up, the room filling with natural light pouring in from above. Holding my side, I waltz to the secret entrance.

"Where the fuck do you think you're going?" Sylas asks, not even bothering to shift his body around.

Now, standing at the mural, I say, "Well, I'm not staying and being harassed after nearly dying. That, and I haven't had any decent food in about... mmm, a full moon cycle?" I say.

"You're already bleeding. You think you're going to make it to the market?" Nyssa chimes in to say.

Hesitating to open the door, I look back down to my side, which is indeed dripping with streams of red liquid. Annoyed that she's right, yet understanding I can't be rash with this decision, I look back to my healer and sigh. "I die of starvation or die from loss of blood. Not much of a difference," I say.

"When did you get so dramatic? Did you pick that up in jail?" Sylas teases.

Snickering, Nyssa speaks once more as she rises to her feet. "Oh, leave him alone before he really does get worked up and loses more blood. Besides, I'm not letting my work go to waste, just stay here and I shall come back with enough food and wine for the three of us," she says. Picking up her brown cloak and looping the string around her neck, it notches into a position where it stays on. She paces to the picture of glass, passing by me as I head for my seat, and leaves. With the two of us in the room looking at one another, I open my mouth, about to talk.

Cutting me off, Sylas says, "Don't."

Caught off guard, my brow tenses. "What? Don't what?" I ask.

"She's far beyond your reach, fella; I wouldn't try to charm her. She's a lion in pants," Sylas says.

"For the gods' sake, grow up," I say, with a slight smirk.

"I know, I know. I'm joking. What is it?" he teases.

"I'm concerned—" I say before Sylas cuts me off. "By the Gods, Amon, I told you I trust her," Sylas returns.

Leaning over the table, I say, "You don't understand, Sylas. 'Tis not her I don't trust, 'tis the eyes and ears around that I'm avoiding," I say,

"Eyes and ears I don't trust," what in the gods' name does that even mean?" Sylas says.

"You really believe they'll let me just walk out of here? With the information I know?" I say.

Raising his eyebrow, my fellow hunter responds, "Amon, I think the blood loss is making you delusional. Make your point," he says.

"I'm saying if the captain of the guard visits me in my cell to punch and stab without consequence, there's no limit to what these people will do. Can do. There's no limit to who's even in on this.

With one wrong word, with one misplaced or drunken sentence, we'll be caught and hanged," I say

Releasing the tension in his face and sitting back in the wooden chair, he says, "I understand your fear—" he begins before I interrupt.

"Fear? No. I fear no man, no god, no devil. I don't fear an end,

I am petrified of a massacre. Not of these people but of our own," I say.

"I see." Sylas nods his head. "I think your heart is in the right place. We can't act on our emotions, however, we must take this one step at a time," he says.

"My emotions? What about the one who wants to play savior for the people in this keep? What about your loyalties to the guild? To me?" I say with fire in my words.

"Amon, don't be so naive. I don't want to be a savior. If we're securing the future of our family, who shall secure the future of the families here? Not out of guilt, not out of the emotion of rage or disappointment, but out of the need for growth. Growth for good in this hold. The hope that this kindness shown shall uproot the wickedness embedded in the cedar's roots," Sylas returns in a kinder manner than I.

With that, I sit silently in contemplation of his words, raking my mind about whether or not there is truth in them. Naive? Me? Naive to what? Safety, security, the want to live? Or the need to secure a future? Alas, my thoughts subside as Nyssa enters the fold once more, coming through the makeshift door. In her arms, she carries two loaves of bread and one bottle of wine. "Ah, lovely!" Sylas exclaims at the sight of her.

Bringing the bought items over to the table, she sets down the loaves and wine, shaking the wood where it sets, and crumbs fall off.

Nyssa pulls the wooden chair out and sits. "Not interrupting anything, am I?" she asks.

"Drink and eat are always welcome interruptions," Sylas returns.

Breaking off the edge of the loaf, Sylas then pours himself a glass of wine using a cup brought over from the cabinet and bookcase of vials. Following suit, Nyssa does the same, and thus so do I, as we each prepare our meal and drinks before dining together. In doing so, our casual conversation begins to flow.

"How did the pair of you meet, anyway?" I ask whilst taking a small bite of the chunk I pulled off.

Raising her eyebrow, she looks at Sylas. "You want to answer this one?" she says.

Sylas chuckles and turns to me to say, "Jail." I start to laugh before realizing he's telling the truth. "You can't be serious?" I say.

"Afraid not," Nyssa says. "Been making friends like him about every time I end up on the wrong side of the bars."

"I was in for theft whilst working in… Lymre? Or was it the Silver lands?" she asks, looking toward Sylas.

"It had to have been Lymre? Maybe? God's what was I there for..." Sylas mutters and shakes his head. "It had to be for Kylian, old fucker always ends up in a state of chaos when he leaves Fort

Kael."

As we converse, the sun above shimmers a little less as dusk draws near. With little thought to the observation I make whilst looking up, I ask, "What were you doing with Master Kylian? I've never seen him leave the grounds of Kael."

Taking a sip of wine, he says, "I can't say I remember. This was years ago, mind you, but if Kylian does ever pick up a bounty, 'tis generally for the big fish," Sylas says, putting his cup down.

"Big fish? Like... the royalty?" I ask. "Mmmhmm," he says, nodding.

"Have you ever been on these bounties with him?" I ask, wanting to probe more about the guild's figurehead.

"No. He does everything alone; simpler that way," Sylas responds.

Shoving another handful of bread in my mouth, I say, "But that must be dangerous, no? We can't just accept our leader goes unguarded to some of these meetings, intel gathering, finding targets, or whatever the hell he's doing for the king. Right?"

Putting his wine down and looking at me, he says, "Amon... the man has a small army under his command, the political backing of the king, and the power to start a war when or wherever he would so choose... to tell a man like this he can't do what he wants is impossible. I've tried and so have many others before me. He's as strong-minded as he is wise."

Wise? How can a man be wise when he puts himself at such a risk? Shaking my head side to side, I crack a smile at the notion.

Piping up and adding to the ongoing conversation under the now black sky, Nyssa asks, "How'd the pair of you meet? You seem to be just the best of friends."

Between the pair of us, both sets of eyebrows raise at the question. My mind churns, thinking about the faraway past, yet Sylas is the one to speak first. "Ah, yes, the day I started to lose my hair," he teases.

"Don't pretend I'm the one who puts stress on the other," I fire back.

"This coming from the same man I just saved from being hanged, then she saved from bleeding out?" Sylas returns.

Smirking, I nod. "Fair enough, but let's not forget about the five times I've done the same for you," I say. "Fucking Five?! What are you on about?" Sylas asks.

"Savar—that's one, Doves Peak—that's two, Savar again— three, and... Daharia, so maybe just four," I say.

Putting his cloak on and standing, he smiles and says, "Absolute shit, you damn well know I saved you in the sea of dunes."

"Guess we'll let the gods be the judge of that. Where are you off to?" I ask.

"I've got to meet my contact north of Cedar Manor, near some taverns, I should be back in a short while. Nyssa, Amon shall fill you in on how long he's been a pain in my ass," Sylas says as he heads toward the glass panes.

As he leaves, my mind places itself into contemplation and unease, but instead of voicing such emotion, I look toward Nyssa to my right. "Long story short, Master Kylian raised me alongside Sylas. The guild found me in a barrel of cabbage brought to the keep from here. Word has it, they took me back here to see if anyone had been missing me... but I guess I wasn't something someone wanted, as no one took me back... and thus I was raised in Fort Kael. Sylas was there as far back as I can remember, like an older brother. We fought each other, or rather, I fought Sylas, as he's always been more levelheaded. Then we grew up, collecting bounties together, fighting together if needed, laughing together, drinking together, and now..." I say, standing up and putting my shirt on as I hit a point of realization. "We always have one another's backs."

I watch as Nyssa throws her hands up and shakes her head. "Lovely story, but where do you think you're going?" she asks.

"Had to give him some time for a head start," I say. "We always have each other's back. I'm going to protect my brother, even if 'tis from a distance."

"Amon, he's fine. He's more than capable of taking care of himself. Not to mention, you are so against the whole idea and now, suddenly, you're on board?" Nyssa asks.

Turning to her as I approach the exit, I say, "He may be an idiot, but he's my big idiot."

"Don't know what the blazes that means, but 'tis obvious you're not going to listen to me, so do as you please," she says, taking a sip of wine.

As the fleeting conversation subsides, I now face the door and push the glass to a smaller opening, only to step through and find myself in front of a chapel. With wooden pews and candles all abound in the place of worship, I take my strides step by step, eventually making my way past the minister's altar and table of incense behind it, where I stand in the aisle between the seats on a red carpet. As I scan the room, I notice the glass ceiling above, the murals on each and every window, and finally spot the priest lighting candles in the window to my left. "Hey!" I exclaim, holding my side.

Rotating his body around to meet my line of sight, the priest stands in his traditional garments—a long black robe and red collar. As he turns to me and furrows his brow, I ask, "Did you see where the man who just came through here went?"

Setting a candle down, now lit aflame, he approaches where I stand in the middle of the room.

"Lower your tone," the priest says, now standing in front of me. "You don't know who's listening in."

Unrelenting in my demeanor, I stare at the priest until he speaks once more.

"A handful of maids come here for service, and in return, we've grown great relationships over the years. He's on his way to meet one of them," the priest says.

"Sylas said they're meeting north of the manor, did he say where specifically?" I ask.

"Afraid not, friend," he says, walking away, back toward the candles.

With little choice, I head toward the large black doors at the combined entrance and exit of the church. Passing by wooden pew after pew, I finally reach them and push open the large opening. Upon doing so, the night sky appears above, with few and far between twinkles lighting up the horizon.

Not getting caught up in the darkness of the sky, I take a left out of the building and onto the stone road lined with torches on each house, church, tavern, and brothel. In doing so, I feel paranoia tickle my skin, as if I am being watched. However, I see no one on the street looking my way. With that feeling setting my skin on fire, I keep my head down as I walk the streets, passing civilians or guards, swiftly aiming north, around the manor, to find the mass of taverns together on one street. However, throughout my entire walk, the keep itself is silent, aside from the noise coming from within the buildings I pass by.

There aren't many guards on the street, nor people, as most have found their destination for the night. With that, I feel cautious, and most notably—I feel vulnerable, as I am one of a handful of bodies on the cobblestone. I push my worry aside and face the challenge ahead of finding Sylas in the dark of night. After dozens of paces, I round the manor's edge and find myself on the northern side of the colossal structure. Here, I find noise bustling out of the buildings, ranging from songs, brawls, or just conversation in each one I pass. Yet, as I pass the third tavern on my left, I spot a brown cloak far ahead turn down an alleyway.

"There he is," I mumble, and so I follow suit with my steps. Keeping a distance, as I am unsure whether or not this figure I follow is my fire-haired friend, I wait a moment before turning into the alley. Now in between two lively places of gathering, I make my way to the end of the alleyway, where it splits off into two directions. Around the corner to the right, I can hear the paces of a figure trailing away. About to follow, I feel a sudden jolt of angst and surprise as a hand falls over my mouth and someone drags me back before I'm able to round the corner.

Fighting back, I throw an elbow into the body behind me, causing a release in their grip whilst I spin my body around to face the person. Shockingly, I stand in front of a familiar figure. I attempt to grip the handle of my blade, only to realize I left it in the Church of Rol. Noticing what I am trying to do, the man throws his hands in the air.

"I only came to help," he says as I hear the Isle of Reed's accent in his voice.

Shaking my head side to side, I ask, "Damn you, what can you possibly help me with, guard?" "You're walking into a trap," the guard says.

With that, I spiral, thinking of what Sylas is about to walk into. My thoughts are erratic, as I can't focus on anything else other than sprinting after my companion.

Running away, the guard who once watched over me in a cage, yells, "Wait!"

Alas, I don't listen to the man as I sprint around the corner, only to see the brown cloak surrounded by cloaked figures, including one I met face to face a moon ago.

"What the fuck is he doing here?" I mumble at the sight of the captain of the guard, the same man who gave me the injury I carry now.

Stunned and standing still in the alleyway behind all the taverns, I watch as the men subdue and beat Sylas. Wanting to take a step forward, the foreign guard grabs and pulls me back once more.

"You saved my life, now I owe you the same," he says whilst bringing me back around the corner.

Fighting him off, I turn to him. "We have to help him; give me your sword!" I demand.

Yet he doesn't as he points to the blood coming through my shirt. "And you'll do what? Fight seven guards and the captain? While dealing with that? I wouldn't be saving you at that point, I'd be giving you a death sentence. Your friend is already lost, for now, there's nothing we can do."

My mind spirals as I peek around the corner to see Sylas being dragged away, surrounded by the keep's insignia on each cloak. In disbelief at the situation, I sit against the wall and put my head in my hands.

BALE
KEY QUESTIONS

The day of judgment

With the leadership thinned, as both Jov and Elder Elovis have left for battle, the tasks needed to be done around the manor have increased. Hearings with local vendors begin my day as I find myself listening to the needs and wants of all sorts. Ever incredible is the greed festering in the hearts of men. All who come in and out during our proceedings ask of one thing: self-interest. Requests of lower taxation, higher taxes imposed on competitors, and those who simply seek power. One who aims himself for that very same goal stands before us. Sir Leroy. He, a well-known and traveled merchant, visits us with his own petition for power in the key room. Knowing him from his repeated pleas in the past, I expect the weaselly man to ask of one thing: coin. Unsurprisingly, he begins to do just that as Valincias and I sit on either side of Lord Hamzi.

Hamzi, delegating whilst the Elder is away, clears his voice before saying, "Our time is yours. Speak when ready."

It takes little time for Sir Leroy to announce himself to the room as he says, "My lords," with a bow and then continues. "Firstly, I must say how refreshing 'tis to see you, Lord Hamzi. I hope your time in the capital yielded you great wisdom."

"Thank you. I am very pleased to be home. 'Tis nice to see a familiar face in yours as well," Hamzi says.

"As is it my utmost honor to see yours. Tell me, I've heard absolutely magnificent things about Doves Peak! Please do tell, is it true what they say about the wine?" Sir Leroy asks.

Hamzi chuckles. "'Tis… great?"

"Ah! Excellent! And the marketplace? Is it true it has the biggest—" he says before being cut off.

"Go on with your request, Leroy," Valincias interjects.

"Oh… hmm… well, my lords, it seems I've come to you three with an offer," Sir Leroy says. "A great proposition for the entire keep to reap the reward from!"

Wary of the coming words from the deceitful man, I ask, "And this proposition, what does this entail?"

"How delightful of you to ask, Lord Bale! This idea is one of many fortunes for... well, the keep... the throne… and perhaps me as well," Sir Leroy says.

Valincias scoffs before he says, "Of course you benefit. Why wouldn't you?"

"Exactly! But not just me! You three shall stand to gain so much

TIRAN

coin you can build a new tower! Or perhaps fix the cracks in the one standing..." Leroy says.

Hamzi leans his weight onto the table, placing his hands down, causing a small thud. "Leroy... I hear a promise of fortune, but nothing of the sort has been spoken in detail. I suggest you spit it out," he demands

"Very well," Leroy says. "My sales of boar have increased over the course of the season. Their fur, their meat, their horns. It seems the town has fallen in love with its soft touch and savory stew. Yet... I don't come for coin but rather... for the assistance of your guard."

Lord Hamzi, with wine pouring into a cup in front of him asks,

"And what is it you would ask of the Elder's guard?"

"Hunting, my lord... one may even call it training!" he says. "More feet on the prowl would not only cause a rise in product but also serve as great practice for your men who have not seen the field of battle."

The captain of the guard lets out a thundering laugh. "Ha! You think chasing around swine would prepare my men for war?!"

Not letting up on his request, Leroy defends his plan. "You would very well be surprised at the sight of these animals! I've seen soldiers smaller than these beasts! Yet another reason not to let them wander the forest of the keep," he says.

The risk involved with the vendor's request seems high, as losing valuable men over personal interest goes against my own integrity. One Elder Elovis would never agree to, let alone entertain; however, my thoughts halt as I feel the weight of the table shift.

"Captain, would you please show Sir Leroy the way out of the manor," Hamzi says.

As Valincias scrapes the chair against the floor, Leroy says, "For every three pelts sold, all the money comes back to the throne. I believe that to be more than generous."

Valincias's voice proclaims, "What a fool! You would have us give you our men in exchange for you to walk away with almost all the earnings?" as he stands.

The captain's paces walk toward the merchant, aiming to end the meeting and escort the man away. However, catching us by surprise, Hamzi intervenes, "Wait!"

The footsteps of the captain halts.

"Half of the earnings in exchange for ten guards. And if, Loria forbid, we lose a guard; we take the full earnings from that hunt," he proposes.

Confused at his want to negotiate, I say, "Hamzi, perhaps we should discuss this." Knowing we cannot afford to lose guards whilst the majority is away with Jov and the Elder, I try to speak reason. However, before I can get the words out, I hear the snake of a man shout, "Deal!"

Not even acknowledging my worry, Lord Hamzi says, "Wonderful, then, Valincias shall escort you to my chamber, where we shall discuss further."

All at once, the movement in the room is bountiful as footsteps tread around.

Getting to my feet and pushing the chair back in, I wait a moment before asking, "Lord Hamzi, may I have a moment?"

"Of course," my friend says as the paces of Valincias and Sir Leroy lead away.

Pausing to ensure the pair is beyond earshot of our conversation, I ask, "Hamzi, you can't possibly be entertaining this? Leroy has swindled nearly every citizen in this keep out of gold, and we're just supposed to trust him? Entrust him with the lives of our men?"

Feeling a firm hand lay on my shoulder, I listen as Hamzi says,

"Bale, 'tis not Leroy I trust. 'Tis you." "Me?" I ask.

"Bale. I would never send our men out alone with a jester such as Leroy. With you there, however, I don't foresee any issue if

Leroy decides to go against his word... or likely try," Hamzi says.

My brow stoops in confusion. "You're asking for me... to hunt boar?"

He laughs, as his steps recede toward the door. "Hunt. Watch. Drink. Fuck. Whatever suits you. Who knows, maybe you'll find it to be more entertaining than at first glance. We shall discuss more after the trial, friend," he says. "As you wish," I say.

All of a sudden, the feet pushing off the manor's floor halt. "Oh! Bale, it nearly slipped my thoughts. There's a man today who supposedly caused quite a violent scene while being transported here. I would like you to see to it that there is no chance of commotion," Hamzi urges.

I nod at the request before the door shuts. The key room is emptied as I'm left with my thoughts.

Noting both of the lords' requests, I push the door open and walk into the hall. Upon exiting, I hear the voice of a familiar handmaid call out, "Lord Bale!" from within the corridor.

Hearing the woman, I reply, "Ramona! How are you on this moon?"

"Good, my lord! I hope all is going well," she says.

"All is well, what can I help you with, Ramona?" I ask.

"Not me, my lord. 'Tis Lady Illia. She's requested your presence," the servant says. "I see. Did she say what the matter is?" I ask.

"No, my lord, she just asked for you to meet her in the observatory," she says.

A pleasant surprise as I respond, "Thank you, Ramona," with a bow of my head.

The manor's floor sends off small vibrations as the woman recedes away, but not before she says, "Of course, my lord!"

I take my strides toward the staircase and Illia. Yet I can't shake the stirring feeling in my gut about the conversation with Sir Leroy and Hamzi. "Might be more entertaining than at first glance, hmm," I mumble. I don't believe Lord Hamzi understands me very well; hunting is the last thing I would find solace in. Honestly, I would find it more enjoyable to hunt Sir Leroy rather than chase down greed, killing something that has never known any better or at least have a say. I would have considered my friend, Hamzi, to be more mindful of me before volunteering me to be his middleman. Alas, it seems his time in the capital has changed him… changed things between us… changed the way he operates. Nonetheless, I shall have another word with the lord after judgment is given to the criminals brought forth during the trial later this moon.

For now, it matters not, as I feel the spiraling spine of the tower come to a halt, slightly saddened, as with all the fresh-smelling flowers and scents of perfume floating on what I presume to be the walkway, I lack the opportunity to fully take in both of their respective beauties. The closest I've ever come is the faint outline of Lady Illia, wrapped in her signature scent of lilacs. Rarely ever getting that close, I am more accustomed to her tone, as I now hear it call out,

"Bale!" she says.

"Lady Illia," I say with a bow. " You mustn't send poor Ramona to chase me down across the keep. Those steps nearly did me in; I couldn't imagine what they'd do to her poor soul."

"Or maybe she needs the exercise," she says.

I laugh before saying, "One day, she'll get you back after all these years."

"Oh bother, she gets spoiled by me. Least she can do is send a message… besides, I wanted to see you before we leave for the capital," Illia says as her voice takes her away from where I stand.

Following the echoing in the passing air, I ask, "First your father and now you and your mother leave the keep? Seems as if

I'm scaring you all away."

"'Tis that sense of humor that eventually shall," she laughs.

"Perhaps, but, if I may, I can't help but be a bit hesitant to have you two leave with the recent passing of his grace's heir," I say.

Pushing past what feels like outstretched limbs and flower buds, I listen to Illia as she says, "You needn't worry about that, Mother and I shall be more than capable of handling ourselves amongst the royals. Besides, with father off, we need to show a strong force in front of the king... oh, these are lovely! Are these new?"

"I see... and what of your guard? Who shall protect you and Lady Elovis while in Doves Peak?" I ask.

"The king, I presume," she says as she turns and calls,

"Guard!"

The jingling of metal draws close before I hear them speak, "My lady! the guard says.

"Would you mind telling what kind of flowers these are?" she asks.

Briefly, silence falls, before the guard responds, "I'm not quite sure, my lady. These were planted after your gala, a gift from Duke and Duchess Arys—"

Interrupting the pair, I question, "Pardon... and if anything were to happen whilst you two are there?"

"And if anything were to happen to us while there, I expect you to be close behind... lurking in the shadows as you usually do... ready to pounce," she quips. Giggling, she thanks the guard before I feel his steps retreat away.

All the while, no more words are said. I stand still with little realization of Lady Illia sneaking into my arms until her hands wrap around me. I pull her close to my chest, embracing in a hug, all the while in shock at the gesture.

Whilst close to my ear, she whispers a request. "I need you to promise you'll be safe. I need you to promise me that when I get back, you'll be here and Cedar Keep shall go back to the way it was before the gala," she says.

Pulling away and aiming to speak into her eyes, I say, "I promise."

With those words, she lets go as I hear her gliding away.

"Until then," she says, leaving me alone with nothing but the heat of the sun and the aroma of lilac that slowly starts to fade.

My lips curve upward into a smile as her words of promise linger in my mind, yet with no light to waste and a date with criminal procedure on the horizon, I head toward the stairs. While descending, passing each floor one by one, an unfamiliar and rather bothersome stench begins to become prevalent. Smells of shit, piss, and dirt fill the stairwell. Doing my best to disregard the smell, I arrive at my desired destination. "My lord!" is what I'm met with.

With a nod in response, I add, "Show me to the man who incited trouble on the path." "Yes, my lord," they say.

Sensing the weight of something rather heavy scrape across the ground—presumably the door, the voices of those detained grow loud. Shouts of obscenity and vulgar prods firing left and right.

Interrupting them, or seemingly paying them no mind, a guard

says, "The Loria smiles on this man, it seems. Two visits in one day."
"What do you mean two?" I ask.

With the steps of the two guards going through the doorway, one responds. "Captain Valincias paid the beast a visit yestermoon," he lets off with a chuckle.

What reason would Valincias have to come here? Him, of all people, wouldn't drag his cape on the same earth as those he considers beneath him. Odd 'tis to hear this, but instead, I say nothing whilst we continue walking. Moans and groans call out from either side of me. Steel being beaten, men and women alike shouting, yet I remain steady. No man, no woman, nor words send chills down my spine, as they pale to the wickedness that put them here: greed. All who shout and spit vile do so out of emotion. These emotions trick them into never being able to satisfy their wants and neglect their needs. However, 'tis not I who judges them, rather 'tis only I who sees through their facade.

Arriving at the end of the hall, I ask, "Is this him?" "Yes, my lord," one replies.

"Very well. Make sure he's secured tightly with steady eyes on his movements," I command.

"Yes, Lord Bale," the guard replies. "However, I don't think he's in any shape to do any damage."

Foolish 'tis to count one out based on one's appearance. Those who are broken are often the ones who rise to become unbreakable. "Even a blind man has tricks up his sleeve. Don't be naive to any up his," I forewarn the two. "Yes, sire," the guards both say.

Turning back from where we came, I say, "I shall be waiting

outside," before pacing away. Walking back through the doorway, I imagine life outside the Keeps walls.

I wonder how the Lord and Jov are getting along. I wonder if they're waging war as we speak. Fighting off hordes of men, galloping on horseback, putting to rest a rebellion against the throne. Or perhaps raising a toast to a swift victory or, perchance, treaty. Nevertheless, I hope for their safety and to receive word soon. As for now, I remain patient and vigilant, leaning against the wall separating the tunnel and dungeon.

Hearing the doors swing open one by one, I await the guard to chain and file the criminals into a line. However, with much surprise, I make notice of the odd sounds and shouts coming from the other side of the stone wall. With rapid steps approaching the doorway, my fingers crawl to the hilt of my blade. In near moments, the tip of my blade finds its resting point on the throat of the rotten-smelling individual. In little time, the guard, along with the serpentine of prisoners, draw close. They find me with a choice of mercy or judgment, yet my morals always overcome.

"Put him back in the cell… his actions shall make him have to wait longer for his judgment," I say before looking back toward the outline. "Consider this mercy, the next time you lay hands on the guard, they won't be as kind."

Taking my sympathy for granted, he shouts, "Damn you!" before the guard tugs him away.

With that debacle resolved, our journey toward the balcony starts. A longer climb but perhaps it shall serve me to process my day. More importantly, process the questions I hold: What could Valincias and this man have in common? If Valincias had thought there was danger abound, it would have been brought up in our gatherings, right? Perhaps 'tis just a grudge, perhaps 'tis a demon from his past... but that would be even more the reason to inform us. Curious. Perhaps he made Hamzi aware, but... why not me? What could be so special about one man that he would personally come to see him? I suppose if I needed to know, Hamzi would inform me. Yet my friend does seem to have his own adaptation of how to lead, a way that is growing vastly different from the Elder's.

Nevertheless, Hamzi was placed in charge with good reason, as the Elder knows him better than most. Practically raising him, same as me and Jov, since early in our childhood, he came to know Hamzi in the streets of the market. At that time, he was just a boy, scheming and tricking the locals with his games of dice. Not one citizen could figure out how he won every turn, not at least until the Elder played him himself. Elovis mentioned briefly before that he lost every single game. When brother asked why he claimed he won, the Elder would say, "With each coin taken, I grew ever so close to the mind behind the scheme. A mind that shall transform this nation." In turn, he took the boy in, and he became my second brother. Alas, many moons have passed since, and that boy is now the man who temporarily leads our people, leads me.

I gear my mind back toward the objective at hand after losing myself in thought. With few steps to go, we soon arrive at the peak of the climb. Exiting the stairwell's doorframe, murmuring finds its way to my eardrums. The chains clink and clatter along the path until 'tis consistent shaking stops. "Damn fool," I hear coming from well behind me as it seems one of the prisoners tripped and fell. Waiting mere moments, the march continues as we arrive out under the sun.

Leaving the rest to the guard, I walk to my place beside Hamzi and Valincias.

"Any trouble?" Lord Hamzi asks. I reply, "None worth reporting."

The lord, along with the captain of the guard, chuckles before the lead guard calls for silence, marking the beginning of the trial. The trial drags on in the usual fashion, with Hamzi leading it in the Elder's stead. His punishments being delivered seem harsh; however, they all lay in accordance with the laws of the land. From losing an eye, hand, foot, or toe—each man or woman is given their consequence. Others found it far easier, as they are let go for trivial mistakes, until the man of mystery finally comes before us. I suppose it isn't the royal announcer calling out the nature of the man's crimes, nor is it the gasps and screams from the crowd that struck a chord of surprise. Rather, a separate shock addresses my mind—the man who claims to fight in his stead. The mystery continues to grow around the so-called 'traitor,' as the one who offers to lay his life on the line seems oddly familiar. His tone and voice I am sure I have heard before... the one from the gala. The one who was exiting my chambers when I arrived only days ago. For now, I shall just observe. "And who are you to this man?" Hamzi asks.

"I am no one, my lord. However, this man is my friend, and I vow to fight in his stead," I hear him say in response.

"Noble. Tell me your name, sire," my friend requests. "Sylas, my lord, Sylas Budd," he says.

Sylas. It seems we meet again. This time, however, I shall never forget. This is evermore the case as I watch the pair duel. His footing, his breath, his heart rate, his reflexes, all show signs of experience you cannot teach. A true master of his craft. He moves fleet-footed and makes rather quick work of Valincias's aggressive stance and tactics. The brute has had the tables turned on him in quick succession as I stand rather vigilantly with Sylas now looking to end the duel.

Before he could do so, Hamzi screams in a panic, "HALT! This trial is over. You may take the prisoner and go. You have until sunrise to be out of this city or be cut down on the spot."

All day, around every corner, something or someone awaited with a bustling and energetic attitude... until now. I sense the atmosphere direly changing as the pair slink away through the crowd. Most stand astonished by the swift fight, some amused, but many fearful to have the two men walking free. No words are needed to understand this, rather 'tis the enlightening fact that there is only... silence.

The wood of the seat Hamzi sits on screeches. "When he gathers himself, meet me in the key room," he says. "As you wish," I say as he whisks away.

I look to where the royal announcer belted from before and give him a simple nod.

Upon the subtle command given, the announcer addresses the people of Cedar Keep. "That concludes today's proceedings! May the Loria bless you all!" he yells.

Thousands of steps echo off the smooth stone of the balcony and into the open air above the keep. All those citizens, all those loved ones, and all of those who seek entertainment file toward the exit. Waiting for the last pace to trail off, eventually the surroundings become quiet—until I hear several coughs from the defeated captain.

Breaking my standing stance, I walk over to where he is knelt down on one knee. As I draw close, I can sense the rage brewing inside this man. My hearing generally serves me better than it does others, and it paints the scene of anger. The painting is one of a man beaten; by another and his own emotions. Knowing this from his heart rate beating tremendously fast, followed by growling and snarling. "Let me help," I offer whilst extending my hand.

He grips the gesture tightly as I pull upward with a heave. However strong I may be, and train all I might, Captain Valincias is a mammoth of a man. "Damned bastard," he lets out as he finds his footing.

Not wanting to provoke him any further—although tempting, I say nothing in return as we both walk toward the stairwell. His heavy steps crash against the stone as we plunge further into the keep. With no letup in our pursuit, we arrive back to the very room where we all started the day. This time, however, the subject at hand consists of far more demanding circumstances than trade and boar. Entering the room, Valincias wastes little time.

"Send me after them. Let me hunt them down like dogs for what they did," the captain says.

"What did they do, Valincias? Embarrass you?" Hamzi says from across the table.

Taking a step toward the edge of the table opposite Hamzi, Valincias barks, "You'll have a traitor free in the city? One who clearly isn't working alone?!"

"No. But I am one who shall honor the laws of this land. Captain," Hamzi responds sternly.

With those words, Valincias offers no response. I, however, make a suggestion. "Allow me to follow them, my friend. We shan't break the deal but rather ensure they commit no further wrongdoing."

Hamzi paces toward us, walking around the table. "Bale, I do appreciate your loyalty and nobility to this land… but I need you here," he says before pausing. "Valincias, calm yourself. Once you do so, find the pair and observe."

"My pleasure," Valincias says before taking steps toward the exit. Yet in the midst of his attempt to leave, he is stopped. "Captain," Hamzi says.

I feel the weight of the floorboards shake as Valincias turns himself around. "Yes?" he says. "Only. Observe," Hamzi demands.

The captain offers no words in return, only the sound, "Tsk," before leaving.

As he paces out the door, I feel Hamzi start to drift out as well.

Stopping him, I say, "One moment, friend."

I wait for the captain's steps to dissipate and then seize the moment. "My friend, I have something I must confess," I say.

I can hear Hamzi's heart rate spikes with my words.

"This day is rather chock full of surprises, it seems. What is it you wish to tell me, friend?" he says.

"I believe the man who calls himself Sylas may have a role in the death of Prince Dedric," I say.

The Lymerian's chest sounds like 'tis about to explode upon hearing those words.

"That's quite the accusation. I trust you have proof of such a claim?" he asks.

I shake my head. "Not necessarily, 'tis a bit more of a theory," I say.

"Well then, entertain me with this theory," he says as the beats of his heart decelerate.

"I know this sounds... quite silly, but I believe the assassin we found after the gala was part of a larger plot," I say.

I feel Hamzi's weight shift as he leans back against the table in the center space of the room. "Go on," he says.

Continuing my train of thought, I say, "I only say this because Sylas was there the night of the prince's death. I followed him around the ballroom whilst I believe he posed as a servant. Not only that, but also I found him leaving my room. Same voice, same scent, same weight pressed down in his steps."

The mood shifts in the room as Hamzi asks, "Hmm... that is quite the theory indeed. I must ask, why wait until now to tell me?

Why not with Valincias here? Why not tell me at the trial?" I raise my eyebrow in response.

"Bale," he says.

"Yes?" I reply. "Do you not trust him?" he asks.

"Do I trust Valincias? In part. I believe we would both be fools not to see that he lets his emotions master him at times. That's why I waited. If I were to tell both of you about this theory, one of which I have no proof, he would seek blood," I say.

"Hmm, interesting," Hamzi says.

My brow furrows. "What is?" I ask.

"That you're right… but as you said, there is no proof, so I agree with you. There is no need to tell him. At least not now, not until you go find more proof," Hamzi says. "What do you mean?" I ask.

He pulls himself off the table and says, "I want you to assist Valincias. Not today, but tomorrow's moon. Allow the captain the night to himself to blow off some steam," he says.

"And if he is unwilling to accept my assistance?" I ask. "That's not an opportunity we can afford him," he says. "I see," I say, hesitantly.

Hamzi's tone shifts to a more serious note. "Bale. I'm asking this of you, because, unlike Valincias, I trust your calm resolve," he says.

I nod in response and say, "As you wish."

With a new task being delegated to me, Hamzi and I leave the key room and go our separate ways. However, after the long day, I feel the need to recoup under my sheets of silk. Yet as I walk toward my appointed room, I can't shake a specific thought.

"Do you not trust him?" rings through my mind. Of course, I do… Valincias has only ever been known to be, whilst many other things, loyal to his vows. Rather, more specifically, loyal to the Elder. But… what was Valincias doing in the dungeon? What about the man is so important to the captain that he'd personally come to interact? I guess

with that on my mind... I don't trust him... or at least I don't understand. Hmm, odd 'tis, and so too is the odd churning in my stomach. A feeling so strong it doesn't allow me to relax in my chamber nor ponder on anything else. I guess since I cannot allow myself reprieve of thought or feeling, I shall try to track down any information on the so-called 'traitor' and his friend. Hopefully, along the way, I shall be able to find Valincias and check his progress regarding the situation as well. Perhaps that's what I am to do after all; ensure he is upholding his vows and honor. `

With my objective set, I rise to my feet, grab a worn cloak, and aim for the servants' tunnels. This not being my first time sneaking out into the city, I know every in and out of the manor. It used to come in handy that Elder Elovis quizzed us about the architecture when Jov, Hamzi, and I would go to the taverns. Alas, that was years ago, and now what I chase seems to be much darker than the ale they served.

None the wiser to my suspicions, I walk past a multitude of maids, servants, and others alike in the underground halls. In fact, none seem to talk at all. 'Tis funny, they actually all stop in their steps when I walk within range. Except one. "Good moon, my lord," the voice says.

Going to bow my head as I walk past, I feel strange. My gut twirls at the voice, that being the reason I listen so close as I continue my strides. Her heart beats erratically. Yet whatever the issue, it matters not for now. Leaving my pursuit of the two traitors and Valincias is not an option, especially not over a matter with a servant of the manor. Pushing on, I reach the end of one of the halls only to find a door standing in my way. Before exiting with my cloak donned, I pull the cloth hood over my head to mask myself.

I then reach out and feel the wooden door. My left hand drifts downward and eventually rests itself on a wooden handle. Pulling and pushing the door open, I find… nothing. A city so lively in its markets, taverns, and homes is dull at this hour of the moon. Perhaps it may be the fact that this tunnel took me directly out into the balcony's shadow. A place with no light from above or below. However, even the beggars who normally rest here for the natural shelter have seemingly found a new home. Peculiar. Yet again, I won't let my quizzical nature deter my goal, so I push on. My feet make no noise as I slide across the stone walkways, wandering for a needle in a very large haystack. With no indication of where the mysterious pair reside, I start to ponder where Valincias would look first. After moments of guessing, I come to the rational and educated conclusion: the taverns.

Having to walk north, where many alike eat and drink, I expect more voices to sound out. Indeed, I am right, as the echoing of drinks and drunks draw near with each step northbound. Though, being much closer now to where I believe the captain to be, I stop my steps. Again, my stomach roars. Not one of need for food but instead one of intuition. I twist my head to the right and hear a clattering of boxes. Walking to the spot where the noise emitted, I tug on my hilt. Alas, 'tis just a boy who cries out. Harmless is the skinny outline who knocked over a stack of wooden boxes.

"Wait! Wait! I'm sorry, my lord!" he pleads, lying on the cobble.

Leaning over him, I say, "Calm yourself. Who are you?" "Ramses Fike," he says.

"Why were you following me, Ramses?" I ask.

"Following you? No, my lord. I'm following the men from the trial. You just startled me, I didn't hear you come up behind me. I looked over from the alley over there to you, and it caused my heart to race and my feet to slip," he says.

Offering a hand out to the young man, I say, "What alley?"

Using me as support, he gets himself to his feet and says,

"Over there, behind the tavern."

"Lest you forget, the blind can't see 'over there,' and there are a handful of taverns," I remark.

"Oh... apologies. He went behind Shrader's Tavern. I can take you if you'd like?" he says.

Shaking my head side to side, I say, "No, I shall take it from here. Can't have you knocking any more boxes over. Go home." "Yes, my lord," Ramses says.

Slowly, almost unwillingly, his paces recede behind me. With him now gone, I head to Jon Shrader's tavern. Jon keeps his places running all moon. Between him and his family, the establishment is always staffed, though it helps they live above it, all twelve of them. Putting my head down and tugging on the cloth, I enter the business, which is bustling with customers, waiters, and ale, and I waste little time mingling amongst those who gather here. My shoulders are tapped and squeezed by locals as I walk to the bar, looking for the owner.

Unsurprisingly, I'm met by a familiar voice,

"My days! Look who we have here! Thought you outgrew sneaking out of the manor? Or did the council want to revisit my proposal form this morning?" he asks, laughing.

"I wish I was here for pleasure, Jon, but neither of those is why I'm here. I need a favor," I say.

Amidst the lively noise, he speaks a bit louder as he asks,

"What's the favor?" "I need to go upstairs," I say.

His tone changes. "Upstairs? My home? What do you seek there?" he asks.

"I can't explain now. Not here. I can only say 'tis urgent," I say.

Exhaling heavily, he waits a moment before saying, "Okay.

But I shall remember this favor." "As shall I," I say.

Tapping the wooden counter, he says, "Hop over."

I swiftly climb over the bar and follow him through the doorway to our right into what smells like the storage room.

However, Jon's steps don't falter as he keeps advancing until we reach a staircase. With each step upward, the noise dissipates below. Wood squeals as he opens the door to his home.

"There's no one here at the moment. We're all serving. Let me know if you need something, but, Bale, I'm trusting you," he says.

With a nod, I thank and reassure him before walking past and through the doorway. Behind me, the wood meets its resting place as it shuts, whilst I stand and wait. Waiting for the feel, waiting for the smell, waiting for... the chill. Slightly, the wind nips my face and I head in its direction. Feeling my way around the unknown rooms, I rely on my senses to guide me. Yet again, they come through, as I can smell the city's open air; scents of cedar, ale, and mud. Then I hear it...

and the chills sent down my spine are vast in number. Valincias's voice echoing in the air.

"Here you are now, mutt. Seems like your friend won't repay the favor of saving you this time," Valincias says from below.

"Seems like you needed a lot more friends this time. I'm blushing, really," Sylas says.

With a thud, I hear the captain crack his hand across Sylas's face. "Quiet, you bastard. Get him to his feet," Valincias barks.

A multitude of footsteps clatter against the stone and off into the distance, yet an alarming crash onto the cobble is made below the window behind me. I slowly crouch and walk over to hear, "We have to help him, give me your sword!" another familiar tone projects before an unknown one says, "And you'll do what? Fight seven guards and the captain? While dealing with that? I wouldn't be saving you at that point, I'd be giving you a death sentence. Your friend is already lost for now, there's nothing we can do."

This must be his partner, but who's the third? No. No… what's Valincias doing? What's the aim here? What's the bigger picture?

And who do I get these answers from? If I confront these two, then I lose Valincias, but if I don't, they get away. Gods… it has to be Valincias, I can't let him kill this man. I must get answers from both of them before I send word to Hamzi.

Racing across the home's floorboards, exiting through the door, descending the stairs and pushing past those in the bar, I find myself on the street.

I hear Jon call out from inside, "Wait! Lord Bale!" but I have little time to lose as I glide in the direction Valincias and his men went. Keeping my ear out for noises in the distance, I track the eight pairs of legs marching back toward the manor. However, I am slightly confused, as the direction the footsteps are headed leads to the north side of the manor, and there is no entrance to get in. Even more baffling is the fact the paces stop and never start again. With little clue as to why, I follow to where the steps halt. To my surprise, I am correct. There isn't an entrance to the keep, above ground. However, it becomes obvious where they are heading after I hear the metal clacks under my feet. I squat down to feel a hatch, one that presumably leads into the waste system below the city. Removing the heavy iron top, I listen as the water trickles beneath my feet and foul smells come from within. However, with the dire situation at hand, I jump down and splash amongst the muck. I straighten my posture, as I have to land on my hands in the waste before focusing on my hearing. With the sound of passing fluid and constant echoes, it makes it supremely difficult to follow the captain and his men. Additionally, the lack of time forces me to act on instinct.

I must consider the fact that this is all carefully planned, and I must walk lightly in order to not get caught. Yet, with nothing to go on, I walk out of the stream and put my left hand against the curved walls. I use my hand to brush across the stone surface in order to help me remember my steps. Heading opposite the eastward stream, I wander into thick noise. However, my ears perk up as I faintly hear something in the distance. Picking the tempo up in my strides, I gain ground on the noise, as it becomes more and more apparent that 'tis the voices of those I seek. "This way!" Valincias barks, far off.

Those words are enough to approximate which direction to go.

Turning left into a new tunnel, I smell the wicker of a torch burn. In fact, as I keep walking, I can hear it flicker. The warmth of the torch, normally soothing, warns me of looming danger. There be no other reason for these to be placed here, furthermore even be lit, then for someone to know they would be coming. Going deeper and deeper into the tunnel system, more and more torches give off smoke through the halls. After a dozen more paces, I catch up to the voices, which are now coming from around a corner to my left.

Shouting, unaware that I can hear, Valincias bellows, "Look at you! Weak and vile, running around my city!"

"Vile? Well, vile I may be, but weak? That would mean you let a lesser man put you on your ass. Shameful for you, I suppose," Sylas chirps back, before laughing.

Not able to see, nor wanting to reveal myself, I can only listen as the captured man is struck fiercely.

With an "Umph," I hear his body fall to the ground before Valincias screams, "Get him up!" Chains rattle as the guard pulls Sylas to his feet, and Valincias continues to talk, "You know what is quite shameful? To even think your little spy would betray us! How truly pitiful she was."

Sylas's tone takes a drastic change. "What did you do?" he asks.

"I did what you do with a pest that gets in your way," he says. "If you touch her, I shall gut you, bastard!" Sylas shouts.

The captain lets out a terrifying laugh. "There's no need to touch the dead," he says.

"You bastard! You can't get away with sacrificing innocent lives!" Sylas screams.

"Innocent? You think anyone in these walls is innocent? In the walls of the manor? What a fool! I'm only sacrificing the lives of those who have done the same before me. The same to an entire nation! You know as well as I that no Elder, no soldier, nor any advisor is clean of evil," he says.

"Elder? What about the Elder and his advisors?! What have you done, you ugly cunt?!" Sylas exclaims.

Valincias lets out a short laugh. "Hmm, it seems you know less than what your life is worth. Amusing. I shall visit your friends to ensure they know just as little as you... then I shall take pleasure in ending their lowly lives," he says.

I hear the noise of saliva being collected before being spat.

"Why, you little fucking prick..." Valincias says. "I'm going to enjoy this."

Hearing the unsheathing of a blade worries me. I know I must make a choice between wanting to save this man from a certain death, while vastly outnumbered, or escaping without being seen in an attempt to share what I have just learned from the captain with Hamzi. However, my decision is made for me and my questions yield no answers as I hear Valincias say, "You know what this is? This is perfectly crafted, perfectly weighted silver from the capital.

Look closer, look how beautiful and pure. Let me warn you, however... just because it looks pure of malice does not mean it is."

With those words and the horrifying noise of the blade piercing the captive's skin. Sylas releases a cry of pain. Short-lived is the noise, however, as I closely listen before the beating of the man's heart stops. A man whose mysterious story shall never be known—aside from his end.

At this moment, I feel something I have not felt since I was a boy on the isle. Panic. The feeling planting itself so deep that my toes feel like they're walking on needles. It matters not, however, as I must push past the emotion.

Sprinting back down the hall and corridors of the sewer, I know I must alarm the manor of a treacherous plot against the Elder and his army. Yet hearing the captain yell, "After them!" only increases my rate of running with little to no chance of them catching me. I make a left, climb the ladder, and resurface, only to continue my sprint.

RAMSES
HOBBLING HOME

Rumbling noises coming from within each darkened alleyway cause me to pick up the speed at which I walk. The town's calmness, aside from those in the taverns, raises questions in my mind. Is it because of the trial? Sylas? Or perhaps an official order coming from the manor? Nevertheless, the silence coming from each street pales in comparison to the questions I now hold since speaking with Lord Bale. Is it possible he is the one responsible for such a quiet night? Or is it pure coincidence? I know one thing for certain. His entire interest was focused on the two men. One I knew for certain to be the man who was placed on trial, the other seemed to be... a guard? Peculiar 'tis, but alas, the lord has his own agenda and needn't explain it to me, yet I still wonder what became of the interaction.

For now, my questions come to a rest as I exit the walls of the keep. Looking down the hill, the moon's radiance lights up the stone path between the fields, farms, and huts. Passing alongside each crop, animal, and torchlit home, I spy a familiar sight. Seeing smoke coming from our chimney, I quicken my pace, knowing Mumma awaits me. She must have been ill with me missing for some time now. Perhaps I should have come straight from the trial to find her... yet my curiosity indeed got the better of me.

Surprisingly, once I enter through the framework, I not only see mother but a lovely sight in Erin as well. With much haste, the pair push their chairs out from the table as they stand.

In tears, Mum-ma exclaims, "Thank the Loria!" whilst rushing toward me in an effort to embrace. She hugs me tight with little to no showing of letting go as she asks, "Where have you been?!"

"I've missed you too, Mum-ma. You're hurting me, though," I say. Grimacing at her tight grasp, she lets go upon noticing my face expressing pain.

"What happened?!" she asks.

Lifting my shirt, I expose the marks and cuts gifted to me by my past cellmate and guards.

Mother's hand goes over her mouth, and she bursts into even more tears, leaving her unable to speak.

In hopes of easing her mind, I place my arm around Mum-ma and say with a smile, "'Tis okay, I'm home now."

Still standing at the table, Erin breaks her silence. "Loria's name, Ramses, you always find a way to hurt yourself."

"Ramses, I've missed you. Ramses, I've been ill with worry. Ramses, thank the Loria you're alive… Good moon to you too,

Erin," I say.

Letting out a short laugh, she curves her lips into a smile and walks toward me. Letting a single tear fall from her glimmering eyes, she says, "I've missed you," before giving me a kiss on the cheek.

"Perhaps I shall go missing more often if this is what I shall return to," I joke.

A punch in the shoulder makes me grimace. "You deserved that one," Erin says.

I laugh off the sting and return my attention to Mum-ma, who weeps onto the hay scattered across the floor. I hold her as tight as my wounds permit me to.

"Mum-ma, 'tis okay, I'm here. I'm okay. I'm not going anywhere," I say.

Her sobbing lets up as we shuffle toward the boar pelt covering the dinner table. "I'm sorry, I'm so sorry. Loria, forgive me," she says.

"Mum-ma what are you on about? Quit that. You have nothing to feel guilt over," I say.

"No, I do. 'Tis my responsibility. I shouldn't have tried to keep you here. I should've let you explore, I should've helped you find a way to see more. Then you wouldn't have run off," she says.

I break out into laughter. "Wait. Wait. You believe I ran away?!" I say

"Ramses! Now is not the time to laugh! We thought you were gone! Or worse; dead!" Erin exclaims.

Staring down at the table, I say, "I'm… I'm sorry. I just… didn't run. I would never run. I would never leave without saying a word."

I hear nothing in return, so I pick my gaze up to see the pair with their brows drooping in confusion. "I think you owe us quite the explanation then..." Erin says.

Sitting back in the wooden chair, I say, "I don't know if you'd believe me, to be perfectly honest... but very well..."

Detailing each step, each interaction, and overarching story, going deep into the night with the entirety of my journey, they sit in disbelief. My tale finishes with my perspective of the walk home, and they sit silent for a while.

"Well, I shall get cleaned up then," I say with the lack of response causing a rise of anxiety.

Grabbing my hand as I rise out of my seat, Mum-ma says, "Wait. Please, wait. I'm... I'm so sorry. I don't have the words to describe... anything right now. Except that I'm so terribly sorry my love," she tears up.

Erin chimes in as well, however her rage spreads thickly across her face. "Damn them!" she blurts out.

"Erin, 'tis ok—" I start to say

However, she interrupts with, "No. Damn those greedy bastards. This is beyond okay. This is beyond a simple wrong or singular act of greed!"

"Erin, lower your tone. The last thing we need is someone to overhear," I say. "Damn them! Let everyone know!" she yells.

With tensions being raised, Mum-ma intervenes. "Perhaps we should take the night to process all of this," she says. "I believe the last thing we all want or need is another draining night. Besides, we need to treat these wounds."

With a nod in agreement toward mother's words, I look at Erin, who still holds a tight fist and frustrated brow. Alas, she reluctantly releases the tension in her face and hands. "Very well. We shall table this conversation for another moon," she says.

"Good. Now that we've got that settled, let me fetch the bucket and water before I heat it over the fire," Mum-ma says, easing herself out of the chair and to her feet. She pushes the door open and walks out into the torchlit street before it comes to a close once more.

Seemingly following Mum-ma's steps, Erin finds her footing. "Where are you off to?" I ask.

"Home," she says, walking toward me from the opposite end of the table. "Or... you can stay?" I propose as she draws close.

Leaning down with a smile, she says, "Perhaps when you're back to full strength... perhaps a day your mother's not home."

With a wink and kiss on the cheek, my face heats up, and I cling to this newfound warmth spreading through me as she glides out the door. My ailments fade into the background, and all I can feel is my heart racing. However, this time, 'tis due to something lovely, something comforting. In this newfound happiness I feel, I stare off into the brick walls, drifting away, thinking of Erin, and don't even notice Mum-ma re-enter. I jolt back to reality with her passing in front of me.

"She wouldn't leave my side while you were gone," she says. "Part of me thinks she just sought to comfort me... the other half believes she sought comfort for her own heart."

"Oh bother, leave me be," I say, smiling.

"I tease, I tease. However, I do think you two would have cute kids," she says.

"Okay. That's enough from you," I say with my cheeks feeling hot once more.

Laughing, she puts the bucket over the flickering flames and says, "Very well then. However, I was pondering; perhaps we should take a day off and go to the market to get your favorite treats?"

"I don't think pudding shall help me heal, Mum-ma. Quite honestly, I would like to return to normalcy. For the first moon ever, I look forward to the market tomorrow. It would be nice to see some familiar faces," I say. "Besides, I don't think the manor shall allow you to take the day away from work."

She lets out a short laugh whilst dipping a finger into the bucket before saying, "Very well. How about we get you cleaned up?"

Rising out of my chair, I make my way to the stump around the back of the house. Mum-ma wastes little time using the first bucket to clean off the dirt. Yet, with her aiming to go inside and warm another, I find myself alone.

Wet and exhausted, I sit on the stump. Trying not to see the weak image I imagine of myself, I avoid looking toward the panes of glass from the house. Alas, I fail at doing so as I catch a quick glance at my reflection. Nearly half of my face is black and brown, my nose still maintaining an open wound, and my locks of hair are matted into patches due to the water and muck. A figure of defeat, a figure bested by the cruelty and corruption this keep affords its own. I feel bested and meager at the sight of my image.

Not needing to torture myself any further, I close my eyes and await the downpour of warm water.

Pour after pour, the grime eventually falls off. Deciding my hair, face, and wound are as clean as they get with the use of a bucket, Mum-ma walks inside, leaving me outside on the stump with only a tattered cloth. I use the rag to clean the rest of myself off, wiping myself from chest to feet, then aim my paces around to the front of the house. Upon entering, I see Mum-ma holding a dark-brown fur blanket.

"Here you go, love," she says, placing the blanket around me. With a warm smile, I thank her before saying, "I do dearly wish

I could converse more, Mum-ma. I am frankly worn to my bones."

"Ramses, you shan't offer any apologies. I am only grateful that you found your way back to me," she says, smiling.

With the fur still encompassing most of my body, I say, "Good moon, Mum-ma."

In response, Mum-ma looks at me and says, "Sweet dreams,

love."

The fire is put out, and both our heads find their resting places for the night. Not long after, I drift away.

Visions of the cells cause my heart to race. Vivid and detailed, and my mind panics at the sight of the dingy room. My eyes look all around, only to find cold steel. Momentarily, I look across from me and into another cell. Seeing a darkened figure in the corner, I call out, "Nyssa?!"

Getting closer to the bars that separate us from the hall, I speak again, "Nyssa, what's going on?!"

Rushing toward the front of the small, square, room, a ghastly sight causes me to awake to the sunlight coming through the window. I feel my brow as sweat rests upon it, and catching my breath, I take my mind back to the startling image. One of Erin. Her face showcasing many cuts, almost as if carved into a symbol. A jester's hat etched upon her fair skin. With not the slightest idea of what it represents, I feel much terror at the thought.

Shaking the dream out of my mind and standing firm in reality is seemingly tougher than I imagined. Even after dressing, eating, scanning the empty house, and packing the wooden crate with vegetables, I can't seem to get the symbol out of the forefront of my brain.

Have I seen this before? What significance does it hold? What about Erin? Is she safe? Does she need me? No, Ramses. No. She's well. She's home. It 'twas a dream, just a dream. Perhaps I should check on her before work. No, no there's no need. Enjoy the day, enjoy the sun whilst it blesses the sky. Something I often took for granted before my stint in jail. Something, I, Ramses Fike, need to cherish this moon, this moment, this life.

However, 'tis quite the damper that today the Loria decides to cry over the keep, letting down drops of water, as the sun quickly flees behind heavy clouds.

With my newfound goal, amidst the horrible weather, I repeat the customary trek to the wall of the keep. Sloshing and shuffling through the muddy path, I am for the gate. Even a downpour of the Loria's tears cannot hide the Great Wall as I draw close. This time, as I approach, I come prepared with an entrance fee—as I am willing to take extra precautions to never end up in the dungeon again. At least not in similar circumstances. So, I wait in line along with much of the other common folk to be permitted inside.

Little by little, the line in front of me dwindles, whether due to admittance or the unwillingness to stand in the cold, until I am face to face with a guard. "Ten silver," he says.

Taken aback by the doubled entrance fee, my heart rate rises. It is unlike me to lose my calm so easily. However, I do my best to gather myself and breathe. Running no risk of irritation, I approach the iron hawk in hopes of appeasing him and myself. "I've got five silver but... how about two beets as well?" I ask.

With a raise of his brow and a glance all around his surroundings, my heart picks up pace.

With haste, I exclaim, "Forgive me! I offer no bribe! I simply only have five silver! I apologize, sire!"

"Shhh! For fuck's sake, gather yourself, son," the guard says. "I accept your offer, now hand it over and get moving."

In a short trance of shock, I snap myself out of my daze and begin to hand him the beets and coin. As I put the beets in his hand, he nods and lets me pass. However, before I get two steps away, he grabs my shoulder. "Speak to no one of this," he demands.

I only offer a nod in response before going through the gate, and entering the city.

Ten silver? First they add a new taxation and now the manor doubles it? It truly is a world belonging to the powerful. Alas, I train my mind toward the objective at hand: selling the shit out of these crops. With having no one in the market for almost half a moon cycle, our profit has surely plummeted. Even on a day like today, where 'tis miserable out, I am sure we shall still make more. Alas, it looks like a daunting task to make coin, as I notice the market is lacking customers. There are a handful of citizens occupying the area, along with fellow vendors, and this sight brings me some hope as I smile at each passerby, though they offer little words. Those who work as vendors all seem to have questions prepared: "Where have you been?" "What caused such bruising?" "Are the murmurs true?" are just a handful of the curiosities my fellow workers have. Alas, even with no intentions ill of heart in their inquiries, my subconscious feels shame. A feeling of being judged and found guilty floats around me, almost serving as an invisible cloak, swallowing my entire being. With these insecurities on the rise, I attempt to shift my focus back toward a day of commerce. That is until I see a cloaked figure already waiting in front of my stand.

With the long black cloth covering the entirety of the being, I can't make out any distinguishable features. Furthermore, the rain only adds to the difficulty of making out the person. The only detail that truly caught me as odd happened to be the very bottom of the cloth, which was ripped and covered in mud. Nevertheless, I turned on my charm, as I wanted to get the day started off early with a sale. "Eager to buy the best crops in hold, I see! How are we on this moon?" I ask. "I am truly eager, but not for this," the male voice says.

Struck with awe and worry as I see Lord Bale tugging the black cloth across his face to hide himself. The Loria must be toying with me, as I have seen the lord thrice in a span of three slumbers.

"My... my lord... what have I done to deserve such a treat that is your presence?" I ask as my brow creases.

"Ease your mind, lad. I only come to ask with curiosity," Lord Bale says, water dripping off his hood.

How can this man know such a thing? Is it that obvious I am caught off guard? Is my face red? Do I shake? Alas, I needn't ask and push my luck. Instead, I stay nimble on my toes. While the lord is calm and known to be kind; I have since learned that the keep is full of wicked and selfish ambitions. Therefore, I word my question with care as I ask, "Of course. How can I assist you, my lord?"

"The men from last night. What did you see?" he asks, getting straight to his point.

"I, uh, only saw the two men that I mentioned to you, my lord," I say.

"Who," he asks bluntly with his smoke-filled eyes.

"The man from the trial and a guard, my lord," I respond urgently.

"Ramses. Be precise and true with your words," Lord Bale demands.

Feeling rather hot and out of breath, I aim to regain my composure.

"Your heart races faster than the wheels on a carriage. I mean you no harm, Ramses. I just seek clarity," he says.

The market around me begins to spin. The lord's face comes in and out of focus as I breathe at a rapid speed.

"You must sit. Your heart and lungs need a reprieve," he says.

I heed his words by turning over the wooden crate and taking a seat.

"Place your hand over your heart," he says.

Following his advice, I rest my left hand over my chest.

Still standing in front of the wooden stand, he says, "Now count to the seventh heartbeat before you breathe in. Then wait again, count till you feel the fifth heartbeat to breathe out," Lord Bale instructs.

Following his guidance, I wait and feel the vibrations of my heart patiently and only inhale on the seventh beat whilst exhaling upon feeling an additional five patters. Upon doing so, my focus slowly returns, and my breathing comes back to a normal rate. "How did you know how to do that?" I ask.

"When I was a boy, my brother would succumb to the same illness. I learned that timing is decisive; not too many breaths, not too little. A structured amount," he says.

With my hand still over my chest, I find my footing. "Thank you, my lord, I had yet to experience such a reaction before this moment," I say.

Unrelenting in his stance and demeanor, he says, "Apologize not for a reaction you cannot control. Yet I still await your words about the men from the night prior."

"Of course, my lord. It was the man put on trial, not the one who fought in his place," I say. "And the guard?" he asks, raising a black eyebrow.

"Not one I've seen before. Shorter, tan, not much else I could tell with only the moon's light," I say.

"I see... thank you. Anytime you feel yourself falling into the same spiral, repeat the steps I told you," Lord Bale says, turning his back to the stand.

My mind, not yet recovered from the inner sensory overload, is scattered. However, I know one thing to be true: my past experiences with the other enigma, Sylas. Knowing the risk of my body falling ill again, I yell out with a mind of fog. "Wait! There's something else," I say.

Stopping his steps and turning back to look at me in his mostly black cloak, he gestures his hands as if to say, "Well then?"

In response, I tell the lord all I know. From the beggars' attempts to steal, Sylas coming to my aid, his advice, his goal of finding his friend, and where I saw him last. Alas, I did leave out the part about running into Valincias. I know not his relationship and wish not to test my health any further.

With explaining everything in detail and honesty, the lord seems rather content with what I tell him as he says, "Thank you," and holds out his hand to shake.

Pulling my palm off my chest, I grasp his grip and give him a firm shake. "I can show you exactly where he went if it would appease you, my lord?" I ask.

For the first time, his demeanor changes. "You nearly faint at the sight of me; now you wish to immerse yourself into the situation? I can't advise that in good mind," he says.

I match his seriousness with a grin and respond with, "Tis a good thing I had not asked for advice."

The lord chuckles. "I see… I shan't stop you from what your heart desires," he says.

"Glad to come to an agreement," I say, starting to pack vegetables back in the crate.

The lord furrows his brow at the sight. "You need not do that," he says.

"What do you mean, my lord? If I leave all of these crops here, they're sure to be stolen," I say.

With a short snicker, he shakes his head whilst tussling with something under his cloak. "Here," he says.

The sound of metal clicking together emits from the cloth as he tugs out a small leather pouch and proceeds to toss it directly into the wooden box. "That should cover it all," he says.

Grabbing the pouch, I can tell just by the weight that the coin inside could buy all our crops three times over. Taken aback by the gesture, I shake my head in disbelief. Alas, I don't notice the lord starting to drift into the crowd.

"Well then, are you coming?" he asks, gaining my full attention once more.

With no words, but rather a burst of excitement in my paces, I aim to catch up to the lord. Upon doing so, we navigate through the wet streets of the keep and toward the cobbled road Sylas had turned onto. Never venturing this way myself, as I typically only visit the market inside the city, I attempt to take in all of the new scenery. However, I am not particularly impressed. Rundown homes, shady characters, and brothels line the streets. The occasional church is also tucked away here, yet they all look relatively lifeless. The streams of water falling from the sky don't help portray the scenery in good lighting either, yet I doubt that to be the main reason for its poor portrayal. Nevertheless, we arrive at the very spot where I last saw the ginger enigma.

"This is where I saw him last, my lord," I say, pointing toward the surprisingly lit-up small church.

"Ahem," Lord Bale interjects.

Realizing my mistake, I say, "Apologies, my lord, the church to our right. Or at least this was the direction he headed." "Hmm, how peculiar," he says.

I wish to ask the lord what he means by that comment, yet I stand silent and watch as he approaches the church's doors, lets go of the cloth covering his face, and, with a soft push, opens the large wooden doors. The light from within reveals a quite delightful scene: one of many dark cedar pews, great and diligent murals, as well as a golden chandelier that helps light the room.

Watching as Lord Bale enters inside and disappears, I make a split decision. One between returning to my stand or even home with a newfound sack of coin or following into the unknown. An easy decision for me as I jolt up the stairs, escape the rain, and go into the chapel.

Excitement washes over me upon entering, or rather; adrenaline. Alas, the feeling flits away as I see the new sights within. A priest to our right, lighting candles on an oak table, and a greatly detailed and large mural of the god Rol. The panes of glass take up the entirety of the back wall. An intriguing picture of the god, one I haven't seen in quite some time… actually, ever. Rol, the deity of truth, was never a prominent figure of worship in my life. I have heard a multitude of stories of tales as I grew up on the outskirts of the keep. Yet all I, and many others, know is the Loria. However, this painting causes my excitement to diminish and confusion to rise. I know not why, but what I do know is that this feels… wrong. It feels... evil. However, the lord seems unmoved by the scenery. Perchance 'tis the fact that he cannot see the great mural, but it seems there's a bit more to it than that. With his hand on his sword's hilt, he remains quiet, so quiet in fact that 'tis as if he is listening to something. Yet, there is no noise aside from the pitter-patter on the roof and windows. Not even the priest speaks to break the silence, that is, until he finally notices us. Turning from lighting the candles on the table, the man walks toward the blind lord.

"Good moon to you both," he says kindly.

Letting Lord Bale take the lead, I stay mute and only observe. "Good moon, father," Lord Bale returns.

"Good moon, my lord. How can I help the pair of you?" the priest asks.

Lord Bale says, "Well, father, it seems I come to you with quite the piqued curiosity," he says, pacing past the clergyman.

"And what would this curiosity entail?" the priest returns, slowly trailing Lord Bale. I watch as the pair walk to the altar.

Inspecting the white sheet and the candles of incense that sit on top, Lord Bale asks, "Father, would you happen to be giving shelter to anyone?"

"No, my lord. We typically only advise all those who come through our doors seeking such to visit the taverns, as they may have a spare room for cheap coin," he says.

Seemingly ignoring the priest's response, Lord Bale walks away from the table and close to the panes of glass depicting the deity. Inspecting it, Lord Bale rubs his hands along the glass.

Noticing his actions, the priest walks up beside the lord and ask, "Do you know the story of Rol?"

Turning to meet the clergyman face to face, Lord Bale says, "I do, father. He was the God of Confession. Or truth, depending on one's perspective. He sought to bring man hope, or what we know as honesty... and for his actions, he was betrayed by those he trusted."

Letting out a small chuckle, the priest turns his attention to the painting. "Indeed. I must say I am surprised at your knowledge of this divine. 'Tis not a tale told often in these times," he says. "I am surprised as well, father," Lord Bale remarks.

The minister's brow raises with confusion as he asks, "By what?"

"With Rol being the God of confession and you being his servant, I would expect you to uphold your vows," the lord says.

The priest's face goes red. "How impudent of you to assume I would break my word... who do you think you are to accuse me of such?!" he says.

Taking off his hood and revealing his longer black hair and light brown complexion, Lord Bale says, "Father... I could hear their breaths from out on the street."

Mine as well as the minister's eyes light up at the lord's statement. Yet in the midst of our shock, a false door in the mural swings open. Rushing out is a silver blade, aiming itself for the lord. Impressive it is to see the lord's reaction time as he narrowly saves himself by pulling his sheathed blade in front of his face, blocking the strike. The one bringing the attack is the man from the trial. He growls at his attempt being blocked and chooses to follow his first attempt with two more. The lord, still using a half-unsheathed sword, blocks the first thrust and takes a step back to dodge the second. Watching as the lord nimbly avoids his opponent, I stand at the ready in case there is a need for my help. However, the lord seems well off, as his dodge causes the attacker's blade to clatter off the altar, knocking off a multitude of candles. This allows Lord Bale to fully reveal his weapon out of his scabbard and ready himself in his stance. One hand gripping the blade as he points it down to the floor behind his right side, preparing himself for any move.

"If you aim to meet the gods today, say such. Otherwise, I have only come to converse," the lord says.

Sneering at his words, the man, dressed in torn brown cloth, races toward his opposition with a lunge. Shockingly, the man never reaches the lord, as he is grabbed from behind. Unbeknownst to me, two more people had hidden themselves in the hideaway. One being the guard from the night prior and the other being Nyssa.

The pair grab one limb each in an attempt to hold the angered duelist back.

"Amon, stop this!" Nyssa shouts as she and the guard pull on the man's shoulders. "Nyssa?!" I say, inching toward the scene of conflict.

Her head whips in my direction. The sight of me must have caught her off guard, as her eyebrows raise whilst she says,

"Ramses? Why the fuck are you here?!"

"You know these people?" Lord Bale asks, sword still drawn.

With my eyes wide with surprise, uncompromising in my stare at the woman, I say, "I do, she's a friend... of sorts."

Upon hearing that, the lord eases out of his stance and sheathes his weapon. Whilst on the other side of the altar, the previously ferocious Amon rips his arms away from the guard and Nyssa.

"What have you done with Sylas?!" Amon says, pointing the tip of his steel toward the lord.

"It is not I who has done anything to him. I only come to you with inquiries, not vengeance," Lord Bale says, his hands open in front of him.

Alas, the man Nyssa calls 'Amon,' the man from the trial, remains unrelenting in his sternness. "Liar! I saw him being dragged away with the captain of the guard! Do not stand here and spew shit in my face as if you two do not work toward the same agenda!" he shouts.

For the first time I have ever seen, Lord Bale seems uneasy. His posture slumps as his head lowers and his eyes, albeit of no use—or at least he says, train themselves on the floor.

"I offer you honesty. I know not the reason Valincias took your friend," Lord Bale says, raising his head back up. "However, if 'tis your friend you stay to search for, I must warn you… it shall only lead to despair." "What do you mean despair!?" Amon asks.

"I was there last night, above the alley. I listened the entire time. To both conversations. Yours," he points to both Amon and the guard, "And theirs. Yet, I couldn't in good conscience let Valincias get away, or at least attempt to stop him. Thus, I tracked them from the tavern to the sewer, where I eventually found them in the tunnels... I must say... I am truly sorry, I had no idea what Valincias aimed to do to him," Lord Bale says.

Growing even more visibly enraged, Amon shouts, "What do you mean?! What do you mean 'aimed to do'?!"

Shaking his head slowly, Lord Bale says, "He's… dead."

Upon hearing this, Amon's outstretched arm drops—lifeless His head falls as well, with his shaggy hair covering his face. Scanning the room, the bodies inside stand in a trance. Nyssa, eyes tearing up, offers no words. The guard, too, stands silent. Lord Bale awaits a response in a hush. Not even the priest opens his mouth at the statement. However, eventually, sound emerges.

Noises that resemble the pellets of water falling outside echo off the hardwood floor. The sound comes from the man I watched stand trial a night ago. He emits even more as he mumbles under his breath. Over and over, it seems as if he repeats the same thing, yet I am too far away to understand. Finally, however, Amon lifts his head to reveal his own tears and chuckles.

"They'll all die!" he screams. "They'll all fucking die for

this!"

He looks straight toward Lord Bale and takes a couple of steps, sword in hand. In response, the lord grabs his blade's hilt.

"I am not responsible. This is not something you want to do," Lord Bale says.

"I think I really fucking do," Amon says, taking himself, and his blade, closer to the lord.

AMON
CONFLICT IN THE CHURCH

Boiling. A sensation so burning hot it feels as if my bones, my blood, my limbs are set aflame. In fact, 'tis the only thing I feel. Not the leather of the priest's sword handle, not the tears that are drying on my face, and certainly not the beating of my heart. 'Tis as if my it beats no more. Instead of the constant thumping, a blazing fire rages inside. Fueling this flame is only one thing—the need for bloodshed. I need not for the civility of words or the trivial nature of compromise. I cannot allow myself anything else than the release of my seething rage. For if I do not, I am afraid I shall never come back from this. In my heated mindset, I hear nothing. I may see the mouths move, the body language change, hands try to explain, or even the rain falling out the windows, but nothing emits noise. Nothing except one thought repeating itself over and over again in the forefront of my mind. Vengeance

Lashing out with a weapon taken from the priest's room last night, I target the man who stands in front of me. Even if he may not be guilty of murdering my mate, he is just as guilty for doing nothing to stop it. Strike after strike, metal on metal, I unleash my anger. However, each and every attempt to take from him what was stolen from my friend is denied. This only ensuring a rise in the wildfire within. For with each attempt matched and deterred, the next grows stronger. Yet my opponent is not one so easily bested, as we continue to duel behind the altar. "Stop this!" are the first words I coherently hear.

"Amon, you're only hurting yourself!" another sounds out, but I do not let up in my strikes.

I take a breath and evaluate my opponent as they stand before me. His blade grasped in one hand, his eyes showing no concern, and his breath as calm as still water. Upon seeing this, I become more irate. Frantically and hysterically, I slash, stab, and hack. Alas, it matters not what form, what stance, or what combo, as all remain unable to crack the foreign lord's defenses.

I scream with one final slash, but it doesn't connect. Rather, I hit the altar once more. In doing that, the metal of the blade vibrates. A sensation so strong it drops out of my hand, and I drop to my knees.

"Shit!" I let out. Ashamed and furious with myself, I put my head down. In doing so, I now see what they meant by hurting myself. The wound on my side had reopened at some point in my fit of rage. The crimson coming from within leaks from me, staining my clothes and the floorboards. Seeing this, I look up to the one I sought to harm. He points his weapon at me as I lay on the floor. His next move holding the fate of my life in the balance.

Coming into my line of sight, Eigor walks beside me and bows, "My Lord, I beg your forgiveness. Spare him, as he spared my life," he says.

"You shall show him mercy? Won't you?" the boy who came in with the lord asks, walking up the steps to the altar.

Returning my gaze from the skinny boy to the lord, I spit out, "Be done with it then! Strike me down as your comrade did to mine!"

Disregarding my words, his demeanor and hand stay set in place, as if he is undecided on what to do next. Yet as the moments pass, slow as the tide, he is forced into a reaction.

The mouth of the church opens wide and clatters against the walls. Heavy are the steps protruding in due to the chain metal. Around fifteen, no, nearly twenty-five guards armed to the teeth slowly waltz through the doors. In unison, half march left and the other march right. Their footsteps halt when they complete the semi-circle, cutting off the exit and standing ready with weapons drawn. Adding to the tally of steel hawks in the room, the ringleader emerges through the center of the shape. "What do we have here?" he bellows.

The sound of the voice causes my being to turn molten. All the blood rushes to my head again at the sight of the giant. His sly grin doing my anger no favors as he speaks again.

"Lord Bale! 'Tis a surprise to see you here," the captain of the guard says, walking toward us. "It seems you have done my work for me. I must thank you. You have saved me the time and strength to defeat this wretched filth."

Odd it is, that the man offers nothing in response to his counterpart. Instead, he stands like a statue whilst the heavy set of steps clank their way in front of me. The lord retreats his steel from my neck and back to his side.

"You shall know justice as well, island dog," the captain says, looking at Eigor. With a motion of his head, two guards gallop up the steps and grab his olive arms.

"No! You shan't! He must be brought back to the tower!" Eigor shouts.

Sneering at the remark, Valincias howls, "Quiet, mutt!" before one of the guards restraining him punches his gut.

Turning his attention to me on the ground, he says, "Here, allow me to do the honor. You needn't stain your blade with the blood of a bandit," to Lord Bale, pulling his silver blade out of its black scabbard.

I look up into the captain's cold gaze, his facial expression showing signs of joy. "I pray the gods tear your tiny prick off," I say.

The captain's facial expression changes into one of annoyance as the leader of the guard raises his weapon. Knowing this may very well be the last time I release my breath, I take one last glimpse around the room. With time, feeling as if it has stopped, I make note of everything around me: Nyssa, pulling out a small dagger from behind her back, is tackled to the floor. Eigor, head hanging low, spitting onto the ground, only able to observe whilst restrained. The priest slipping away toward his chambers. Lastly, an unfamiliar boy, standing in shock, holding his hands over his heart. Taking it all in, I turn my head back to where the malicious intent looms. Unwilling to shut my eyes or give the satisfaction of being weak in my last moments, I stare sternly into the man's eyes. Watching as the steel descends toward my line of sight, I can't make internal peace, knowing the end is now. Rather, all I feel is hate, anger, and a lust for revenge. It feels infuriating knowing I shall never get word back to Fort Kael. Furthermore, it shatters my core, knowing

I shall never get vengeance in the name of my friend. Nevertheless, I grip my bleeding side and await for judgment to fall.

"May the Loria damn your soul," the captain says before descending his blade. Cutting the air, slicing the tension, and aiming to end my days, the captain makes the sword fall.

Yet it is interrupted by the singing of echoes and vibrations bouncing off the cathedral walls. The collision is so fierce that it feels as if it shakes the mural of Rol as the captain's blade is repelled.

Utter astonishment creeps over the bloodthirsty guard's face as his ambition is blocked. His evil deed is put to an end.

My head stays motionless, but my eyes wander upward as I see the lord's expression is firm, whilst the captain stands in disbelief.

"No," Lord Bale says. His steel inches above my head, acting as a barrier.

"You would side with traitors?" Captain Valincias asks.

"It seems I have already been doing so," Lord Bale remarks. The captain furrows his brow in disdain. "Then you too shall be put down like the mutt you are," the guard says.

"Hamzi shall hang you off the tower for this," the lord says.

Letting out a small chuckle, the captain responds, "You are indeed much more of a fool than I thought, Lord Bale."

Whilst one duel had concluded moments ago, another is set to ensue, their blades still locked over my head, eyes gleaming with disgust, and their body language showing anger. "Kill them all!" the captain shouts.

With swift response to the command, the clanks of steel sound out in plenty. Every guard, aside from those holding my associates, unsheathes their blade and stands at the ready.

This can't be who I lose the fight of life to. Not this hate-filled man, not these greedy bastards disguised in uniform. I lunge toward my sword on the floor. Groaning due to the sharp pain, I still carry and grasp the weapon. Looking up, I see the one who saved me battling his foe ferociously. I notice, however, his stance has changed. Using two hands to unleash more power behind his strikes on the bigger man, he clashes steel. Striking downward toward the captain, the lord has his attack deflected. The collision causes him to lose footing and take a step back.

Upon seeing this, I make a split decision, as the lives of Eigor and Nyssa are in dire circumstances. Deciding to leave Lord Bale to his own defenses, I turn to the guards holding my friends, gripping my blade tightly with my left hand as my right holds my side. I must make my movements quick, as the guards circle in; however, with the condition I am in, it becomes increasingly difficult. Trying to run, I endure the agony in my steps and push past the physical pain, relying on my mental aptitude. Two of the four guards holding my pair of comrades release their hold and advance toward me.

Fools.

The first of the two lunges straight. Sidestepping the deadly intent, I drag my blade upward. His hands serve him no longer. The second, with fear in his eyes, seems to learn from his fallen brother. Yet his emotions overcome him. Running toward him, he hesitates to deal a blow. Poor soul, had he even attempted to block in my weak state, he may have had a chance. However, he too falls to the hardwood—neck opened. My steps are not quick enough, however, as four more guards surround me. Even if I were to dispatch all of those, more and more rush toward me.

Circling around, I hold my blade pointed out in an attempt to maintain distance from those who seek me harm. Constantly having to rotate and only being able to scan with one eye, I notice the other fight. 'Tis Lord Bale grabbing the young blonde and swinging the boy behind him, away from the steel that was inches from taking his life, whilst repelling attempts on his own. In front of them is a multitude of guards and the captain leaning against the altar—bleeding from his nose. "Ramses! Breath!" the lord shouts.

The boy looks in shock, stuck in one time with his hands clasping his chest. Yet, whilst the pair deal with their own impending demise, I, too, face a daunting task. Swinging and slashing to warn those who draw near that they shall be cut down, I slowly backpedal toward the mural. Carefully taking small steps, whilst eyeing the guards sneering all around, I find myself next to Lord Bale and the boy. Like animals, they poke and prod at us. Each guard trying to find the right angle to put us down. Creeping ever so close, they march slowly in unison, step, step, step. Coming within a spear's length away, me and the lord dashed our blades across the air. Yet it matters not. Trapped like rats in a cellar, our fates are sealed.

"Halt!" the brute of a captain calls out.

Pushing aside his subordinates, the proud man of the law smiles. "I must admit. You have always been the fleeciest fighter," he says, looking at the lord. "However, today, the mighty lord Bale shall too fall."

"I wonder what they shall cut off first when they find out you've betrayed our Elder," Lord Bale says.

"Hmm, how humorous. It seems you know much more than you should," the captain barks.

Valincias flicks his hand and turns to walk away. "Kill them and hide the bodies," he says. "Bring me the other two! I shall take that delight myself!"

How violently sickening is the understanding of Valincias winning. The man who stole blood from me. The man who stole a brother from me. Now, a man who shall steal everything. From myself, from the lord, from Eigor, from Nyssa, and from those in the keep. It doesn't add up, however, why this man does this. Why does he seek to slay us? Me? The lord? Sylas? But I'm afraid this shall never be known. The men of the guard close in and appear ready to strike.

"Gods! C'mon then! At least do not be a coward about it!" I scream, not knowing whether I say this in the want to antagonize or perhaps the need for it to be over. My efforts are dismissed, however. "Halt!" a voice careens throughout.

Not wanting to give any chance of letting my guard down, I stare deeply into the eyes of the men around me. Each and every one of those men turn their heads almost immediately. It's shocking how naive people can be with their projected words and the conviction in their tone. With them in front of me, clueless to my next move, I plot. This must be used as an opportunity to strike and reduce the odds. I step to strike at the cost of my own soul but am tugged back. The lord grasping my shoulder catches me off guard. Confused, he nods toward the front of the altar. "I suggest you stay very still," the priest says.

In awe, I watch the old man hold his right arm in the air. In his hand, he grips a small glass jar full of black insects fluttering their transparent wings.

"I would hate to see these get out, or worse, get nervous and drop it," he continues.

Valincias, casually, striding toward the center space, says to him, "Father, you would send us all to damnation? A man of the gods killing dozens with phantoms? Not to mention if they get onto the streets. Tsk. Tsk. I don't think your god shall speak to you then, and I certainly do not believe you shall take that chance."

The priest laughs before putting his hand on the jar's lid. "Then you, my friend, do not know what I am willing to do," he says.

With those words, I see Valincias hesitate in his steps. Yet I focus my eyes on the scene as he continues on.

"May the gods have mercy," the priest says, releasing his grip.

The eyes I stared so intently at before, ones that peered on with malice and curiosity, turn to something much darker. Terror.

Death with wings abound in the chapel. No matter if there were ten thousand hands to swat at them, half would perish. With sixty-two, we surely shall all die. Flocking to the bodies in the room, I watch as many men get stung. Cries echoing throughout. Bodies in hysteria. Men in tears. All running.

Amidst the sight of hysteria, a nip on my neck grabs my attention. My reflexes cause me to swat at the spot. Feeling a squish, I pull my hand off and look down. The body resembles a phantom. Its sleek color in my palm is a sign of impending doom. Next to me, I hear the same; this time, ill fate finds the boy behind me. However, as all the guards run out the open door, so do the insects flying into the open city. I suspect in mere hours, hundreds shall fall ill.

"Why… why did you do this?" Nyssa asks.

Sheathing my blade, I add, "You have condemned us all." "No. He has saved us," Lord Bale says, sheathing his weapon.

"What in damnation do you mean we're saved? We're all going to be dead by the time the new moon comes up!" I say.

Meanwhile, I hear the snicker of the old man. "Oh bother. You best calm yourself, son," the priest says.

"Calm? You want me fucking calm?! After you just poisoned us and gods know how many innocents?!" I shout. "You should be giving him your thanks," the lord says.

"Thanks?! For postponing certain and agonizing deaths for a short period of time?! For ensuring it?! I shout.

The father laughs. "Ha, no one shall die. I drained those bees a long time ago of any poison they had," the priest says.

"And being stung shall have no consequence?" Eigor asks.

"All you felt was them giving you a kiss, or rather, a little nibble. I swear it, no harm shall come to you. All the poison in their tail is long gone, I give you my word," the father says.

"It was a facade," Lord Bale chimes in.

Raging and confused, I ask, "You knew?!"

"No," he says, helping the boy find his footing," I did know that Valincias was right, however. A man of the gods could never turn on his vows."

The priest laughs. "Indeed!" the man exclaims. "You are truly a wise one, son," he says, looking at Lord Bale. "I must say, however, those insects shan't live long outside. They won't last out of their habitat. I had to keep them under the floorboards to avoid too much heat. I only ever keep half of what I catch alive. Nevertheless, might I suggest we get you out of here quickly then."

"But.. We have nowhere to go, father. Nowhere they won't find us, at least," Nyssa says.

Chuckling and nodding his head, the priest walks toward the mural and enters the hideaway. "Come along then," he says.

Shaking my head, I walk toward the false door. Crossing the threshold between the church and back room, we five follow the man.

Passing by the tables and chairs, he takes his strides toward the steel surface top that was used to stitch me up. Stopping at its edges, he places his hands on top. "Help an old man out, would you?" the priest says.

Putting my hands on the table, he starts pushing it back, scraping the floor, metal creaking. Straining myself and my side, I let go. Having moved it just enough, a staircase hides below. "This shall take you into the crypt. From there, you shall find a gate at the end of the tunnel.

Open it, and you shall find it leads to the sewers," he says, handing Nyssa a key. "You can find your way out of the city from there."

Looking over, the robed lord asks, "What shall happen to you, father?"

The man turns and heads toward the panes of glass, smirking. "I shall pray, serve, worship, and teach. The same as every other day until my last," he says.

"Thank you, father," Nyssa says.

Not looking back to match our gazes, he says, "May the gods guide you," and shuts the door.

Turning my head back, I look at the descending staircase. Not being able to see the bottom, as 'tis shrouded in darkness, I say, "There must be flint somewhere here," before heading to the room where I slept. Entering the square space, I notice a small pouch lying on the floor. 'Tis not mine, as all my belongings were taken by the guard upon my capture. This means it must belong to either Sylas or Nyssa. With intrigue, I grab the pouch and pull the string, allowing the material to open. Looking inside, I make a saddening discovery and grab a small metal band from within, sorrow falling over me. I hold in my hand a silver circle, one that used to serve the purpose of wrangling my fallen mate's beard.Looking at it closely,

I shake my head. "You cheap bastard," I mumble at the sight of the bronze showing through parts of the silver coat. "Amon? Did you find any?" Nyssa asks.

Pulling myself back to reality, I stick my hand inside once more. Feeling a small rock, I pull it out to find exactly what we need: flint.

Heading back to the stairwell with the flint in one hand and Sylas's pouch in the other, I see Nyssa grabbing vials, needles, and thread, then proceeding to place them in her satchel. I grab two torches off the wall, handing the first to Eigor. "Here," I say, placing it in his palm, then light the wood, cloth, and oil once 'tis in his grasp, using the flint and my sword.

"Let's get going then," I say, looking at the bodies in the room. Motioning for Eigor to go first, Nyssa follows in tow. The pair descend the steps and into the void.

Following behind, the boy hesitates. "Are you confident in this?" he asks the lord, eyes filled with fear,

Releasing a deep breath, the lord responds, "I do not foresee any other way or any other choice."

"Very well, I trust you," the boy says, before walking down. I walk next to the lord as the boy disappears under the floor and say, "He shan't see the new moon."

His darkened gaze looks into my vicinity and says, "Then I shall do my mightiest to prevent that from happening."

"Then that is the reason for you joining us? Leaving everything you have ever known behind?" I ask.

"Tis not all I've ever known. Certainly not all that matters," he says, before taking steps down as well.

Arrogant and naive is this lord. One who acts as if he is invincible, one who knows no pain, who fears no evil. Ludacris. Yet this is what I have to work with, what I have to put up with in order to survive. Then I descend as well.

Reaching the bottom, the rounded halls are dimly lit by the flames. To our left and right are the markings of names and offerings to the gods. Purses of coin, letters, swords, spears, and axes lay over tombstones. Lining the entire hall in my field of view and our trek into the darkness that seemingly does not have an end. Having no choice but to proceed into the unknown, we walk, grouped together, while I stay ready in the rear with my hand over my hilt. It feels weird to palm the unknown steel oval at the end of the sword. Nothing special about the standard weapon, as common iron and steel were used to forge the blade. Yet, it shall serve well for now in my venture and may very well be needed in these dark chasms.

Venturing onward, we pace past a plethora of resting places for the souls that have moved on, walking in a straight line, those ahead of me at the ready. Eigor grips his sword, Nyssa rests her hand on the dagger that resides in her waist belt, and then there is the lord. Seemingly at ease with his surroundings, he walks with his hands by his side, ever so casually. The only one without a weapon in hand or close by is the boy; Ramses. The very same one I question being here. The lord acts as an inquisitor and even a helping hand. Eigor, who feels he owes me a debt from saving his soul, and Nyssa, who has only offered help and advice since first meeting her. Yet the young man is a mystery. A soul who knows no such consequences of spilling blood or, worse, amongst a band of rebels and outlaws. I suppose it matters not, and surely not enough to keep my attention, as Eigor whispers, "Wait... stop..." and halts his movement. "What is it?" I ask from the back.

His torch flickers and illuminates a small fraction of the air in front of him. "Do you hear that?" he asks.

We five stand silent, my own heart racing amidst the suspense and apparent sounds coming from ahead.

"I don't hear anything," Nyssa says, moments after we pause.

The man in front of me, Lord Bale, says, "Water," and starts walking once again.

I know not if the lord speaks the truth, yet I have zero reason not to believe him. I do not trust the royal, but I do know he does not seek us harm. Therefore, I follow behind him with a torch in hand and motion with my head to those we pass as if to say, 'come on.'

As we advance, the sound becomes clear: running water. A sign we are close to the sewers. Soon enough, the bright light of the hot blaze reveals metal bars.

"We're here. Nyssa, the key?" I say, reaching my outstretched arm back. In return, she places the small iron solution to the door lock in my hand. Using the torch, I shine light on the keyhole, place the blades inside, and turn. With a clank and push, the barrier separating the crypt and sewer is swung open. I don't know what I hate more, however, the sight that was the burial ground or the smells of shit and piss filling my senses. It seems I am not the only one who reacts with much disgust, as the young man heaves.

"Keep quiet. You must keep it together, Ramses, before someone above hears us," Nyssa says.

Alas, after a few more heaves of whatever the boy ate before coming hits the ground, we start discussing which way to go.

"We must follow where the water leads," Lord Bale says.

"And what if that leads us directly to someone waiting for us?" Eigor asks.

"Then we kill them," I say. "Hmm," he grunts and nods in reply.

"Besides, any guard, other than their captain, shall be far more interested in the runaway lord than any of us," I say with a sly grin toward the group.

"Cheerful to be of service," the lord says, starting his walk downstream.

Following suit, we all dredge through the muck behind him, with myself bringing up the rear once more. With daylight along with the rain coming through the metal bars of the few and far between lids above, we needn't carry open flames any longer. Not wanting to emit smoke, either, through the sliver of an opening, I toss my torch into the water and advise Eigor to do the same. With both lights put out, we rely heavily on the rare rays and pellets pouring through to light the path as onward we go, slushing through and doing our best to minimize any noise. The gray tunnel of stone and mortar is the only thing in sight aside from the four in front of me. Yet, whilst the dull pattern takes up the entirety of my line of sight, the noise above gives me a bothersome feeling.

"Search every tavern and home! Search every church, chapel, and cathedral! Bring them to me on their knees! You! Bring me that priest.

Damned fool, his phantoms dropped dead at the sight of the sun's rays," the muffled shouting of Valincias continues.

Looking above, I see the captain through the bars of the lid. Standing so proud and mighty, barking orders to his subordinates. A man they think of so highly. A man I shall bring to his knees and force him to watch as I make his world burn. Tempting 'tis to climb the wooden ladder and strike him through his heart.

"Amon?" Eigor whispers, but my focus remains on my enemy.

"Amon," he says again, this time much closer to me, putting his hands on my shoulder.

Inciting my reflexes, I quickly turn my head to see the hand and familiar demeanor.

"Not now. His time shall come, but not now. Let's go," he whispers once more.

Indeed, he is right. My emotions would have me open the lid and sacrifice myself, and them, in order to get revenge. A choice I won't make, not today, at the very least.

Forcing myself to keep going, we make dozens and dozens of more strides through the disposal tunnels, wandering aimlessly, and come across a bright light with reflections of shadows on the water below. "It seems the clouds gave way," Eigor says.

The illuminated trickery of the sun reveals long and pointed edges. Yet, with the light blinding us as it reflects off the water, I cannot make out what it is. Is there to be danger or freedom, I wonder. Do we meet salvation or damnation? I prepare myself for the latter by unsheathing my sword, and, being the only one to pull out a weapon, I stand idly by in the back to see if the cause for concern jumps out. However, the lord disappears into the brightness, and for once, I imagine 'tis useful to have two blind eyes instead of one.

I notice Ramses' hand trying to block the light as he calls out, "Lord Bale?" but there's no response. Again he tries, a bit louder this time, "Lord Bale!"

"Quiet!" I whisper. "You don't know what's ahead, don't go screaming about it."

Echoing from ahead, Lord Bale calls out, "Take it easy on the boy. There's no one ahead. Just the cedars."

Upon hearing this, we four pick up the pace in our steps. The sound of rushing water only increases as we approach where the lord's voice came from. Pushing through the disorienting light, it eventually fades in its harshness and reveals a relieving sight. A stream of waste exits the tunnels and falls toward a large and wide hole in the ground. Even farther out, however, there seems to be nothing but the open wilderness, just past the farms and huts. Though there surely await in the thousands of trees dangers that reside within, the current smell, however, is as harsh as whatever might befall us in between the leaves. I place a cloth over my nose, as all those around me have or are doing so as well in response.

Speaking up, the boy remarks through his shirt, "Is this... the soil reserve?" "The... what?" Nyssa asks, muffled.

The boy walks to the edge and peers through the human-sized opening. "This is where we get manure for our crops," he says.

The thought of what the boy is implying causes an unease in my stomach. Wishing to never eat again, I say, "Who's first?" in hopes of moving things along.

We all stand around looking at each other, aside from the lord, who trains his eyes through the bars. Alas, none speak up, and therefore, I say, "Very well," before kicking the boy, who stood on the edge, into the pit.

Ramses screams on his way down before smacking into the mountain of waste. I briefly gaze down at the sight of the boy pulling himself up, before turning back to the others. Rotating around, I see the three, even Lord Bale and his grayed vision, sending me glares.

"'Tis not like he was ever going to jump. Don't lie to yourselves','" I say before adding, "Who's next?"

Stepping up to the bars, Eigor still gives me an annoyed glare. I put my hand on his shoulder, and in response, Eigor says, "If you kick me, I shall cut your thumbs off," before taking a deep breath and jumping. With a thud, he lands on top and helps Ramses climb out of the pit. Looking back once more at now two, Nyssa and the lord, I motion with my hand as if to say, 'Well?'

Chuckling, Lord Bale says, "A lady must be given the opportunity to go first."

"Ha! No, love, please. I could not go before we make sure the blind find safety," Nyssa counters. "I insist," the lord says, smiling.

"No, my lord. I insist, 'tis my honor," she returns, raising a golden brow. "Oh for fu... both of you can just jump together," I say.

Whipping her head toward me in dissatisfaction, she squints her eyes and says, "Fine."

They walk up to the bars and look below. Jumping simultaneously, the pair land immersed in the waste. Coming up all the way to their knees, I watch them shuffle to the side before making my own leap. Plunging into the muck, I land in such a horrific stench I cannot control my stomach any longer, and as I pull myself out of the reserve, I bend over and empty my guts onto the earth. In the midst of this, the heaving causes pain to my wound. The adrenaline and emotion of the moment drowned out any sort of ache and I nearly forgot about my stitched-up side. Grasping it, I walk over to the group circled just beside the pit.

"Are you well enough to travel?" Eigor asks

Nodding, I say, "I'm fine."

Their eyes look upon me with worry, but I brush past, walking toward the looming cedars, saying, "Let's go then, it won't be long before they find the crypt."

From church floors and sewage slush to long grass and small huts for homes. The common man and woman, slaving away tirelessly just for the right to live, just for a day, as that work only ever lasts one moon's light before you must repeat it again. It sickens me, passing by these farms and small huts, how pitiful it is. Not the matter of those above taking advantage of their diligence in their trade but rather the men and women themselves. For the powerful to be greedy is not surprising. However, for the common folk to naturally accept that this is the way things are and cannot be changed is entirely disappointing. The guild, however, treats everyone equally, everyone with respect, with equal food portions and equal opportunity. A place I must return to, and with haste—or else risk the fall of Fort Kael. Alas, for now, we stroll through the community, aiming for the land that lies behind.

Sure to be caught out or noticed by those working in fields or with cattle, I intend to stop for not a single thing or conversation. It seems we are all in like minds with that intent, as we all keep our heads down. The lord Bale even dons his hood over his head, whilst Eigor, Nyssa, and I walk steadily forward, trying not to draw attention to ourselves. Yet the boy does not follow suit. I notice he instead stops his tracks. I, not being one to care much for him, keep walking. However, my colleagues and the lord stop in their tracks upon noticing that the young man is not keeping up. "Ramses? What are you doing?" Nyssa asks.

The shit-covered blonde stretches out his finger and says, "I know her, I know her," almost in disbelief. Following the direction of his finger, I see a young farm hand. A girl, picking onions. "I have to speak with her," Ramses says.

For the first time, I hear Lord Bale raise his voice, "No," he says, "We must leave."

"I… I have to give a message to her..." Ramses trails off.

"If they see you together, if anyone sees you together, they shall tell the guard and she shall be killed. Or worse," Lord Bale says.

"Listen, son. He's right, but do as you please. Get yourself killed. Or come with us, but either way, we shan't stay here," I add in, looking at the lord and then toward the saddened boy's glare. "We need to keep moving. We are already putting ourselves at more risk by standing here conversing." "Come along, love," Nyssa says.

Turning himself around, his arm deflates to his side as he quietly mutters.

We continue our journey eastward, still five strong. Reaching the end of the farmlands, we arrive at the tree line. The overhanging limbs cover the sky above with green. Within resides safety and harbor for now.

Turning back around, to the place that supplied the opposite, before entering the forest, I take in the city. The farms, the huts, the great stone wall, the bustling life inside, and its centerpiece: the manor. Equipped with flags, guards, and the keep's crest, fluttering in the wind. Beside it, a looming tower. A tower that strikes me with surprise. A place set for gathering and deliberating justice garnishes three bodies hanging off its edges. A servant. A priest. A brother. The sight doesn't bring fear but instead reminds me of my conquest, one that the manor so proudly boasts on its walls. Vengeance.

Knowing I must plot my revenge carefully on those who slayed my partner, I enter the woods.

BALE
BRUSHING PAST LIMBS

Odd it is, how I do not know all their names and yet we sprint away together. Yet, as one, we flee, our breaths coming heavy, the rush of adrenaline runs rampant through my veins. Five strong, we race through the snapping twigs, and brush past the bushes and leaves, all the while rain pours down through the canopy above, running away from pursuers, who grow louder even as we push our pace forward. With the guard now on our heels, we have not let up in our steps, nor has my inner turmoil over my choices let up. Yet the scent of bark, fresh air, and wet grass fill my nose as we aim to go deeper and deeper into the cedars. The combination is nearly overwhelming, as I haven't been this deep into the forest since the day my brother and I were brought to the keep as children. Nevertheless, our five distinct sets of paces charge on, into the unknown to escape a certain fate.

Whilst fleeing, the woman whom Ramses called 'Nyssa' within the walls of the church asks, "How'd they find us?"

In response, the man I dueled, Amon, replies, "They must've ripped one of our scents off something. Keep running!"

It's hard for me, however, to keep stride with the others. Being used to echoing off wood or stone to locate and identify my surroundings, the wilderness presents a challenge. Now, instead of following noise reverberating off surfaces, I listen closely to the crunching of leaves and what direction it comes from. I only hope, amidst the heavy reliance on my ears, I do not run into a tree or trip over any manner of things. Yet, I try to match their speed and attempt to stay close to the sounds coming from their heavy breath and steps. Meanwhile, chasing us down comes the daunting howl of dogs from behind. In reality, I don't fear the hounds, but rather what trails behind them. Captivity. This is something I simply cannot allow, at least not until I gain full insight into the corruption of the guard.

With so many questions about the manner of Valincias's treason, my mind runs rampant: How long has he been plotting against the Elder? Who does this extend to? The king? Lady Sylvia? Hamzi? Rylan? Illia? Jov…? No, I would know if my brother were to do something like this—he would tell me. Right? No. No. I shake my head, as these curiosities matter not. At the very least, they don't concern me at this moment, as a different task is at hand. Escape.

Breaking my inner trail of curiosities, however, is a foreign accent. "We need to mask our scent!" he says, taking a sharp right turn.

Not wanting to get separated, I change directions and ask, "How?"

His response is one that causes confusion. "There's a river we can use, this way!" he says

How is a river going to mask our scent? 'Tis not as if the hounds chasing us shall get thrown off by simply dousing ourselves in water.

In fact, with the rain falling from above, that would surely already have happened.

As if she could read my mind, Nyssa asked the former guard, "How is a stream going to help us, Eigor!?"

Eigor. Finally, I can put a name to the voice of my fellow Isle native.

"'Tis not the water that shall help us! 'Tis the mud!" he exclaims.

"How are you certain there's a river that flows this way?!" Amon adds.

"You have to trust me! We came through these woods at least a hundred times transporting prisoners! I know there's one this way!" Eigor says.

Eigor shows he's good for his word, as after running a dozen more steps, the crashing of water close by becomes abundantly clear. However, equally as notable, gaining ground with every step, are the barks and snarls of the pack hunting us. Upon hearing both, the quickness of our sprint rises. Amazing, it is, that while being chased, my mind races as fast as my feet with observations. Within these mental remarks, a disturbing thought comes across my mind; these hounds couldn't be released without Hamzi knowing. Furthermore, he would have to give the order for the hunting party. Even Valincias himself doesn't hold such power. 'Tis solely up to the Elder of the keep to decide such things.

Perchance he doesn't know I am here, however? Or perhaps Valincias went behind his back? It wouldn't be the first time, it seems, yet I can't imagine my friend giving the go-ahead after our conversation last night.

Whilst pondering this, I hear Ramses cry out, "Ah, Loria sake!" breaking my train of thought as his body thuds, hitting the ground.

"Cmon! Get up!" Amon tells him, unwilling to slow his steps. I, however, am willing to help the boy as I come up behind him and pull him to his feet. "Are you alright?" I ask.

"I just tripped over a log. I'm fine," he says.

Nodding to his response, we both return to a sprint and gain ground on those who pushed ahead, approaching the rushing water. In little time, we catch up, as I hear the splashes of my counterparts.

"Grab the dirt from the bottom and rub it over yourself!" Eigor says, sloshing the water.

Making my way down the bank and into the stream, it becomes impossible to retain awareness. The cold of the water, splashing, rain falling, the roar of the river, and the smell of the mud I'm smearing all over my once pristine robes. All of these together cause me to lose track of any other noise or scent— including the hounds. This proves to be costly, as Amon says,

"Shit. Don't move."

Stopping my hands from wiping my body with any more dirt and water, I stand still. In doing so, I regain slight insight into my surroundings. That's when I hear the rattling of metal and the sniffs coming from above the riverbank. The twelve paws that linger, almost an outstretched arm away, start to draw close. Their low growls come in a trio, but a new noise blooms behind them. One even more startling than the beasts close by. The clattering of hooves and men distinctively talking comes within earshot. I can tell they're not close enough to spot us, but we haven't much time until they come within range of sight. However, knowing they follow the hounds and their howls, I start to bend down into the water. "What are you doing?" Amon whispers.

Putting my hand below the stream's surface, I say nothing. Moving slowly to avoid triggering the animals, I pick up a smooth rock, pulling it out of the water. I then feel around the lining of the bottom of my robe to find a spot not covered in muck. Eventually, I discovered a small piece untouched by mud and ripped it off. Tying the cloth around the stone, I heave it as far as I can into the neverending cedars. Hearing the hounds howl, I start to think I have doomed us, but dismissing that thought is the crash of the paws striding away. Just in case, I stand still. Eigor scoffs. "How'd you know that would work?" he asks.

"I didn't," I say, dredging through the river in the opposite direction of where I threw the stone.

Exiting the water, we keep a steady pace, darting toward freedom. Knowing the guard won't venture too deep into the forest or too long into the day, I start to slow myself. Yet the strides of the others with me stay at the same rate until, eventually, I stop moving entirely. I can tell this causes hesitation in their steps as they ease their pace.

"What are you doing?!" the angered Amon calls out.

Holding up my hand, I request for silence as I listen closely.

"Damn it, you're going to get us captured or killed," Amon says, starting to drift away with Ramses, the former guard, and the woman.

Ignoring him and standing still, I focus solely on my ability to take in noise. Standing there for dozens and dozens of heartbeats, I hear nothing, not even the rain that once pelted the trees and soil, as it must have stopped recently.

"They're gone," I say, causing Amon and the others to stop walking away. "How can you be so sure?" Ramses asks.

I walk over to him and place my hand on his shoulder, "If the guard or their dogs were within a fort's range, I'd be able to hear them," I say.

"That's a neat trick, love, but I'm not willing to bet our lives on it," Nyssa says.

Interjecting and surprisingly backing my point, Amon says,

"No, he's right. Listen," he pauses before continuing. "We could hear the hounds when they first released them in the keep. Now there's nothing."

"I think I know why. Look at the sky; we've been running till dusk. No guard wants to be this deep in the forest when 'tis completely black in the sky," Eigor says. "Why's that?" Ramses asks.

"Bandits, wildlife, stories of the other creatures that dwell in here, take your pick," Eigor says.

Hesitantly, Ramses followed up with another question, "What creatures...?"

"The only creatures we should worry about are ourselves at the

TIRAN

moment. Let's make camp for the night and try our best to warm up," I interject. The last thing we need is to spread fear or give the poor boy another heartache. He's been through enough heart-wrenching experiences already, some of the things he's seen and done having been my fault. If I hadn't sought him out or let him accompany me to the church, perhaps he'd still be safe within the walls of the keep. Yet I do not know if being within those stone structures does, in fact, keep the people shielded from danger. It seems the clear and apparent danger is those designated to protect them.

However, I needed to know if Ramses knew anything further about Amon and Sylas, and I don't feel as if I had much choice after I witnessed Valencias murder a man. Nevertheless, all I can do now is keep the boy safe and one day return him back to his home in one piece. That very same young man, breaking my thoughts, asks,

"What can I do to help?"

In response, Amon says, "Try not to keel over dead."

"There's no need to be a prick, he just wants to help," Nyssa says. "You can help me gather some dry wood for a fire, love." The boy pulls away from my hand on his shoulder, his steps moving to meet hers as they aim to gather fuel for a flame. With the two going off with a task at hand, I hear Eigor devise his own plan.

"I'm going to see if I can find any berries. If we're lucky, there'll be some on trees or their cones," he says, pacing off.

With it now just me and Amon, the man who sought to end my life, left standing, the tension becomes increasingly apparent. Neither one of us forced any words to break the tension, and I can tell he's standing

249

still, staring at me. I hear his hand grip his blade's handle. In turn, I do the same with haste.

"Hmm," he remarks, "If I were to strike you down right now, there would be no one to hold me back anymore."

"I don't believe they were holding you back. I believe they were saving you from choosing a fight you couldn't win," I say.

He sneers at my comment. "I don't give a damn that you saved us. I won't forgive you. Only a coward does nothing when an innocent man is put against the blade," he says.

I shake my head and release the grip of my sword. "I couldn't imagine you ever forgiving me… in fact, I'm sure one day you'll try again to get what you think is justice… but we both know that day won't be today. We have things we need to understand and accomplish before we do this again. I am, however, sorry. I wish there was more I had done," I say before walking past him.

He lets out a deep sigh before I hear his body plop to the ground. I, however, reach my hand out with the aim of finding a tree. Eventually, after feeling around the air long enough, my palm finds a resting place on bark, and I sit on the soil, using the cedar as support for my back. My only objective now is to listen carefully in case the guard or any threat comes within a distance while we wait for the others to return.

Not having to be patient for long, Nyssa and Ramses walk back, jostling an abundance of something in their arms.

"This amount of bark should get us through the night," she says as she and Ramses release control and drop the wood to the ground.

With what they gathered clattering down to the soil, I can hear the three arranging materials.

"Put some dry leaves underneath, it'll help ignite the flame," Ramses says.

Rummaging of the earth ensues as I hear the snapping of branches, and Nyssa asks, "Can I see the flint?"

A short clinking noise occurs before Amon replies, "Here," after digging through his pouch.

Following his words is the scraping of a short blade against stone, ringing throughout the forest. Smelling the smoke emitting from the now-lit kindling, I pick myself up and walk closer to the warmth of the burning wood, then sit myself down in between the voices of Nyssa and Amon and stretch my hands out in the hopes of heating myself and my wet clothes. As we three sit around the flame, Eigor's steps draw close as he joins us once more. "Any luck?" Amon asks.

"I was able to find about two handfuls of berries. That should be enough to hold us over for the night. Plus, we wouldn't want to eat too many of these; they're poisonous if eaten in abundance," he responds, sitting opposite me around the flame.

"But they're safe to eat? Right?" Ramses asks, sitting himself down between Nyssa and the former guard.

Teasing him, Eigor says, "I guess we'll find out. Who would like some?" "I would like a few, please," Nyssa says.

I hear her shuffling and Eigor stands. She says, "Thank you," before the former guard seats himself once more.

"How about you?" Eigor asks.

In response, Ramses says, "Maybe just a one or two." Eigor chuckles. "Very well," he says. "Amon?" "I'm not hungry," the bounty hunter says.

"Amon, you must eat. Your body needs it to heal. You're still not in good shape," Nyssa interjects.

"My body has seen worse than this and survived. I'm not hungry," he says again.

The man handing out food now turns his attention to me.

"Lord Bale?" Eigor asks.

I shake my head to indicate I don't want any. "Thank you, however," I say. "Suit yourself, more for us," Eigor teases.

As Ramses, Nyssa, and Eigor partake in the berries, we four sit quietly around the open flame. That is until Eigor speaks up, "Who was that farm girl you were pouting over?" he asks.

Letting out a sigh, Ramses says, "Someone I was hoping I could ask to let my mother know I'm safe. She's a friend."

"Didn't seem like a regular ol' friend, love. What's her name?" Nyssa chimes in. "Erin," he says.

"Well, I'm sure Erin shall miss you dearly while you're gone, your mother as well. Hopefully, one day, you'll find a way to get back to them," Eigor says.

With a tinge of sorrow in his voice, Ramses trails off, "Yeah, hopefully..."

Sensing the boy's spirits are low, I decide to jump in. "How about you? Who are you leaving behind, besides the guard?" I ask Eigor in the hopes of bettering my understanding of him.

He chuckles before saying, "Not a soul, I'm afraid. I was in Cedar Keep alone. You see, when I was taken from the Isle as a child, I was sold to slavers. I don't have the slightest clue who my parents are or if I even have other family members. The only semblance of family I ever knew was my fellow slaves, owned by the Millard Silver Traders. With them, I grew up mining in the Silver Lands until I reached twenty-odd years. Then, one moon, I woke up and had been sold again. Taken from my family once more... This time, I was sold to a kinder man. A leader... The Elder. Or at least I was bought under his sigil and put to work in one of the garrisons of troops. 'Tis been about five or so years that I've been in his Elder's barracks, and I sought to serve him well. That was until I came across this brooding muck," he says as I hear him tap on Amon's shoulder. "Saved my life, and then, well, you know the rest of the story."

"Well, you're not alone anymore, Eigor. You have us, for better or for worse," Nyssa says.

The Isle native laughs. "Definitely for the worse," he says.

Piping up over the wood, cracking under the flame's weight, Eigor returns the question, "What about you, Nyssa? What people did you leave behind?"

"Ha, I promise I'm not that interesting, love. I don't have much of a story," she says.

"That's hard to believe, considering the company you kept in me and Sylas. Everyone has their own tale. Tell us," Amon breaks his silence.

Taking a deep breath, Nyssa says, "Very well," and then pauses before continuing. "Never knew my parents, to be quite honest. I grew up in an orphanage close to the capital until I was sixteen, and then I ran away. I've been healing, stealing, and traveling ever since. Not really an honest life, but 'tis one I've made for myself. So, to answer your question and be completely frank; I don't have family in the keep, I don't have friends there either. In fact, I didn't know anyone until Sylas sent word he would be visiting."

I can tell there's more in the way her breath shakes and her heart beats. She's not lying, but she's definitely not telling the entire truth.

For now, however, I don't push for answers as I turn to my right and look in the direction of Amon, who says, "What did he say, exactly, when he reached out?" he asks.

"Well, honestly, he didn't even reach out. He just showed up to the church, saying he would need my assistance. That's when he told me about you and how he's been searching for you ever since you two split up," she responds.

Her words lay heavy on the man's heart, as I feel his breath grow staggered and his heart beats accelerate. I can tell the man is growing upset, and his words do not do well in hiding it.

"He was always looking out for me, it seems. Always there when I needed him the most..." Amon trails off.

Whether intending to or not, Eigor stifles the tension by asking, "What about you, Amon? Anyone special in the keep? Or in general?"

Swiftly, he shuts down the question almost as quickly as it was asked, "No. I'm not delving into my past with you lot. Especially not with him around," he says.

Nyssa raises her voice, "What are you so afraid of? The man saved our lives!"

"And that justifies trust? Forgiveness?!" Amon says. He shifts his body weight in my direction and remarks, "Why? Why me?

Why not Sylas? Why decide to put your life on the line for us but for Sylas, it was considered too dangerous?" "Amon..." Eigor trails off.

"No! Let the blind bastard answer! What reason could he possibly have! You lose your title, you lose your home, you lose everything you knew! Why?!" he exclaims.

Feeling the abundance of warmth against my open palms, I think back to how we got to this moment. How I got here. Wondering if I made the right choice, asked the right questions, chose the right side, or if there was anything I could have done to prevent being an outcast. Prevent being hunted.

With all of this in mind, I answer the angered bounty hunter, "When I heard Valincias kill your friend, it sent shockwaves down my spine. I knew he was temperamental; I knew he was furious after the trial, but I never thought he would go that far. Even in the moments building up to it, I never could have imagined him murdering him. That is until your friend questioned why he intended to murder the innocent and the captain revealed his true nature. One of which was willing to sacrifice your friend, the elder, my brother, or anyone who stands in his way.

'Tis shocking how little I actually know of Valincias and what he is capable of, as he talked about sending Elder Elovis to his death. When I heard that…

I was stuck in panic… so, maybe you're right, maybe I am a coward," I look over to Amon. "But even in my stunned state, I contemplated saving him. Yet I needed to get word to the manor about this treason. In fact, I did… or at least, tried..." "And look where that got you," Amon quips.

"Amon, for the Gods' sake… what do you mean, 'tried,' my lord?" Nyssa asks.

I take a deep sigh before continuing, "When I got back to the Manor, I ran straight to his room. I knocked over servants, spilt wine, and fell a multitude of times. However, when I eventually got to his chambers, the lord was fast asleep. I shook him until he awoke and told him everything I had witnessed. From meeting and spying on all three of you, tracking Valincias into the sewers, explaining what he said, and ultimately what the captain did to your friend. Yet, Hamzi told me it wasn't enough," I say.

"What do you mean not enough?! Is witnessing a murder and hearing a confession to treason not enough to warrant justice!" Amon yells.

"In his eyes? No... He said that I had no way of confirming it was Valincias. It certainly didn't help that when I forced him out of the manor in the middle of the night to go down into the sewer with guards; there was no trace of your friend. There was no proof of anything that I claimed to have occurred. In fact, when we returned to the manor, Valincias was there, standing guard."

Amidst the flames flickering, and the story being told, Ramses speaks, "That's why you came to me, isn't it? You needed more proof."

I nod my head. "I was hoping to gain more insight from you, bounty hunter," I say.

The air goes silent as the howls of the wind and the crackling of the flame are the only noises being made.

"I don't have any insight, I'm afraid," he says.

Catching me off guard and countering his words, Nyssa says,

"Loria's sake, Amon. Tell him what you found out." "Nyssa, stop..." Amon says before she cuts him off.

"The keep's in danger. A royal servant discovered a treaty between Savar. I don't know how Valincias fits into this, but there's something bigger going on," she says.

"For gods' sake!" Amon bellows.

Ignoring his griping, I say, "I'm afraid I don't follow."

"The king has agreed to an alliance with Savar. In return for trade, military aid, and ongoing peace, the Savarian council demands land. Specifically, Cedar Keep is to be given to the refugees from Daharia, Lymre, and the Isle," Nyssa says.

In utter shock, I say, "That... that can't be. My brother and the Elder are taking some of our bannermen to wipe them out per the king's request. I... I don't understand, why would he ask such a thing of us if he agreed to an alliance?"

"Tsk. The king lied to you. He probably knew your Elder would never agree, or maybe that he would and just didn't care. Either way, the king gets rid of the figurehead of the second largest and second most profitable hold. Maybe he felt threatened, or he felt as if he couldn't control your Elder? And we all know that would drive King Arys 'The Just' mad. The only way to deal with that? Get rid of him. Whatever you thought your brother and leader are heading toward is wrong. I'd wage a hefty amount of coin that 'tis a trap," the bounty hunter says.

"Amon! Can you be any more of a snake-tongued bastard!" Nyssa scolds the man.

"No," I say. "He's right. The only reason the king has for doing this is to get rid of the Elder and his influence. Valincias must be taking orders from him. Trying to help get rid of Elder Elovis from the inside... I must get word to them before 'tis too late." "How do you intend to do that?" Ramses asks.

Unsure of my next move, and frankly still taken aback by this new information, I mask my lack of confidence by saying, "I shall head for the border east of here. That's where my brother and the

Elder were going, last I knew."

"Then I shall come with you," Ramses says.

"This shall be too dangerous for you. I can't allow it," I say.

In my time knowing the young man, he has never raised his voice or shown much of a backbone. However, he surprises me and most likely everyone around the fire as he raises his tone, "You don't get to rip me from my home, get me nearly killed by the guard, and be hunted by hounds to turn me away now! I'm coming with you, and not even The Loria can stop me!"

"Look at you, growing a set of balls. About time, aye?" Amon says.

In my head, I know the boy shall slow me down. Yet, as I am the one who got him involved in all of this, I am the same one who must protect him with all my might. That is until I can at least get him back home or somewhere safe. Therefore, I nod my head and say, "Very well, Ramses. We leave at first light," before rising to find my footing. Shockingly, though, Ramses isn't the only one offering assistance. "I would like to join you as well," Nyssa remarks.

In a state of confusion, much as I and everyone around the fire, Amon exclaims, "What?!"

"Why wouldn't I?" she returns. "No one would need my assistance more than those heading toward a battle."

"What about us? What if we need your aid?" Amon says.

She scoffs before saying, "Then I shall lend you elixirs for your travels."

Amon sneers, "Tsk. I surmise you'll be joining them as well?" Caught off guard, Eigor says, "Uh... no? I don't believe I've paid off my debt to you. Besides, I mean this with no offense, Lord, but I owe this keep nothing more than what I've already given."

"I understand, I thank you for everything to this point," I say in his direction before turning to Nyssa. "As for you, I welcome your company; however, I must insist you are set on your decision. I shan't imagine the next few moons shall be easy on the mind or soul."

The woman to my left grabs my hand and says, "Love, if I wasn't confident, I would never offer." "Very well," I nod.

With the break of conversation, I walk back toward the tree I once sat against to do the same again.

As I stroll over, I hear Ramses ask, "Where shall you two go?"

To which Amon responds, "To warn my other brothers and sisters in arms." "And where would that be exactly?" the young man inquires.

The bounty hunter chuckles, the first time I've heard any emotion other than anger or disdain leave his mouth. "If I told you, boy, you'd either have to join us or be put against the blade," he says.

"Hmm... two shit choices. I think I'd rather not know then," Ramses says.

The young man's comment incites laughter from Nyssa, Eigor, and even a bit from me. However, Amon returns to a flat tone as he responds to the boy's tease.

"That's it. I'm going to sleep," he says. "Aye, me as well," Eigor says, still chuckling a little.

Sitting against the rigid bark, I say to Ramses and Nyssa, "I shall take the first watch. You two should get some rest as well, we all have long journeys ahead of us."

The pair say nothing in return, and I soon hear the shuffling of dirt and leaves. The only noises now apparent are the flame still flickering and the wind brushing past the outstretched limbs of the trees.

As I sit amongst nature and bodies dozing off, I can't help but contemplate a number of things. First, the trajectory of our trek to find the Elder and brother. If they were heading to the border of Savar, they must pass through Leafs Edge to rally our forces there, pick up supplies, and rest for the night. Heading there shall allow us to gain insight into what direction they marched next and hopefully, we'll be able to purchase horses to catch up with Jov and the Elder. With them having a head start on us, it shall be difficult to reach them. I can only hope we don't reach them too late.

However, even with thinking through this intimidating task, it isn't what bothers me the most. 'Tis the wickedness that I have shared a home with for far too long and I can not help but wonder if it extends beyond Valincias.

With these thoughts weighing heavy, I continue to analyze the past couple moons and even far beyond that. I shall get to the bottom of this treachery and save those I hold dear, even if it costs me everything.

LADY ILLIA
THE CARRIAGE WHEELS TURN

Two moons have passed since we left the manor and Cedar Keep as a whole. The coachman, who steers the horses westward, has navigated us through countless roads, rivers, and villages on our way to the capital alongside our eight-guard caravan. Therefore, we sit in our elegant silk gowns, mine green and black, whilst mother dons white with a green leaf pattern, waiting to arrive at our journey's end. An ending that shall be much welcomed as we have grown weary of our coach and travel. I do not remember the trek being this dull, even if I had only done it once when I was ten years of age. Perhaps I was too fascinated with the changing future and new opportunities in front of us as we came to see King Arys name Father an Elder. This came fresh off of father winning Elium, the final battle on the isle, resulting in the nation triumphing in the Red War. Thus, he had been dubbed Elder of Cedar Keep and made protector of its respective hold. Such a joy-filled time, unlike now, as, this time around, I find myself to be at odds with utter boredom. As a result of the apathy, mother and I have attempted to keep our wits about us on this journey by often taking breaks. These include stretching, smelling the fresh air, seeing the sights of the awfully flat grasslands, and even exchanging coin for more wine in the towns we pass through. At times, it has helped with the travel, the wine certainly doing so. Yet none bring me the same relief and joy as knowing that our ride is at a near end.

"How much farther do you think we have to go, Mother?" I ask. "Impatience is not befitting you, Illia," she returns.

I sigh before saying, "I would just like to get out of this cramped wooden crate."

"We shall be there soon enough, my dear. Remain patient," Mother says.

"Patience is near impossible when all I have had on my mind is a cherry tart the entire journey. I'm looking forward to visiting every pastry chef in the capital," I remark.

Mother snaps her head away from looking out the glass window and looks at me sternly. "Illia. Remember why we are here. This is no time to quench our appetite with desserts... not when we face the judgment of the king," she says.

She's right. I've often lost sight of the reasoning behind our travels. With father and his men going to fight a battle to the southeast, we must be the ones issuing apologies to his grace. Even if we are not at fault, with the Savarian assassin causing the demise of the prince, it was in the walls of our home. Something that I never would have conceived happening, something only a great plea and show of loyalty shall fix. Even then, 'tis up to the king to decide whether or not we shall be punished. I pray to the Loria that he has mercy, for I cannot imagine the repercussions that shall await us if he decides we are at total fault. Perchance, with father carrying out the king's request, the handed-down decree may be less brutal than first thought. Yet we soon shall see what is to become of us, become of father, and become of our home as Mother, looking out the coach's glass window, speaks.

"I nearly forgot how grand and glorious this sight is," she says.

Hearing her words stirs curiosity inside of me. Peering out the glass panes separating the open air and us, I see what draws such awe out of her. My eyes take in the lush forestry trickling into grasslands and rock, watching as we slowly leave the colorful bark and leaves behind and voyage into the hot and arid land on the cobblestone road. Within the habitat that the greatest city of Elium has to offer lies trees with palm leaves reaching down from above, bushes that stand few and far between, and behind it all, the Aging Sea. The deep blue ocean ranges across the horizon, as the only thing breaking the sea apart is Doves Peak. The hold is not actually sitting in the water but rather cuts the sea in two, as it sits in front of the shoreline. Its colossal, white, stone walls stretch wider than the moon, whilst the additional homes and farms outside its gates consume even more of my view of the sea. Pulling my eyes up to the stone barrier's top, I see hundreds of guards and dozens of shelters on its ramparts. The sight provokes a sense of security, as I have never seen such a vast defense.

"Safe to say we'll be more than protected whilst here," I say at the sight.

Mother sighs. "What some view as protection, others come to know as endangerment," she says.

Her words disturb me, as all I can remember now are the words Bale said to me. It seems he's not the only one worried about this visit, as mother clearly is on edge. Nonetheless, I push the trail of thought aside as I bring my gaze back down to the giant bronze gate. Slowly, it becomes larger as we approach our final destination. At this sight, I pull myself away from the glass, lean back into the plush green and yellow seats, and take a sip of my silver cup. After a couple more sips of wine, the wheels halt and the guards converse.

"Who are you to seek passage within the king's sacred walls?" a faraway voice calls out.

In return, through the wooden wall, our carriage driver says, "Lady Sylvia Elovis of Cedar Keep, wife of Elder Duggan Elovis. Accompanied by her daughter, Lady Illia Elovis, heir to the cedar throne."

"I would hope you have proof of such a claim?" the capital guard asks.

"Of course, sire. Here you are," the driver responds.

I hear the faint shuffling of parchment before the letter is read aloud, "I, Elder Elovis of Cedar Keep, hereby offer my sincerest condolences to his majesty, King Jacque Arys, Lord of Elium, keeper of all its bountiful lands, and protector of all its endearing citizens. Delivering my apologies in the flesh are my wife and daughter, Ladies Sylvia and Illia Elovis. Signed, Elder Duggan Elovis… very well, we shall have a member of the guard escort you to Doves Rest," the guard of Doves Peak says.

In response, our driver replies, "Thank you, sir," before using the reins to slowly spin the carriage wheels once more.

Odd, it is, having to announce ourselves to the guard. Even more abnormal for myself and mother is having the guard carry a written document signed and sealed by my father to prove such. Yet these are the necessary requirements and precautions, as we were warned by father not to exit the carriage until we arrived at the king's palace, Doves Reach. "The streets of the capital may seem glamorous and full of opportunity to explore. However, if you find yourself in the wrong place, you may discover you are the opportunity for others to take advantage of," he warned before he left. In actuality, father was against Mother and me going before the king alone. However, Mother is quite strong in her will and words, unrelenting once her mind is set. I have always admired that quality in her, wishing and striving to accomplish the same mindset. Perhaps now is the best time to practice such a characteristic, now that we stand to face an unnerving task. One that we edge ever so close to as the bronze gate creaks open.

As we move along, the guard who spoke with our driver flashes by the window. Being much closer than before, I can easily make out the attire of his majesty's loyal soldiers. The protector wears a sleeveless, white, buttoned shirt underneath a golden chest plate, with the dove insignia etched into its center. The armor is accompanied by bracers made of gold, reflecting the day's light. Additionally, the guard wears a leather strap over his chest, his sword in its scabbard on his back latched to it. However, out of all the apparel different from our own guard, what strikes me odd isn't the golden helm he wears but the leather kilt and sandals. Perhaps 'tis to stay cool in the humid grass-lands, perhaps it allows swift movement, or a combination of both. However, it matters not, as the guard goes out of view whilst we roll on, passing under the wall.

The shadow of the stone droops down over the carriage, blocking out the sun, and leaving us to ride in darkness. The absence of light, however, does not last long, as an abundance of rays pour down as we enter the city. Through the glass, I can see a multitude of stables, stone buildings that serve as places to sleep, places to drink, places to watch, places to indulge, and places of work, filled with people that are too many to count. These individuals range from the guard, all in the same uniform, and the average citizen, in their dirtier cloth garments. In groups, they streak by the window, as a handful stare at us whilst we pass. The majority, however, go about their life, paying the carriage and our escorts no mind as we trot along. Amongst the noisy city, we sit silent. Taking it all in, the new sights and style of life, and I reminisce about what we left behind. A life of color amongst the trees, a life of comfort amongst loved ones, and a life of certainty. The latter, something Mother and I no longer have as the carriage halts. The window, allowing us limited vision to the outside, only shows ascending marble steps. At the sight of this, Mother raises her cup.

"May the Loria watch over us," she says, before taking a sip.

I have never seen her this way. She is typically the picture of independence and strength. Yet even her hand trembles subtly as she drinks her wine, causing me to be fearful of the interactions approaching. Nevertheless, the door separating us from the open air is opened, and Mother exits first, picking the bottom of her dress up as she steps down. In turn, I follow and do the same, only to make three very distinct observations. What hits me first is the profound stench in the air; a scent of salt, waste, and body odor. The salt in the air is emitted by the nearby sea; however, the rest is bound to be due to the massive population. Secondly, what truly draws the most attention from me is the massive castle that had been hidden from afar by the looming walls. It stands giant before me, the framework different from the typical castle, fort, or tower. It bears dome roofs instead of jagged walls, with marble columns, adding support to each of the six dome tops. It boasts three towers to the left and right, along with countless windows, balconies, and flags that don the dove emblem on each floor. All of which are entirely made of gold and marble from top to bottom. Even the entrance is made of white rock, as columns span across the entire bottom. Yet, my attention to the king's chosen place of residence is shaken as my third observation begins to speak.

In her Daharian accent, she says, "How lovely 'tis to see the two of you again."

"And so good is it to see you as well, Duchess," Mother responds.

"I hope the journey was kind to you both," Duchess Arys looks at me.

"As kind as a two-moon trek can be," I say.

Mother grabs my arm. "Illia! Mind yourself. No journey is too great in order to see our king," she says before turning back to the golden-skinned royal. "Please forgive her. The trip seems to have made her forget her manners."

The duchess snickers. "'Tis alright, my dears. I promise I won't tell anyone," she says. "Nonetheless, welcome. Let me show you to your chambers. The guard shall show your driver and escorts to their place to reside for the night."

As those words exit her blue-colored lips, the carriage wheels away, and we start to climb the steps.

Walking upward, the duchess says, "I remember the last time you graced us with a visit. Seems so long ago now."

"Indeed. I wish we were visiting for another celebratory occasion," mother says.

"Ah, yes. It seems this time the wine shall be used to grieve the dead rather than commemorate them," Lady Arys says.

Her response causes a slow rise of tension within my body.

"How are his and her majesty taking the news?" Mother asks.

"The queen has not left her chambers since the pigeon arrived with the news. The king, however, has remained steadfast in his demeanor," the duchess says.

I do not know what is worse; The queen likely being deeply wounded or the king showing no sign of sorrow. Either one alludes to no certain forgiveness, no certain understanding, and, definitely, no certain mercy. Unable to take my mind off the situation, I clear my throat before furthering the conversation. "And their other children?" I ask.

"A pigeon was sent north to Snowdrift Keep. Nothing has been received back yet, but we expect a response from Princess Orliena any moon. Meanwhile, Prince Alaric is still here in the castle, helping his mother ease her grief. He often brings her wine or other sorts of gifts to soothe her mind," she says.

I ponder what she means by "gifts," is it jewelry? Is it clothing? Or is it elixirs? Medicines? It may help knowing what she has been using to relieve her spirits when we come face to face. That confrontation is just a slumber away; however, the place in which we shall find out sits in front of us. We reach the top of the flight of steps and walk through a row of thick columns, only to find a plethora of guards and a large wooden door in front of us. Walking past the protectors, who provide security with their axes, swords, and javelins, we approach the door, and as a result of our advance, the door is pushed open by the golden defenders. With a long creak due to the stature of the great frame, a peek of what lies inside is shown. Floors made out of hand-carved white stone is the base, whilst a layer of fabric lays atop.

The royal blue carpet, matching the duchess's lips, lays on the floor of the foyer. It extends from the door we stand at all the way up the split staircase straight ahead. The stairs ascend upward before coming to a landing. Paintings of past rulers, the capital, and battles hang on the landing wall. Yet the stairs continue on, going off in two directions, left and right. Marvelous is the art and architecture, as every single detail is perfect and made of marble. From the floor, the railings, and the stairs. Each expertly placed and crafted to create such a beautiful scene. One we haven't even set foot inside of. Once we do, however, only a little more is revealed as we stride forward.

To our immediate left and right are more guards, but more columns are also used as support for the second floor. As I look up, I see a grand, golden chandelier with lit candles illuminating the entrance as well as the second floor, having its own beams of support for the floor above it. This makes me believe the entire castle is designed this way. Nevertheless, I pull my gaze back down and look through the separation of the columns to find a doorway on either side. I wonder what they lead to...

Breaking my digestion of the scenery is the Daharian accent. "Lady Illia?" Duchess Arys says.

"Yes, my lady?" I reply, noticing Mother and her have stopped their steps. She chuckles. "Did you not hear me?" she asks.

Caught off guard, I reply, "No. My apologies, I must have been distracted by my new surroundings."

"No apologies are needed, my dear. I, too, was taken aback when I first took in Doves Landing and its beauty," she says. "I did, however, ask if you would like anything to be brought to your room?"

I look at Mother, who sternly holds a certain look in her eyes. One I know all too well, as I have been given it many times before in my life. One saying 'Don't' without actually speaking.

Therefore, in accordance, I say, "My thanks, but no."

"Hmm, very well, my dear, but this is where I shall leave the two of you. The guard shall see to it you are escorted to your chambers for the night," the duchess says.

"You have our thanks for this warm welcome. We look forward to meeting again tomorrow, perhaps for a stroll in the gardens with wine in hand," Mother says.

Duchess Arys laughs. "You may not speak my native tongue, but you do certainly speak my language. May the Loria watch over you," she says, bowing and then leaving.

I watch as the duchess takes a left and walks through the marble pillars, opening the door, walking through, and closing it behind her. We, however, are instructed to walk up the steps, take a right at the landing, and walk straight. The second floor is more of the same, with a blue carpet walkway, closed wooden doors, and windows scattered throughout the hall. A noticeable difference, however, is the stairwell that lies at the end of the hall. As the guards push forth, I can only imagine this is where we are headed, and indeed, I am correct. We reach the spiraling steps, much like the ones at home, and follow our escorts on their climb. Passing two floors, the guard exits the well on the third and paces forward.

Eventually, they stop at one of the many doors in the hall and look at me.

"My lady, this shall be your chambers whilst you stay in the capital. The maids shall be by soon to escort you to a freshly drawn bath," the gold-plated guard says, pushing the door open.

I nod in response to the guard before looking at mother. She gives me a slight nod, and in accordance, I walk through the doors to my chamber. In doing so, the door behind me is pulled to a close, and I find myself in very different settings than what I am accustomed to. 'Tis far from stark or bleak circumstances, rather 'tis just odd to be in a new place of slumber. The room itself is bigger than mine in Cedar Manor; however, there are a few small differences. Where I would have a fire pit is replaced with a marble wall. Where I would have books on a large desk to sit and read is replaced by a smaller one with wine and grapes on top. However, the dresser is slightly bigger, and the bed is vastly larger, with a white, sparkling canopy overtop. Even the chairs and table are larger but made out of the same material as mine at home, imaginably due to us supplying the capital with our cedar products. Yet, even with all our trade with the largest city in Elium, I find myself frustrated with the fact that I have no books in my room. I walk over to the stand next to my bed, which holds grapes and wine on top, and indulge. With each sour grape eaten, I sip on the delectable red liquid. After a dozen or so grapes and sips of wine, there is a knock at my door. "Come in," I say.

In turn, the door opens, and in come two younger ladies dressed in brown linen gowns and wearing white bonnets.

The pair curtsy in my direction before one of them says,

"We've been instructed to show you to the bathing room, my lady."

I nod my head in their direction and reply, "That would be quite refreshing, thank you."

Following the two of them out of the room and into the hall, we aim for the stairwell at the end. Only descending one floor, they show me to the first door on the left. One maid opens it, and the other enters inside. I follow their lead as the maid holds the door open for me, finding a wooden bathtub filled with steaming water. "Here you are, my lady," a maid says.

"We shall take all your garments to wash them after we help cleanse you. The queen has picked out a dress for you to wear in the meantime," the other says, pointing to the right of the room.

Her finger aims at a blue silk gown hanging over a chair, with white slippers underneath. It looks quite elegant, with its thin straps and shiny color. Eager to try it on, I take off my dress, shoes, and undergarments, handing them to maids, and step into the hot bath. The pair place my things down and help wash me clean of all the dirt and grime I had collected over the course of our trip.

For the first time since we arrived in Doves Peak, I feel at peace. I feel comfortable. Yet the sight of the dress to my right reminds me of my want to try it on. Thus, I step out of the bath and put on the gown and slippers. Fitting me perfectly, I feel the stress being relieved from my body due to the hot water, and I am ready to return to my room and retreat to my dreams. A maid knocks at the door, and once it is opened, a different pair of maids wait outside the door. The two are dressed identically to the ones before; however, one is much older than the other. "This way, m'lady," the older one says.

Following her instruction, I walk with them as the pair guide me back up a floor and to the door of my designated chambers.

Before I go inside, I ask, "Would it be possible for me to request something to read?"

The two look at each other, almost as if they are confused.

"Were you not shown to the library? Typically, all our guests are shown every nook and cranny of the magnificence that is Doves Landing," the older maid responds.

I shake my head from side to side, now wearing the same look of confusion they bear. The two look at each other again, raising an eyebrow at one another, before the other young maid looks back at me.

"Very well. We shall show you to our library if you'd like. This way, you can pick what you'd like to read rather than us bringing back something at random," she says. "I would very much like that," I respond.

Consequently, the pair walked me back toward the spiral of marble slabs, and traveling all the way back to the bottom, we exited onto the second floor, Mother, and were on not an hour ago. This time, however, the windows that were once filled with light are now darkened, as the moon has come up, and torches line the hall to amplify warmth and illumination.

Walking past the flames and doors, we walk back down to the landing and descend the great marble staircase in the foyer. To my surprise, the maids take me to the door opposite the one the duchess exited through, the very same one I was caught wondering about. The older maid opens it, revealing a vast and grand library. The large, candle-lit room is filled wall to wall with bookshelves and tables. Both holding parchment were glued together, and the words were written on them.

"Welcome to King Jacque Arys III's Arsenal," the younger maid says.

Taken aback by the name, I question, "Why is it called an

'Arsenal' and not a library?"

"If you take one pebble from the ocean, you only have one pebble. If you obtain a multitude of pebbles, then you have a collection," the older maid says.

Very confused, I ask, "What does such a saying mean?"

"King Jacques III believed there was no greater weapon than what's written by those who come before you. He knew the only way to overcome it was to learn. Not only from his own success and failure but from others. Not learning from just his pebble but by taking others as well," she says. I squint my eyes at her. "I see..." I trail off.

The other maid laughs in return. "Don't mind her. Seems her age is getting to her. We shall wait for you out here until you are done," she says.

"Thank you," I say, and I walk into the library in the hopes of finding something good for the night. The door shuts behind me, and I am left alone with my thoughts, a map on the wall of Elium, and an abundance of reading material. As I go over the books one by one, I encounter a title that catches my eye, 'The Isle Water Ran Red.' Opening it up, I hope to find out a bit more before I commit to it.

Suddenly, a voice came from the corner of the shelves. "I see you're partial to the history of the Red War," he says.

Startling me, I whip my head up from the pages to where the voice projects from. Standing across from me, in between two bookshelves, is a younger, blonde-haired man. The sides of his head are shaven, but the top is shaggy. His skin is pale but covered up by black leather cuirass and pants. He stands tall in his brown boots, looking at me with hazel eyes.

"You shouldn't be sneaking up on a lady like that! Or anyone, for that matter!" I say. "I could've died if I had a weak heart!" He chuckles a little before bowing. "My utmost apologies, my lady. I hope you shall forgive me," he says.

Looking him up and down, I size him up. "That may depend. Who are you?" I ask.

Smirking, he says, "My name is Ali. I'm the royal librarian."

Still a bit on edge, I keep my distance from the man but ask,

"Well then, Ali, what can you tell me about his book?" He draws close and offers his hand out.

I pass it over and wait for his response, watching him in the dimly lit room as he reads the title.

"Hmm," he says. "What is it?" I ask.

"Nothing, it just details the last battle on the Isle. Odd 'tis you wish to read this," Ali says.

Slightly offended, I say, "Why's that? Because I'm not a man and shan't educate myself on such things?"

He gently laughs. "No. No, not at all. Just that this was written from the perspective of someone who lived on the isle," he says. "Oh..." I say.

"Nonethematter, 'tis a good read. I've read it myself a handful of times," he says, handing the book back over.

I take the book from his outstretched hand and nod. "Very well then, I shall be going back to chambers. Thank you for your help,"

I say.

I start to walk back toward the door, but the man asks one more question.

"May I inquire? Why do you wish to educate yourself on what happened in the Red War?" he asks.

Turning back to face him, I say, "Someone I care deeply about was there when this occurred. Someone who should have never been put through such terrible conditions and circumstances. I wish to learn as much as I can in order to be able to understand them more. Perhaps along the way, I shall be able to understand people more and why we do what we do. Starting with why we choose war. Why do we choose to harm others and, ultimately, ourselves in the process? Maybe once

I know the answer to these questions, I can truly understand their pain and be able to help them through it."

"And you believe those answers to be in that book?" he proposes back.

I sigh. "No, but if I can understand a little bit more than what I already do, I consider that growth. Growth I shall need one day to rule my people justly, to love fiercely, and, perhaps, to understand fully," I say.

With those words, I leave the room and am escorted back to my chambers. Once I arrive, I lay in bed and read deep into the night. However, sometime under the moon's light, I fall fast asleep, only to be awakened by Mother. Rays shine in from the balcony behind her, as she shakes me.

"Illia, hurry. You must get ready quickly; we are to see the royal family within the coming hours," Mother says.

Urgently, I rise out of bed and start to prepare myself for the meeting. From doing my hair, putting on my necklaces, silver bracelets, and a green dress, I ready myself for the appearance before the most powerful family in the nation.

With all that taking much time, by the time I finish putting on my shoes, there is a knock at the door. Mother and I exit the room to be escorted by four guards, two in front and two behind. We ascend the stairwell all the way to the top. Coming out, we find ourselves in a large, open air space with a dome roof above. The sun shines through the marble columns holding up the white covering, creating a stunning scene below. One can see the entire capital through the space between the columns, and it all looks so small from this far above. Hard to believe there are tens of thousands who live in its walls. Even harder to believe is the golden throne that sits in front of us.

Looking toward the king, who sits on the throne, dressed in his blue and gray royal garb, I notice an astonishing sight next to him. Not the man sporting a gray beard, hazel eyes, and a golden crown that bears doves instead of pointed ends like the king. Not the queen, wearing a gold circle, violet silk dress, blonde braided hair, and blue eyes who stands next to him. And not the nameless keys to the capital's palace. Rather, 'tis the one who called themselves a librarian, standing on the opposite side of King Arys. Instead of his black leather, he now wears blue silk robes and a golden dove pin on his chest.

My brow stoops in confusion as I whisper, "Ali?" However, mother gives me a nudge to the side, indicating for me to be quiet. The guards disperse from us to find their places next to Queen Arys. Once they do so, there is an eerie silence, until mother speaks. "Your Grace," she bows, and in turn, I do the same.

Looking back up to the king, he nods and opens his hands as if to say, 'Speak.'

In return, Mother continues, "We come before you to offer our humblest condolences and apologies. We can never forgive ourselves for such a tragic accident happening within our walls."

Silence comes over the room once more as the royal family offers no words in return, rather they all stare blankly at us.

Taking a deep breath, mother says, "Furthermore, my husband

has decided to deal with those who we believe did this to your son, personally," she says.

For the first time, King Arys speaks, "Tell me, Sylvia. Who do you believe did this to my blood? My kin? My boy?"

"After the… untimely passing of your son, we found the assassin hiding in the stables. A Savarian, who had masked himself as a servant," mother responds.

King Arys takes a deep breath. "I see… inform me, then, why is it that Savar would assassinate my son after I agreed to a treaty, giving them everything they asked for?" he says.

"Treaty?" mother mumbles. "I… I do not know, your grace."

"Hmmm. No answers, rather you come to me with blood on your hands and tell me that Elder Elovis is on his way to spill more?!" he asks.

The king then waves a finger to one of the guards. At a flick of his finger, the guard nods, and the golden protector walks toward Mother and me, unsheathing his blade.

In a panic, Mother screams, "Wait! Wait! Your grace!"

Those are her last words, as I watch the guard cut her down, opening her neck. Her killer then walks over to me, sword in hand, about to strike, before the king calls out. "Not her," he commands.

At his order, the guard stands down and moves aside to reveal Mother on the floor. Blood rushing onto the marble, creating a terrifying contrast of color. I fall to my knees, eyes wide, breath heavy, and nothing but horror on the forefront of my mind.

Fueling that terror, however, is his majesty as he says, "One of my most loyal friends sent a pigeon a day prior to your arrival. It details the entirety of a sickening plot. One I would never believe your father, my friend, was capable of. Yet the evidence and eyewitness testimony is simply too much to ignore. Tell me, why would your father plan to kill my son? Why then blame it on the Savarians and start a war?" King Arys asks. "I shall tell you why. Power! Enough power to gain popularity amongst the people to take the crown! Your father, the war hero, is a coward! A traitor!

How dare he send me his wife and daughter to lie to my face! As if I am so blind and naive to his tricks and actions! But he shall soon meet the fate of all who dare to cross me. As your mother did!" the king shouts, his words echoing into the open air outside.

"And you," he says, much more reigned in. "Do not mistake me keeping you alive as mercy. I am only doing so at the request of Prince Alaric. Otherwise, I would see to it that you are filled from your toes to your head with the very same coral snake venom he killed my son with! I promise you, though. Make one misstep, and you shall meet that fate."

With those words, I offer no response. Instead, I shed a single tear, feeling it stream down my face.

RAMSES
THE EDGE

It seems as if the Loria has deemed me eternally unfortunate in this life. From being born into a close-knit family, one that had to work hard every single moon in order to put food on the table each night, to being driven away from the only place I've ever known. I've been beaten, cast in the dungeon, put on trial, and chased by guards and dogs. Now I march toward certain violence after wandering with two fugitives through the never-ending woods.

Yet, through it all, I have found a way to keep my life and not put the lives of those I truly care about in danger. One day, I shall return to them a stronger man and clean of my accused crimes. For now, that is what drives me forward through the branches as, according to Nyssa, we approach the town of Leafs Edge. Lord Bale mentioned whilst on our trek that this place is the last civilization in Elium before reaching the lands of Savar. In other words, the last time we shall have to dodge the guard in Cedar Keep's territory. 'Tis here I hope to find Father, as I pray to the Loria that he did not go with the Elder into battle. With my luck, however, he has already left to go back home, where I'm sure he shall find mother in a state of distress, as my disappearance the first time made her weak of heart.

"Ramses," Lord Bale says.

My train of thought breaks at the sound of his words. "Yes?" I reply.

"Are you alright? Your heart rate is rising faster than the moon," he says. "I'm fine. Just thinking of home," I say.

In front of me, the moon's light pokes through the trees, and illuminates the blonde woman as she teases me without turning around. "Thinking of that girl again, aren't you, love?" she says. I say nothing in response; however, she continues to laugh.

"You shan't worry yourself; you shall see her soon enough. Once we reach the elder, that is. If he'll believe us, of course-" she adds.

I whip my head over to the lord as he interrupts Nyssa. "He shall," he says.

"Hmm, we shall have to wait and see. Good thing we're not too far away now," she says, stopping her steps.

Looking past the backside of Nyssa and the satchel she bears, light shines from torches in the distance.

Finding myself a bit paranoid, I ask, "What's that?"

Lord Bale, continuing to stride past the both of us, says, "Leafs Edge."

Indeed, he is right, as when Nyssa and I follow him closer, the sight of the village becomes clear. The light we see emits from torches hanging on the wooden posts of the entrance gate as well as the homes within the low stone wall. 'Tis hard to make out the entirety of the civilization in the dark, but from what I can tell, there is a decent number of houses, one large tavern, and a stable. Squinting my eyes, I see that each building is made entirely out of stone, with glass windows, and topped off with a chimney poking through straw roofs. Yet, seeing it all from a distance makes it look minuscule compared to what I am used to in Cedar Keep.

Taking my attention away from Leafs Edge, Lord Bale stops his paces at the tree line and says, "This means we're only a day's ride from the border."

The Lord starts to take a step out into the uncovered sky before Nyssa grabs him by his shoulder.

"Where do you think you're going, love?" she asks.

Turning his head back to her hand that rests on his shoulder, he sounds almost confused. "Into the village…?" he says.

Nyssa giggles. "Not in those royal robes. You shall be recognized within a moment's notice as long as you wear those," she says.

"And what would you have me do? Sleep in the woods whilst you two sleep in the tavern?" he asks.

Nyssa shakes her head. "Myself and Ramses shall go into town and fetch you new garments. It shan't take us long," she says.

With a slight nod, the lord agrees. Upon him doing so, Nyssa looks back to me and motions her hand as if to say, 'come along.' Following her instruction, I walk past Lord Bale and head toward the small civilization, walking side by side with Nyssa as we eventually hop onto the dirt path made from carriages and horses coming in and out and make our way to the entrance. Upon passing underneath the wooden gate, we are met with a stone path. One not made of cobblestone but rather of large and small granite. Alas, this is the only thing accompanying the two of, us as the town seems empty aside from the lights coming from within the nearby homes. Therefore, we walk aimlessly, without any idea of where to go.

"Don't believe anyone will be out in the market this late… if they even have vendors here," I say, mid-stride. My comment prods Nyssa to laugh. "Oh, love, I didn't intend to buy anything," she replies.

Her words cause a stir of confusion within me. "Where shall we find clothes then? Especially now, under the moon's light," I ask.

"Ramses, do you remember what I told you when we first met?" she asks.

"If I recall correctly, you told me I am confused and naive," I say.

"No. Well, yes, but no," Nyssa replies as we walk toward the tavern in the center of town. "All any and every man wants is to have coin and someone to bed."

My brow stoops in further befuddlement as we come upon the tavern doors. The stone building has a bit of noise coming from the inside, but none compared to the taverns back home. Alas, it matters not as we stop our steps at the entrance.

"Let me see if I have this right. You are going to bed someone… for a shirt and pants?" I ask.

Nyssa doesn't respond but instead shakes her head and laughs. Whilst doing so, she pushes the door open, looks back at me, and signals me to follow. Deciding to obey, I walk two paces to the right and lean up against the wall. I'm not able to help but think she can't be serious. Is she really going to seduce a man in order to acquire mere clothes? Is this also the same way she procured a way out of her cell the night I met her?

My curious mind gets the better of me as I peer through the window to my left. Through the glass panes, I scour the inside to find Nyssa. At first, I look left, where, inside, four tables sit relatively close to a fireplace. Instead of seeing her blonde hair, I find the heads of men and women sitting around, conversing and drinking. Unable to spot her outline, I pan to the right. This time, at a long wooden bar, occupied by patrons sitting on stools and a man serving them drinks, I'm able to pick her out of the crowd. She stands next to one of the few townsfolk at the wooden ledge, looking as if she's conversing with them. Smiling and sipping their ale, the two look to be enjoying their interaction with each other. So much so, the man rises to his feet, draws closer and closer to Nyssa, and grabs her hand. The two leave their drinks behind and scamper off toward the steps to the left of the bar. As they go upward, I pull myself away from the window and sit down, placing my back against the tavern's outer wall. Anticipating I may have to wait for longer than I'd like, I start to ponder how I ended up here. What have I done in my life to have been given such a fate? One of constant panic in my heart, of being torn away from everything I know. Alas, 'tis the fate I have wanted for so long. A fate of knowing much more than what I was accustomed to.

However, I didn't foresee it to be this difficult, this dangerous, this heartbreaking. I can't help but wonder what Father would think of me if he came to find my current state of being?

A voice breaks my inner state of contemplation as it says, "Ramses."

I turn my chin up to my left, and standing over me is Nyssa with a perplexed look on her face.

"Lost in thought, love?" she asks, reaching a hand down.

Grabbing her outstretched arm, I pull myself up and find my footing.

"Passing the time is all. Speaking of the matter, that went by rather quickly, no?" I ask.

Nyssa giggles. "Poor soul didn't realize the situation he got himself into when he invited me to his chambers. He never would've surmised I could put him to sleep with one whack of a candle stick," she says. "So... you didn't..." I raise my eyebrow.

Nyssa rolls her eyes. "You think so low of me, Ramses. I'm not going to whore myself out. Just because men want coin or comfort doesn't mean you give it to them. Rather, you make them think you shall. Then, you get creative..." she says.

"Then, in the dungeon? That's not how you were let out?" I respond.

This time, she looks away from me and eyes the road in front of us. "No, love. Instead of what he was desiring, that guard received a swift kick. I only hope it did enough damage to where he shan't have any offspring in his image. Now, we really must be going, as I left a man unconscious and have his garments tucked underneath and between my shirt and pants," she says.

Rather than giving words of response, we both start walking toward the gate. With little to no life on the granite paths, it doesn't take long to exit the village and navigate toward where we left Lord Bale in the forest. Whilst walking through the grass, I start to wonder about my newfound friend. Nyssa is a woman I have come to know as tough, charming, caring, and intelligent. All the more reason to ponder what causes a woman like her to be disdained with a certain memory or experience, as she seemed to be a bit on edge when asked about the guard. Perhaps I shall never know the full extent of her change of behavior, but I can only imagine it to be caused by something of significance. Alas, as I look over to her as we near the tree line, she carries a glimmer in her eyes and holds her head high, a picture of strength and confidence.

As we reenter the land of limbs and leaves, we start to hear shuffling on the soil. With no torch and the canopy of green above blocking the moon's light, 'tis very difficult to make out where the noise is coming from.

"Lord Bale?" I call out into the darkened forest.

But no reply is made.

I call out again, "Lord Bale!" and this time I'm met with a response.

"I'm here," he says, walking out from behind a nearby cedar trunk. "Something in the distance caught my attention, but it matters not. How did the pair of you fare in the village?"

Nyssa giggles. "As well as one can imagine. I wouldn't say it was easy finding clothing in the middle of the moon's presence. However, Ramses and I were able to figure something out," she says.

Nyssa slightly raises her dirty, buttoned, white shirt, revealing a cloth shirt and cloth pants underneath, both colored black. The two items are tucked underneath her own waistband until she pulls them out and throws them on the ground.

The Lord stands still, solid in his demeanor and blank stare. "You both have my thanks," he says. "I shall change before we head toward the tavern in search of rest."

"I don't know if that would be the wisest decision..." Nyssa says. Lord Bale furrows his brow. "And why is that?" he asks.

"Nyssa may have seduced a man, sent him into a deep slumber, and stolen his clothes in the upstairs of the tavern," I reply.

My female associate punched my arm. "You make it sound as if I did wrongdoing. The man had it coming with how touchy he was..." she says.

Lord Bale shakes his head. "This makes things a bit more difficult," he says.

"What do you mean?" I ask.

"If word gets to any guard about the incident, they may send more to query about the woman who looks near identical to the one who escaped Cedar Keep only a few days ago," the lord says.

Nyssa speaks up upon hearing Lord Bale's words. "Considering there wasn't a single metal hawk on the streets or around the village, I do not think it likely for the keep to send more guards here," she says.

"You would be surprised at the lengths a scorned citizen shall go through to get what they believe to be justice. For now, however, let us make camp for the night," Lord Bale says.

Nyssa gives an agreeable grunt before saying, "I shall gather firewood," and wanders off behind a couple of trees.

I turned toward where she took her strides and start to follow. That is until the lord asks a favor of me.

"Ramses?" he asks. I turn back to face the man. "Yes, my lord?" I say.

"Would you be so kind as to bring the clothes over to me? I am having trouble navigating amongst the never-ending crunching of leaves," he says.

Having originally set out with the idea of taking my paces toward finding fuel for a flame, I now use them to gather the shirt and pants on the ground. I walk where I can lean down and gather the garments before bringing them over to the lord. Placing the pair in his hand, he offers me his thanks with a nod and walks off behind a tree.

Now that I have given the lord what he asked for, I start on the next task of gathering branches for a fire. Pacing around the nearby trees, I nab a multitude of fallen, broken, or twisted pieces of wood. As I return to where we three gathered before, so too does Nyssa with an abundance of sticks. We both place the kindling down and start to worry about how to create a flame.

I look at Nyssa. "Any chance you carry a piece of flint in that satchel of yours?" I ask.

She shakes her head, indicating she doesn't, before saying, "Perhaps a stone shall do. Hopefully, if we scrape it fast enough against a blade, it shall create a spark, as a grinding wheel would."

I furrow my brow before shrugging. At this point, we have nothing to lose; therefore, I look around the dirt before grabbing a nearby rock. I hand the stone to her whilst she pulls out her dagger, harshly sweeping the two against each other, but with no success.

"Perhaps I may find luck. The Loria owes me this at least," I say, offering out my palms. She places the dagger in one and the rock in the other. As I rake the pair against each other, small sparks disperse from the conflicting forces, but they don't catch the pile of leaves and sticks. Again, I scrape the blade against stone, and this time the sparks land on a leaf, causing it to catch aflame.

I laugh out of disbelief and turn to Nyssa. "It seems, for the first time, the Loria granted me a favor," I say

She gives me a pat on the shoulder as we both crouch down and says, "So proud of you, love," before giggling.

Suddenly, coming out from behind a cedar trunk, Lord Bale says, "You shan't tease the boy too much. Well done, Ramses," he says as he now stands in his new black shirt and pants.

"Look at you! The spitting image of a commoner. Must be a strange sensation for you," Nyssa says.

Lord Bale raises his eyebrow. "Perhaps if I could see; however, we both know 'tis not the clothes that separates a noble from a commoner," he says.

I watch as Nyssa stands up perfectly straight, looks at the lord, and says, "You're right. Perhaps 'tis simply the unjust criminal accusations that make you more and more like a commoner each day."

Her words cause my body to snap up straight.

"Nyssa!" I interject.

"What?! 'tis not like he's unaware of his circumstances," she exclaims.

In the midst of our interchange of words, I faintly hear the lord laugh. So strange 'tis to hear him break his calm and blank demeanor, and so I train my eyes back onto him.

"Ramses, whilst I appreciate your support, 'tis okay. She speaks the truth. However, I must admit I am sad to only have come to know this truth as of recent," he says. "But now that I know it, I shall see such injustice uprooted and replaced with a better way."

Nyssa takes a seat next to the fire, and I look in her direction.

"Those are noble words, love, truly," she says, opening her satchel and pulling out a glass bottle. "For now, however, let's wash down such harsh truths."

Taking a seat next to her, I ask, "You haven't been seriously carrying that with you this whole time, have you?"

She giggles. "I swiped it from the man's room in the tavern. I surmised it was the least he owed me, besides the clothes, of course," she says.

Nyssa pulls the cork out and takes a prolonged drink. When she swallows, her expression changes to surprise. "That is actually quite lovely," she says.

Her hand reaches over toward me with the bottle in her clutch. At first, I'm hesitant as I look down at her hand and then back into her eyes.

"Gods' sake, Ramses, go on. Live a little, especially while you still can," she says.

With those words, I grab the drink from her and take a deep swig. Not knowing what it is, I find it to be sour and rough to take. The liquid causes me to squeeze my facial features and let out a cough.

"Loria, what is this? 'Tis dreadful," I say. Nyssa lets out a laugh.

"Have you never tried wine before, Ramses?" Nyssa asks.

I shake my head. "'Tis not something we could afford. In fact, we hardly ever even had ale in the house. Even then, I've only had that a handful of times, as Erin and I would sneak out late at night on special occasions and go to the taverns," I say.

Nyssa snickers. "You really are an innocent thing, aren't you, love?" she says. "I guess this calls for celebration then. We have to commemorate your first bottle of wine by finishing it all tonight." "Ah, I don't know about this, Nyssa..." I start to say. "No, no. Come on! Get another sip down, love!" she says.

I look up to my right at Lord Bale. "Why don't you take this drink instead of me, my lord. 'Tis my honor to offer you this over taking it all myself," I say.

Lord Bale takes a seat to the right of me, faces the flame, and says, "Flattery does not suit you, Ramses, just as drinking wine or ale does not suit me. 'Tis best to keep my wits about me in these times. However, I urge you to indulge yourself, as in the next moon, we shall be heading into quite a violent atmosphere."

He's right. Throughout the past nights, as my heart and mind adjusted to my new company and circumstances, I have forgotten about what lies ahead. Alas, as I start to think about the expected brutes, barbarians, and ensured death before us, my heart starts to race. Whilst it beats fast, I consider using the technique Lord Bale taught me. Yet I fear they would see me as weak, or weaker than they already think if I were to do so. Consequently, I seek refuge in the cool glass that I hold in my hand. As I do so, my racing mind and nerves do not settle in their quickness. Therefore, I take two more large gulps in the hopes of easing my concerns. "Easy there, love. Save a drop for me," Nyssa says.

I hadn't realized the pair were staring at me with shock, or at least Nyssa was. I can never tell what emotion the Lord holds. I chuckle. "My apologies, 'tis starting to grow on me," I say.

"Aye, I'd say so," she replies, pulling the bottle from my clutches.

As she takes another sip, I decide to ask a question. "If you could lead any life, what would it be?" I ask.

Straight away, Nyssa swallows the wine in her mouth, as I can hear the gulp, and speaks up. "That 'tis easy. I would like to be a lotus dancer in southern Daharia," she says.

Struck with shock, I ask, "Are you being quite serious? You? A tropical dancer?"

"Why do you say it like that? Am I not pretty enough? Do I not have the figure, Ramses?" she snaps back. "No... no..." I start. "No?! How cruel of you," she says.

"No! I mean, uh, yes! Yes, you do! You're beautiful! I just meant—" I say before Nyssa cuts me off.

Her demeanor quickly changes from one of anger to one of playfulness. "I know what you mean, love. I'm simply fooling around," she teases. "But I must thank you for calling me beautiful.

Your courtship is unmatched."

I can feel my face heat up and start to change color. However, Nyssa upended her toying with me as she smiled and handed me the wine.

As she passes me the glass, Lord Bale chimes in, "Why there?"

"'Tis where the land meets the Glass Sea. The water is said to be so clear, 'tis as if you are looking at the ocean floor through a windowpane. Not to mention the sun is never ending," she says. Nyssa looks at me. "How about you, love?" she asks.

"I'm unsure, to be quite honest. I've always dreamed of more, I just never knew what that would look like," I say before taking a sip and continuing. "My father is a soldier, so perhaps I should follow his lead."

"Oh, love, I can see you be many things, but a warrior 'tis not one. Besides, we shan't have your pureness of heart be blotted by the malice of war," Nyssa says as I pass her the wine before continuing. "You strike me as a, hmm, harpist? No, a poet!" she teases.

I roll my eyes at her whilst she laughs, drinking from the glass. Looking to my right, I ask, "And you, my lord?"

"Oh please, he has already lived a life most would die for," Nyssa says.

The lord remains even-keeled, as her comment seems to have no effect on him.

"Many have died for me to be where I am. Many that I cared for deeply," the lord replies.

Nyssa stutters, "I'm... I... I apologize, I just meant it as a joke."

I keep my eyes focused on Lord Bale, who stares blankly into the flames.

"I know you meant no harm, but perhaps this shall teach you that power and reputation is as much a burden as 'tis a blessing," he says.

The mood takes a deeper shift until the lord breaks the silent tension. "I would be a sculptor," he says.

At first, I assume he is joking and start to smile. That is until he does not proceed to laugh, therefore I look at Nyssa, who holds the same confused look as I do. I look back at him, "A sculptor?" I ask.

Lord Bale smirks. "I don't need eyes to see the faces the two of you are making," he says.

"Forgive me, but you must know why we are surprised," Nyssa says. "Not necessarily," he replies.

She laughs. "Ah, yes, I've met thousands of blind artists," she says.

The lord raises an eyebrow. "Tell me, Nyssa. Do you need your eyes to feel? Do you need your sight to imagine?" he asks. "No," she responds.

"Indeed, you need only the will to carry out your creativity. For most who wish to inspire, they can't see the true change they first wished to occur. Rather, they instead feel as if change is needed, imagine what it would be like, and, the very few, act in their will. 'Tis not eyes needed, only an active mind," he says.

On account of him imparting his wisdom on us, I grab the wine from Nyssa.

"Cheers to that," I say, having another drink and passing it back to my left. Our female companion giggles. "Cheers," she says.

After a few quiet moments pass around the fire, I stand up as I feel the need to piss. As I do, my legs become weak, and my balance becomes loose. My entire body sways like the leaves on the trees during this clear night. "Whoa there. Are you okay?" Nyssa asks.

I start to blush. "Um, yes. I suppose I'm just a bit new at this," I giggle.

Both of my fellow travelers start to laugh. "Oh Gods. Do you need a hand?" Nyssa asks.

"Nyssa, I'm flattered but I'm afraid my heart belongs to someone else," I slur. She sighs. "Men are so naive," she says.

I shake my head from side to side, shrugging off her comment as I walk off toward a nearby tree. Pacing behind it to where they cannot see me, I relieve myself of my heavy bladder. As I finish, I pull my pants up and wrap around the tree, bumping into the wooden trunk. However, I stop my strides once I see a frightening sight. Close by the flame, Nyssa stands close to Lord Bale. The pair stand with their weapons drawn as they are encircled by bandits. The men and women who challenge them don leather armor, except for a few who have chosen to wear no protection at all. Pointing their assortment of weapons at them, ranging from bows, swords, daggers, maces, and morning stars, the group outnumbers us fivefold. Indecisive as to what I need to do or how to act, I stand still in horror. That is until I am grabbed from behind and a tan arm puts a knife against my throat.

"Don't fight," are the words whispered into my ear.

My breaths quicken and my heart races, as newfound danger is close to ending my life.

ACKNOWLEDGMENTS

Firstly, to my readers, thank you for embarking on this journey with me. I am grateful for the time you have invested in these words. Secondly, I would like to thank my family and friends, as many have cheered me on, pushed me to be better, and shown me much love while writing this novel. Lastly, a heartfelt thank you to those who helped me with the publishing and editing of this book. Marni Mcrae, Ana Hantt, and Josie Baron, I am forever in your debt.

Made in the USA
Monee, IL
06 February 2025

11722417R00184